EDUCATING THE WORKER-CITIZEN

EDUCATING THE WORKER-CITIZEN

The Social, Economic, and Political Foundations of Education

JOEL SPRING

University of Cincinnati

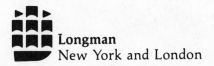

Longman
New York and London

EDUCATING THE WORKER-CITIZEN
The Social, Economic, and Political Foundations of Education

Longman Inc., New York
Associated companies, branches, and representatives
throughout the world.

Developmental Editor: Nicole Benevento
Manufacturing and Production Supervisor: Kris Becker
Composition: A & S Graphics
Printing and Binding: Fairfield Graphics

Manufactured in the United States of America

Library of Congress Cataloging in Publication Data
Spring, Joel H.
  Educating the worker-citizen.

  (Educational policy, planning, and theory)
  Includes index.
  1. Educational planning—United States. 2. Educa-
tional equalization—United States. I. Title.
LA210.S67 1980   370.19   79-17415
ISBN 0-582-28075-3

CONTENTS

INTRODUCTION

The major role of the school in modern society is to provide equality of opportunity in a hierarchical occupational structure. The theme of equality of opportunity permeates the political and economic structure and functions of the school. In the United States it has provided the justification for shifting the control of political institutions, including the public school, from elected representatives to a bureaucratic structure dominated by professional experts. The ideology of equality of opportunity puts the professional in control of the social system and creates a closer relationship between training in educational institutions and entry into the job market. Understanding the ideology of equality of opportunity is important for an understanding of the political and economic structure of schooling and the relationship between schools and the modern welfare state.

This book begins with a description of nineteenth-century political goals for developing systems of modern schooling. These goals, which included the development of patriotism, nationalism, and good citizenship, have not disappeared from educational systems but have become secondary in importance to the economic goals of schooling. Chapter 2 begins the discussion of the economic functions of schooling by describing attempts in the United States, China, and the Soviet Union to use the school to overcome the alienating effects of industrialism. The relationship between education and the welfare state is described in chapter 3 in the context of the ideology of equality of opportunity. This theme receives further elaboration in chapter 4 in a discussion of the relationship between schooling and social mobility.

One theme of the book is the increasing political power of professional experts in a society that attempts to provide equality of opportunity through educational institutions. As a result of this process, all occupations become professionalized (i.e., require expert training and certification from an educational institution), and the status of occupations becomes dependent on the status of the educational program. It is in the context of this theme that chapter 5 discusses the professionalism of teachers and school administrators.

Chapter 6 extends the discussion of teacher-administrator professionalization by linking that process to the increasing control of educational systems by professional experts in bureaucratic structures. The description of the control of modern educational institutions is related to political theories of democratic elitism and representation. This description is expanded in chapter 7 to include educational research, or the social production of knowledge. This chapter argues that significant control of educational systems is exercised through educational research sponsored by the government. Understanding the politics of educational research is important for understanding the politics of education. Of equal importance are the issues surrounding educational finance. Chapter 8 discusses the central issues in the political economy of modern educational systems.

Each chapter of the book integrates history and theory with descriptions of the functioning of educational systems. The general goal of the book is to provide the reader with the broadest possible perspective of the social, political, and economic foundations of modern systems of education. Each chapter is also designed to raise major questions in the reader's mind about the validity of the functions of the modern school. The major argument of the book is that the ideology of equality of opportunity has made the school one of the central institutions of society and that when this ideology is examined in terms of its meaning and consequences for political and economic institutions, serious issues arise regarding its effect on contemporary life.

1

POLITICAL
THEORIES OF EDUCATION:
NATIONALISM, REPRESENTATION,
AND BUREAUCRACY

THE ROLE OF EDUCATION AS IT RELATES TO political control and the modern state is ambiguous and often contradictory. On one hand, systems of schooling provide the knowledge and skills that will give the individual the means to control the political system. On the other hand, the political system uses education to control the individual. The degree to which either role is emphasized in an educational system varies with the political system. Obviously, the more dictatorial systems emphasize control of the individual. But, even in representative democracies, a combination of these two functions exists within the school system.

Another way of expressing these dual political functions of education is through the concept of citizenship. It was the education of the future citizen that made systems of schooling important components of political systems in the nineteenth and early twentieth centuries. Contemporary studies of political socialization make a major distinction between the individual who is an active participant in the political system and the passive citizen. This distinction is largely dependent on how people define good citizenship.[1] Some people might define a good citizen in active terms: a good citizen is one who votes, works to improve the country, and participates directly in the political process. Others might define a good citizen as a person who obeys the law and is loyal to the government.

1

The educational system designed to allow greater control of the individual by the political system would emphasize the passive concept of good citizenship. This educational system might stress patriotic exercises, obedience to authority, and the teaching of a highly nationalistic literature and history. The educational system geared to the active form of citizenship might stress the teaching of the means of political participation, knowledge about different political systems, and the encouragement of political activity. Educational systems that stress active or passive citizenship traits are not mutually exclusive. In fact, most educational systems teach a combination of traits with varying degrees of emphasis.

In addition to concern about the citizen's relationship to the political system, an increasing emphasis in the twentieth century has fallen on economic duties. Modern governments have increasingly intervened in the economic affairs of their societies. Economic planning has become a part of the welfare states of North America and Europe, as well as communist countries like the Soviet Union and China. Involved in all these economic plans have been concerns about the educational systems that prepare individuals to meet the needs of the plans. These concerns include ideas about the specialized training and shaping of the individual who exhibits cooperation with the country's economic plan. The integration of the individual into the economic system has been a central educational issue in the twentieth century.

This chapter explores relationships between the state and the educational system by examining the role of schooling during the rise of the modern state in the nineteenth century. Chapter 2 deals with the economic state in the twentieth century.

The development of representative government in the Western world in the nineteenth century gave birth to modern systems of schooling. The modern economic state has provided further justification for the expansion and integration of schools into society.

Representative Government, Nationalism, and Education

Representative government and nationalism were concurrent developments in Western society that contributed to the development of educational systems. Nationalism was rooted in concerns about popular sovereignty and resulted in arguments for national systems of schooling to create national languages, literature, and loyalties. Representative government induced both fears and hopes about mass participation in government. Those who were fearful supported schooling as a means of controlling the activities of individual citizens. Those who were hopeful saw the schools giving citizens the tools for participation.

Understanding the relationship between nationalism and representative government helps in understanding the dilemma facing educational systems as they try to produce loyal citizens who are not so blinded by loyalty and obedience to the law that they become servants of power. The problem is not only a continuing one for most representative governments but one that might not be solvable unless some basic changes are made in political structures.

Nationalism in the nineteenth century was part of the concept of popular sovereignty. The nation was to reflect the will of the people and not that of a monarchy or aristocratic class. The people were to be the nation, and the nation was to be the people. To worship the nation was to worship the people, and vice versa. The phenomenon of nationalism occurred in both Europe and the United States.

Nationalism developed almost as a religion with a liturgy and symbols to be worshiped. Flags, monuments, architecture, songs, literature, and ritualistic ceremonies became part of nationalistic movements. To be patriotic and loyal to the nation, and to participate in nationalistic rituals, became the mark of the good citizen and an expression of loyalty to the people. The school was to become a central institution for training people for nationalism.

Nationalism and representative government are not contradictory. Representative government requires a population that believes the nation is an expression of the people's interests. Representative government does not involve direct control of the actions of government by the people: it involves the election of individuals to represent the people's interests in government. This means that people have to believe that their government represents their interests even though they do not directly control the operations of government. This means a willingness to be loyal and obedient to laws passed by representative parliaments or legislatures. In other words, representative government does not provide the complete democratic control demanded by political movements for popular sovereignty. Nationalism creates the belief that representative government does represent the will of the people.

The link between nationalism and popular sovereignty can be seen in fascist movements in Italy and Germany during the 1930s and '40s. Historian George Mosse has argued that what Hitler and Mussolini promised the people was a form of participation in government that was more meaningful than representative democracy.[2] Representative democracy, they argued, was only a device for allowing bourgeois control of government. Fascism, with its extreme emphasis on nationalism, was to give more meaningful expression to the will of the people. School systems were to be obvious vehicles for the nationalism of the modern representative state.

In the late eighteenth and early nineteenth centuries Noah Webster expressed the relationship between representative government and nationalism in the United States. Webster's importance is magnified by the success of his *American Spelling Book*, published in 1783. This book, which was to train Americans in the spelling and pronunciation of a national language, eventually sold over 100 million copies and earned Webster the title Schoolmaster to America. Webster, an ardent nationalist and supporter of represenative government, saw his spelling book and his work on the standardization of the American language as vehicles for promoting his beliefs. The importance of Webster's work for the United States cannot be overstressed. At a time when the total U.S. population was only around 10 million, his book sold 1 million copies a year.[3]

In his introduction to *Dissertations on the English Language* (1789) Webster wrote that political harmony depended on a uniformity of language.[4] That uniformity, which would be accomplished through a national system of education and his spelling book, would link self-interest with national interests and create a strong union of the people. Webster's idea of nationalism was related to his concept of the power of the people. He believed that the ultimate power of the people was in the ownership of property. In 1787, discussing the federal Constitution, he wrote: "In what then does real power consist? The answer is short and plain—in property. . . . A general and tolerably equal distribution of landed property is the whole basis of national freedom."[5] A strong union would protect that property, and a strong union depended on the identification of self-interest with national interest.

For Webster, as for most promoters of nationalism, linking individual interest to national interest meant strengthening the government. As he expressed it, "The citizens of this new world should enquire not what will aggrandize this town or this state, but what will augment the power, secure the tranquility, multiply the subjects, and advance the opulence, the dignity, and the virtues of the United States. Self-interest, both in morals and politics, is and ought to be the ruling principle of mankind, but this principle must operate in perfect conformity to social and political obligations."[6]

Linking individual interests to those of the nation meant emotional involvement along with reason. The issue was not simply a matter of citizens understanding their interests in terms of national interests: they must also have an emotional attachment through the power of love. Patriotism is the emotional attachment to, or love, of the nation. Webster believed that "every class of people should know and love the laws." Attachment to the laws "may be formed by early impressions upon the mind."[7]

One result of nationalism and the development of representative government, reflected in the previous quote from Webster, was the politicization of childhood. Children were viewed as future citizens who had to be molded in the interests of the nation. They had to be taught to love the nation and the nation's laws. Their future character had to be shaped to meet the needs of government.

The politicization of childhood placed qualifications on the concept of liberty within the framework of a republican society. People were to have liberty as long as they acted in the "right" manner. One goal of the national educational system was to assure that children were trained to act correctly. Or, as Webster put it, "Education, in a great measure, forms the moral characters of men, and morals are the basis of government. Education should therefore be the first care of a legislature. . . ."[8]

In addition to his work in standardizing the American language, Webster helped form a national consciousness through the creation of a national literature. He wrote a comprehensive history of the Revolutionary War and promoted George Washington as a symbol of Americanism. Webster helped create a national mythology, which was essential to the promotion of patriotism. In young minds, love of country can be formed around a galaxy of national heroes. Webster epitomized the ideology of nationalism with his attempts to wed individual interests and emotions to the nation through language, a national literature, and history. The moral stories in his spelling book would inspire moral and patriotic citizens of a representative government.

Preparing children for future participation as citizens in a nation controlled by popular sovereignity was clearly stated by the French political philosopher Jean-Jacques Rousseau in the eighteenth century. Rousseau, although not a supporter of representative government, believed that the ultimate control of the state should be in the hands of the people. The people were superior to the government, and the government existed to serve the people. The expression of the people's interests was in what Rousseau called the "general will." The education of children would prepare them for participation in the general will. Carried to its logical conclusion, the concept of the general will could become one of the strongest statements of nationalistic fervor.

Rousseau had an important influence on political and educational theory. In 1762 he published his *Social Contract* and his educational treatise *Emile. Emile* became a classic statement of Rousseau's views on education in accordance with the laws of nature. It has had an important influence on child-centered educational movements in the twentieth century.

Rousseau's political and educational thought exemplifies how a concern for popular sovereignty can result in an educational system that submerges the individual's will and interests into the interests of the nation. In a 1755 article on "Political Economy" that foreshadowed his ideas about the general will, Rousseau gave clear statement to the role of pariotism and education in his concept of government by the people. He wrote: "If . . . we train them early in life never to think of their individual interests except in relation to those of the state as a whole, and never to regard their own existence as having any meaning apart from the state, they will come in course of time to identify themselves in some fashion with this grand Whole and be conscious of their membership in their fatherland. . . ."[9]

The politicization of childhood was an important part of melding the identification of individual interests with those of the state. For Rousseau, the child must be trained early for the citizen role: "A man . . . shares in civic rights as soon as he is born, the moment of birth ought to be the beginning of the performance of his duties." Rousseau in fact argued that the education of children was more important to the state than to the parents because parents often die before their children are fully mature. "But sooner or later," Rousseau stated, "the nation feels the effect of it. The state abides, the family passes." Rousseau went on to claim something that has been echoed by writers on education and government to the present: "Public education . . . is therefore one of the fundamental requirements of popular government."[10]

Like Webster and other republican writers, Rousseau gave public education the role of training for obedience to the law and creating a love of the nation. Rousseau compared the love of the nation with the love fostered by a tender mother. This was the emotional attachment to the nation that he wanted developed in the child. If children were to become citizens, they must be "imbued with the Laws of the state and the maxims of the general will" and "surrounded by objects that unceasingly remind them of the tender mother that fosters them . . .

they will learn to cherish each other as brothers and wish only what the community wishes. . . ."[11]

The sublimation of individual interests to collective interests was central to Rousseau's proposals for an educational system in Poland. In 1773 Rousseau gave full expression to his belief in the importance of patriotism and its likeness to motherly love: "A child ought to look upon his fatherland as soon as his eyes open to the light, and should continue to do so till the day of his death. Every patriot sucks in the love of country with his mother's milk. This love is his whole existence."[12]

To develop this love, Rousseau proposed for Poland an educational system that would prepare the child to work for the common good. Rousseau particularly stressed the importance of group activities in developing mutual interests. For example, all games would be group games performed in public "so that there may always be a common end to which they aspire, and by which they are moved to rivalry and emulation."[13]

The naturalistic education proposed by Rousseau in *Emile* does not contradict his emphasis on using education to wed individual interests to group interests. The child Emile is educated in the country and in accordance with what Rousseau believes to be a natural development. At adolescence Emile is introduced into society. Early isolation and a naturalistic education have not neglected the issue of individual versus group interests. Emile learns trades as a means of teaching that which is useful, for he has been taught that society is useful because it makes people interdependent and able to provide aid to one another. At a later age Emile travels and makes a decision about the form of government he wishes to live under.

When Emile returns from his travels, he concludes, "The more I examine the work of men in their institutions, the more I see that in seeking independence they make themselves slaves." To which Emile's tutor responds, "It does matter that you should be where you can fulfill all your duties as a man, and one of these duties is to be loyal to the place of your birth."[14]

Popular sovereignty, nationalism, and a system of education designed to mold the individual in the interests of the state were all part of Rousseau's political philosophy. They were not mutually contradictory because his whole concept of popular sovereignty was bound up in the general will. The general will was an expression of the interests of all people in a society. It expressed the welfare of the whole as opposed to a particular individual interest that might be disadvantageous or harmful to the public good. The general will, or popular sovereignty, was supposed to act for the preservation and benefit of the entire society.

It is easy to understand how the concept of the general will could lead to educational systems that would teach patriotism, obedience to the law, and subordination of individual interests to collective interests. If the government expressed the general will, then obedience to its laws accomplished the greatest good for society. Any desire to break the law would reflect a false understanding of individual interests in terms of the rest of society. According to the theory of the general will, the true interests of the individual lay in conforming to the will of the government as proclaimed in its laws because these laws expressed the general will. The individual also must be trained to see collective interests as more important than individual interests. This is a preparation for citizen participation and the understanding of the general will. In addition, patriotism—love of the people and the nation—emotionally attaches an individual to supporting the general will.

A concept like popular sovereignty, taken to its extreme point, could obviously support a dictatorial government and educational system. Even in societies that claim a high degree of liberty, a tendency exists for school systems to train for obedience and patriotism, using the argument that the government expresses the will of the people; conformity to the law and love of country is in the best interests of the individual and society.

Patriotism as a means of promoting service to the community has continued to be part of the rhetoric of nationalism in the nineteenth and twentieth centuries. During that time, one of the ways of serving the community has been the willingness to fight in the country's military forces. The nineteenth century witnessed the growth of the modern military with its use of the citizen-soldier. One requirement of the modern military was a citizen population with sufficient emotional attachment to the nation to be willing to fight and die for nation and flag.

Johann Fichte, in arguing for compulsory education and support of a national system of education for Prussia, claimed that with mass schooling Prussia would have the greatest army the world had ever seen. Fichte's proposals included not only the teaching of a national history and literature, accompanied by nationalistic ceremonies and songs, but also the use of the community of schoolchildren as a training place for service to the state. Fichte argued that in a system of national education, children would not only gain a knowledge of the law and learn how to obey it by obeying school laws but would also learn to go beyond mere obedience of the law in their service to the state. Children would learn to relinquish their individual interests for the interests of other children. This training in service to the community of children could then be transferred to service to the nation and the military.[15]

Even free-trade and minimal-state economist Adam Smith saw the primary function of a national system of education as preparing the population to support and participate in a national army. Smith, the great English economist of the free marketplace, opposed most government intervention that might disrupt competition and the workings of self-interest in the economy. But when it came to the education of the poor, he was willing to have the government provide partial (not full) support of a national education system. He believed that full support would take away some of the incentive for teachers to do a good job.

Smith's arguments are important and interesting because of his general unwillingness to allow government a monopoly over any institution. His argument regarding schooling was that modern industry required a specialization of the work force that often resulted in the destruction of intellectual and social understanding. (As we shall see in the next chapter, this specialization of labor, and its resulting effect on the intellectual development of the worker, was a major concern of the late nineteenth and early twentieth centuries.) Smith felt that industrial specialization resulted in a lack of understanding of the relationship of individual interests to the interests of the nation. Smith said of the modern worker: "Of the great and extensive interests of his country he is altogether incapable of judging; and unless very particular pains have been taken to render him otherwise, he is equally incapable of defending his country in war." For Smith, the major purpose of national education was to maintain a martial spirit in the people. Inherent in this spirit was the concept of the modern citizen army. Smith claimed that an advantage of a martial spirit was that "where every citizen had the spirit of a soldier, a smaller standing army would surely be requisite."[16]

Patriotism played an important role in the development of the modern military, and national systems of education played an important role in developing nationalism and patriotism. Thus one must conclude that national systems of education helped develop the modern military system. Indeed, most celebrations of patriotism in school systems are permeated with a martial spirit. Patriotic songs and ceremonies are often conducted with martial music and marching. Heroic figures of a nation's history are often associated with war or military achievements. Patriotic oaths often include statements about love and a willingness to defend the nation.

Such patriotism may be compared to a religion. The symbols and ceremonies of patriotism often take on a mystical flavor. In essence, the individual is taught to love abstract concepts of nation and people. It is as if something called "the people" actually exists separate from the individuals who make up the nation. But there is no general will, no popular consent of the people. "The people" is not greater than the sum of the individuals in the nation; nor is there a single will or interest that expresses the will or interests of individuals in the nation. Concepts of the general will and popular consent are mystical and mythical concepts. This is why the primary focus of patriotic exercises must be on flags, symbols, monuments, and music. These are the abstract symbols of abstract entities. Attachment to these symbols is not rational but emotional. A major purpose of modern schooling has been to forge an emotional attachment between the individual and the abstract concepts of the people and the nation.

Nationalism and patriotism have been among the most destructive forces in modern civilization. Fighting to protect flag and nation has resulted in a large-scale loss of human life and untold anguish in the nineteenth and twentieth centuries. World War II was the result of nationalist extremism in Germany and Italy. Germany, it should be remembered, had one of the finest national systems of education in the world; Germany used it to increase the patriotic fervor of Nazism.

Patriotism as an attachment to mythical concepts can further the interests of those who control the government for their own ends. Because the attachment is emotional and symbolic, a person may be willing to die for interests that in reality are not individual interests but the interests of those who control the government. This is what happens to the concept of the general will when it becomes linked to emotional patriotism. People may be told that the government is working in their interests and thus it is necessary for them to give up personal interests for the good of the nation. This is what happened in Germany; and it can happen in any country.

Another often heard argument is that national systems of education build the patriotism and nationalism needed to protect the country against aggression. In discussions of deterrents to warfare it is argued that an aggressor will not attack a united country or that people must be patriotic so that they will be willing to defend themselves. There is no concrete evidence that patriotism is necessary for self-defense. If an individual points a gun at me, I do not need an emotional feeling of patriotism to protect myself. If another country invades my land, I do not need patriotism to fight to protect myself and my property. The only person who requires the emotion of patriotism to fight a war is one for whom the persuasion of reason is not enough. And if people do not see a war as reasonable or in their self-interest, then maybe the war should not be fought. It should be remembered that patriotism and nationalism have killed more people in the last two centuries than they have saved.

Education and the Political Community

It is possible to talk about unity without appealing to patriotism and nationalism. One argument that has recurred through the nineteenth and twentieth centuries is that a political community is needed to maintain representative forms of government. One of the major institutions that has been called on to weld this political community is a national system of education.

A *political community* refers basically to a group of people who share political values. People are kept from destroying one another and society by sharing a consensus of beliefs about how the political system should work. For instance, a basic requirement for the stability of a representative government is an agreement to obey laws legislated by representatives that one might not have supported during the previous election. In other words, one must accept the consequences of a system that allows people to be unrepresented in government if their candidate fails to win an election. Within a politcal community, one accepts and works within the framework of beliefs about how law should be legislated and executed.

In the United States an excellent articulation of the school's role in building the political community was made by Horace Mann, the Father of the Common School, in his 1848 report to the Massachusetts Board of Education. Previous to Mann, many Americans had called for some form of political unity through common teachings in the school. Even President George Washington had proposed to Congress the establishment of a national university that would attract people from all sections of the country and create a common national identity.

Horace Mann's arguments for the creation of a political community reflected his concern with the potential for violence in the representative system. Mann warned Massachusetts of instances "where the voter, not being able to accomplish his purpose by voting, has proceeded to accomplish it by violence. . . ."[17] Mann worried that the introduction of political teachings in the school as a means of eliminating the potential violence of republicanism was turning the schoolhouse into a political battleground where different political doctrines battled for control of the child's mind.

Mann envisioned overcoming the political strife within and outside the schoolhouse by "teaching those articles in the creed of republicanism, which are accepted by all, believed in by all, and which form the common basis of our political faith. . . ."[18] This political faith taught in the schoolhouse would provide the framework that would guide debate within nonviolent parameters of republicanism. Discussing disputes about the meaning of the Constitution and partisan topics, Mann wrote: "No man is qualified, or can be qualified, to discuss the disputable questions, unless previously and thoroughly versed in those questions, about which there is no dispute."[19] A firm grounding in the republican faith would be both qualification and remedy for disputes among republicans.

Several problems arise regarding Mann's construction of a political consensus reached through schooling. First, what precisely are these undisputed political principles that will constitute the political faith of the common school? Who is to decide on this faith? How is it to be decided on? One obvious possibility is that the political creed of one faction in the community may dominate the teachings of the school. That this was a possibility seems to be admitted but not openly stated by Mann. The key to this issue lies in the sometimes slippery rhetoric of Mann's argument.

For example, consider the following questions. If there exists a "creed of republicanism accepted by all," why is it necessary to teach it in the common school? If such a faith exists, why is it necessary to worry about political strife resulting from a lack of consensus? The answer to these questions, an answer implicit in Mann's argument, is that this faith does not exist, but the common school will bring it into existence. This, of course, does not answer the question of whose republican creed will eventually become the political faith of the common school. One can only assume, since Mann believed such a creed existed, that Mann and others with similar political principles would define it.

To suggest the existence of undisputed political doctrines is a political argument in itself. Even a description of the workings of government is open to dispute. Among political scientists and historians there is a wide variety of interpretations and controversies about political systems. To suggest a single creed of republicanism would silence the very disputes that supposedly are the heart of the evolution of government forms.

Mann called for the removal of all controversial political doctrines from the school. "When the teacher, in the course of his lessons or lectures on the fundamental law, arrives at a controverted text, he is . . . to read it without comment or remark. . . ."[20] Essentially, this would teach the student to function as a republican in a ritualistic way and treat most issues in a bland, noncontroversial manner. Mann's school would produce a generation of republicans who avoided political conflict and debate.

Mann's arguments were based on his fears about how individuals would act, given the opportunity to elect their own governors. In calling for the teaching of a republican catechism, Mann was essentially saying that a republican society could function only if people acted the way he thought they should act. Or, stated another way, people could be free as long as they acted in a good manner and endeavored to do right. "Right" and "good" were to be defined by people like Horace Mann.

To say that you cannot have a free society unless the schools' shape the behavior of individuals is essentially to say that you lack belief in a free society. Rather than the government having direct control over individual actions, the school controls future actions by shaping the conscience and character of the individual. Promoters of the common school believed that schools had to shape particular patterns of behavior in order for society to function. Mann wrote: "It may be an easy thing to make a Republic; but it is a very laborious thing to make Republicans; and woe to this Republic that rests upon no better foundations than ignorance, selfishness and passion."[21]

Much like defining the republican creed, defining ignorance, selfishness, and passion cannot be done without a great deal of dispute. Mann calls for the shaping of character around basic moral principles; this would create a moral consensus. But Mann does not explain how and by whom the moral objectives of the school will be defined.

If schools had the educational technique to actually shape behavior, a public system of education whose purpose would be to shape political character and creed could be a more effective engine for dictatorial control than control through the law. The important thing for understanding Mann's argument is the mechanism by which to define the shape of the republican character.

The important issue becomes the political structure of the school, for the political structure of schooling defines its political content. If the school system has as a goal molding republican character, then the definition of that character must be made by those who control the schools.

In any representative government, governance is impossible

without the granting of power to a few individuals. It is always possible that the individuals who operate the government may claim to represent the collective desire or the community interest when in fact their actions reflect the fad of an individual bureaucrat or a tyrannical administrator. Similarly, an educational system that consciously attempts to shape political character may find the nature of that character defined by an official who claims to understand and reflect the values of community. A teacher, school administrator, or elected official in charge of schools may believe that his personal values represent the general values of the community; worse, he may think that his values should be adopted by the community.

Even when the values that guide the molding process of the school reflect the majority of the community, there is still the problem of the suppression of other political values. As John Stuart Mill pointed out in *On Liberty* (1859), people often confuse representative democracy with "self-government" and "the power of the people over themselves." "The people," Mill wrote, "who exercise the power are not always the same people with those over whom it is exercised; and the 'self-government' spoken of is not the government of each by himself, but of each by all the rest."[22] What the will of the people actually meant, Mill argued, was either the will of the majority or the will of the most active part of the population. The distinction between "the majority" and "the most active" is important when you consider that in many representative democracies, only a fraction of the eligible population votes. What often seems to be the will of the majority is in reality the will of the most active.

In either case, the will of the majority or the most active part of the population might oppress and attempt to destroy the political and social values of the rest of the community. As Mill pointed out, it is an error to think that representative government always leads to political liberty. Majority rule can be just as oppressive to some as a system controlled by a single individual or a small group. Even equality before the law is not a guarantee of liberty; it means only that all people are treated equally by the law. The law can be either limited or can exert extensive control.

His concern about control by the will of government administrators, the majority, or the most active led John Stuart Mill to a different conclusion from that reached by Horace Mann. Mill said: "A general State education is a mere contrivance for moulding people to be exactly like one another: and as the mould in which it casts them is that which pleases the predominant power in the government, whether this be a monarch, a priesthood, an aristocracy, or the majority of the existing generation. . . ." For Mill, an educational system run by the government "establishes a despotism over the mind."[23]

Mill believed education to be an important element in maintaining political liberty. His concern was that a national educational system could become an instrument of government oppression. Mill proposed that government make education compulsory by requiring public examinations of children to determine if they could read. It would be the responsibility of the family to have their children instructed. Mill proposed that state aid could be provided to defray educational expenses. If a child failed the public reading examination, the father would be forced to pay a fine and the child forced to attend a private school at the parents' expense.

Mill also proposed public examinations on a wide range of subjects; passing them, an individual would earn a certificate. One of Mill's main provisions was that the state not be allowed to exercise influence over the knowledge required to pass the examination: "The knowledge required for passing an examination (beyond the merely instrumental parts of knowledge, such as languages and their use) should, even in the higher classes of examinations, be confined to facts and positive science exclusively."[24]

The important difference between Mill and Mann was that Horace Mann wanted to mold the republican as a means of controlling the use of liberty, whereas John Stuart Mill wanted to give the republican the tools to use liberty fully. It is possible to argue that Mann would have agreed with Mill's statement that "all attempts by the State to bias the conclusions of its citizens on disputed subjects are evil; but it may very properly offer to ascertain and certify that a person possesses the knowledge requisite to make his conclusions, on any given subject worth attending to."[25] Mann argued that disputed subjects should not be dealt with in the common school, but he assumed that government could define common political principles. Mill would have considered these principles to be the despotism of the state over the mind of the child. Mill would not have removed from education discussion and study of controversial subjects if education was not controlled by the state. For Mill, the choice of education would be in the hands of parents or children.

Another important distinction between Mill and writers like Webster, Rousseau, and Mann is that Mill viewed such concepts as popular sovereignty, the will of the people, and the interest of the community or nation as mere abstractions that in reality reflected the interests of particular groups. To use government-controlled education to promote nationalism or the interest of the people was in reality to use the educational system to promote the interests of specific individuals or groups who claimed to represent the will of the people. If one rejects these concepts, then the major concern about education in a representative system is that all people gain the tools to make political decisions.

The Professional as Representative of the People

The issue of representation of the people has grown more complex in the twentieth century with the expansion of government social services and government involvement in the planning and management of the economy. More and more of the actual governing of nations takes place in countless government bureaus where government experts and professionals orchestrate the vast powers of the modern state. The rise of the administrative state has occurred to varying degrees in most countries of the world whether they call themselves communist or capitalist. Most government bureaucrats are not elected to office but hold lifelong positions based on their claims to expertise.

Some attempt has been made to create the impression that these bureaucrats are selfless individuals who primarily use their expertise for the good of the people. The terms "civil servant" or "public servant" are meant to conjure up images of a person dedicated to the service of others. A claim is often made that government bureaucrats can be more dedicated to the interests of the people because, unlike politicians, they have no obligations to particular political factions and interest groups. This argument is used especially in countries where government hiring has been removed from a political spoils system through the use of civil service examinations. In these situations one often gets a picture of the public-oriented bureaucrat battling the special-interest-oriented politician. If one accepts this picture, then the representative of the people is no longer the politician but the civil servant.

All these arguments have been used to justify the increased power of professional educators, as opposed to elected representatives, over public school systems. Part of the argument for increased control by professional educators is that they represent the interests of the child, whereas elected officials represent special-interest groups whose primary concern is not the child.

One of the characteristics of the modern administrative state is to rely more and more on the expertise of the specialist. When today's politicians draft legislation dealing with public works projects, welfare, defense, and education, they constantly seek the advice of experts in the specific field. After the law's passage, administration of the legislation often depends on the same experts. This situation has resulted in the belief that the proper role of the politician is one of representing broad economic and social policy; hired government officials will give meaning to that policy.

In education the argument is used that professional educators should have major control of the school system because they represent the interests of the child and have special training and knowledge about education. The claim to expertise has resulted from the actual expansion of the field of education. The nineteenth-century study of education, aside from the actual study of subject matter to be taught, was limited to methods and examples of teaching. In the twentieth century the study of education has expanded to include the study of the psychology, sociology, administration, politics, and economics of education. In other words, people can now claim to have expertise in the methods and organization of educational institutions. Armed with this expertise, educators can now say that they have a greater understanding than elected officials about how things should be done in schools.

In the United States these claims were used to justify a decreased role for school boards in the control of schools and an increased role for educational professionals. Beginning in the early part of the twentieth century, the argument was advanced that boards of education should be concerned primarily with broad educational policy; details and specifics of policy should be in the hands of the professional educator. This resulted, as we shall see in a later chapter, in actual shifts of power from elected representatives to professionals. One extreme view of this position was given by the educator Charles Judd in the 1930s. He wanted all boards of education eliminated and control of the schools turned over to professional educators.[26]

Claims of representing the interests of the child and special expertise have been used to justify the expansion of teacher organizations and their increased control of the schools. One important example of this argument was given by George Counts in the 1930s when he said that schools should participate in the restructuring of society.[27] He felt that most school boards represented conservative economic interests and that teachers were a special social class concerned mainly with the interests of children. As a group dedicated to humanity, it was logical that teachers control the schools if schools were to be a means of social change. Counts' involvement with, and leadership of, a teachers' union in the United States reflected his philosophy.

Beliefs that the government bureaucrat represents the interests of the people and the professional educator represents the interest of the child seem as difficult to defend as the view that an elected official can represent the interests of the people. But at least the elected official might be said to represent the majority or the most active part of the population. In the case of the expert or the professional, there is no mechanism like an election to assure control over that representation.

Part of the claim by professional educators that they represent the interests of children is based on their special training. In considering this training one must make a distinction between techniques and ends. Techniques, which are based on the findings of psychology, are methods used to teach the child and shape behavior. Ends, or objectives, define what materials should be taught and what character traits should be developed. Professional educators and government bureaucrats can be trained to become experts in techniques but not in ends.

The objectives defined by experts might be representative of part or all of the population; or they might not. What must be recognized is that when individual educators choose a particular objective toward which to direct their techniques, that objective represents only the choice of those educators. Any community agreement on that objective is purely accidental. It is possible for teachers as a group, through unions or professional organizations, to establish objectives; again, however, those ends represent the views of those organizations and do not necessarily represent the views of other members of the community.

Ideally we could have elected representatives establish objectives and experts use their techniques to accomplish them. In this way the professional educator or government bureaucrat would function as a technocrat who applies techniques to accomplish predetermined goals.

This model, efficient as it may sound, won't work. At this point in time it is not possible to get people to act without involving their personal values and goals. The model of the bureaucrat who would follow orders handed down by elected representatives conjures up the image of a government system run by machine. The experts would function like robots who have been programmed for certain techniques.

The model of the technocratic representative government can be used for self-protection and concealment. A government bureaucrat or professional can claim that he has no power over goals when in fact his judgment directly affects goals. Or he can claim no responsibility for outcomes except in terms of technical details. This can create a situation where real centers of power can hide behind a structure of representative government and make it difficult for members of the public to locate power and bring it under control.

Applied to education, this model allows professional educators to hide their own values behind the official pronouncements of goals. Teachers can translate their values into system goals and choose techniques to accomplish those goals. The general goal stated by elected representatives might be the education of active democratic citizens; teachers might translate this in terms of their values to mean "it is good to be obedient and orderly." The "obedient and orderly" might reflect the teacher's concept of good citizenship, whereas "it is good" might reflect a merger of personal values with technique. The teacher can argue it is good because it is supported by expert knowledge of child development, learning, and classroom management.

The above example is not too far removed from reality. Sociologist Dan C. Lortie found in his study of .the American schoolteacher that although some teachers "stressed the desirability of independence of mind, most allusions to moral outcomes and citizenship emphasized compliance and obedience." Lortie saw most teachers' concepts of good citizenship as directly related to their self-interest in classroom management. Within this framework the ends chosen can be hidden and justified by techniques; they can also reflect the self-interest of the expert. Lortie reported: "Connecting compliance with classroom norms to future citizenship authenticates the teacher's control effect. Thus discipline becomes more than mere forbidding and ordering; the dross of classroom management is transformed into the gold of dependable citizenship."[28]

Conclusions

A major reason for the expansion of the number of experts and professionals in government has been the attempt by government to manage social and economic problems. The degree of this management has varied from the socialism of the Soviet Union and China to the welfare state of the United States and England. This has resulted, as we shall see in the next chapter, in a concern about schools developing political and economic citizenship.

There has never been a resolution of the problem of what political values should be taught in schools. The issue of representation has been complicated not only by the claim of bureaucrats and professionals that they represent the interests of the people but also by the claims of fascism and communism. The Communist party developed by Lenin was to be the vanguard of the proletariat and represent the interests of the people because of its ownership and control of the means of production. In socialist countries the claim to representation of the people is based on economic ownership. Hitler and Mussolini stated that they expressed the will of the people in their expressions of nationalism. They represent the extreme point of the nationalism that emerged in the nineteenth century. In the welfare states of other industrial countries, representation is still claimed by the actions of the majority or the most active part of the voting population.

In all three forms of government—fascist, communist, and welfare—bureaucratic and professional power and representation have competed with the claims of the different political parties. In all cases, national systems of schooling have continued to be used as a means of shaping the individual in the interests of national policy. The major difference between the nineteenth and twentieth centuries is that today citizenship has been expanded to include economic rights as well as political rights.

Consequently, tension has developed between the demands of individuals to use education to expand their economic benefits and the demands of government to use education to control the economic system. This is similar to the nineteenth-century conflict between the individual's desire for knowledge as political power and the government's use of education to control political power. These conflicts will not end until the individual has direct control over the government, as opposed to representative control through elected officials, bureaucrats, party leaders, and those claiming to represent popular sovereignty.

In the twentieth century the issue of individual interest in education as an instrument of power versus the interest of government in education as an instrument of policy seems to have been lost in the growth of an almost religious faith in education. Faith in education often obscures the fact that education is not a good in and of itself. The value of an education to the individual depends on the educational content. Merely to embrace schooling without considering its content or purpose can make a person a victim of economic and political control. Public systems of schooling linked with nationalism, popular sovereignty, a community of interest, and building a political community have been used to gain political and economic power by politicians and government officials who claimed to represent the interests of the people. The expansion of the use of the school as an instrument of economic control has made these issues even more acute.

2

POLITICAL
THEORIES OF EDUCATION:
THE ECONOMIC STATE

THE MOST CHARACTERISTIC FEATURE OF EDUCATIONAL POLICY IN the twentieth century has been the concern about social consciousness—the individual's relationship to the group and participation in the economic system. In 1897, just before the opening of the new century and his rise to prominence as America's best-known educational philosopher, John Dewey wrote: "I believe that education is a regulation of the process of coming to share in the social consciousness; and that the adjustment of individual activity on the basis of this social consciousness is the only sure method of social reconstruction."[1] In the 1930s the most popular educational thinker in the Soviet Union, Anton Makarenko, echoed Dewey's opinion when he wrote: "The profound meaning of educational work . . . consists in the selection and training of human needs. . . . A morally justified need is, in fact, the need of a collectivist, that is, a person linked with his collective by his sense of the common aim, of the common struggle, by the living and certain awareness of his duty toward society."[2] And in the East, at a kindergarten in the People's Republic of China in the 1970s, visitors were greeted by a sign over the bulletin board that reflected the major socialization goal of the school: *Serve the People.*[3]

These educational goals were stated in dissimilar economic systems, but they all originated from a similar concern about the effect on the individual of modern industrial life and inequalities in the distribution of the economic benefits of industrialism. The nineteenth century saw an almost universal concern that the modern industrial system was alienating the individual from the community and fragmenting his experience of reality. The blame for these conditions was placed on the specialization caused by the factory system, which reduced human action to machinelike repetitive tasks in which the individual never produced a whole finished product. Because of this system, it was felt, the individual was unable to relate his work to the functioning of the rest of the world. Isolated in the specialization of the factory, the alienated individual lost a sense of common aims and the interrelatedness of society. For many in the twentieth century, the aim of the school was to restore this lost sense of community.

Concern about the inequalities in the distribution of the economic benefits of industrialism resulted in the rise of the welfare state in capitalist countries where the school came to be viewed as an instrument for providing equality of opportunity. In these settings the school was to encourage the redistribution of wealth by giving rich and poor a similar chance in the school so that they could compete on equal terms in the economic system. It was hoped that the school would become a major means for promoting social mobility.

In socialist countries, where there was common ownership of the means of production, emphasis was placed on providing equality of opportunity within the framework of a socialist economy. In this situation the school was to give everyone an equal opportunity to work for the good of the entire society and not for personal economic gain. The concern was not with equality of opportunity as a means of social mobility but with equal opportunity as a means of enhancing the benefits of collective ownership.

These new roles of the school in society reflected a general shift from the nineteenth-century concern with the distribution of political control. In the nineteenth century some people wanted to use the school to control the political power of individuals through political teachings and nationalism, whereas others wanted to use the schools to gain knowledge and skills that would enhance their political control. In the twentieth century some people wanted to use the schools to increase their economic control, whereas others wanted to increase their economic benefits.

This meant that many issues regarding education and the *political* system were translated into education and the *economic* system. For instance, concern about teaching the individual a sense of the interrelatedness of society, a feeling of community, and common aims raises the same questions that surrounded the teaching of patriotism and nationalism. If these things have to be taught or formed in the school, then they do not result from the free interaction of society. Some person or some group must define the common aims and describe the interrelatedness of society so that these ideas can be developed in the school. Who is to make these decisions? The problem arises because they may be defined in terms of the self-interest of the definers.

The Chinese kindergarten maxim Serve the People is a form of economic patriotism that is very much like political patriotism. It assumes that because there is collective ownership of the means of production, the system works for the benefit of all the people. To serve the people means to work for the benefit of the economic system. But collective ownership does not necessarily mean equal or just benefits. To assume that state ownership results in equality of economic benefits is much like Rousseau's argument that the general will represents the best interests of all people. Collective ownership works only if mechanisms exist by which the individual can exert direct control over the production and distribution of the economic system. One problem in socialist countries is that the ideology of service, community, and interrelatedness can obscure the necessity for individual control of the economic system. A bureaucratic system in a socialist country can run an economic system for the benefit of the bureaucracy and at the same time convince the people that they must and should cooperate through a system of schooling that preaches social service and community and presents the goals of the bureaucracy as the common aims of society. The economic and social goals of schools can pose a great threat to control by individuals of collectively owned systems of production.

In the same manner, the school under welfare capitalism can be used to build allegiance to an economic system that does not function in the interests of the individual or allow for individual control over the system. In addition, the argument that the school is providing equality of opportunity can obscure the fact that economic benefits are not being redistributed.

Education and the Effects of Industrialism

One of the first statements of concern about the effects of industrialism on the individual and the role of education in remedying those effects was made by economist Adam Smith in his *Inquiry into the Nature and Causes of the Wealth of Nations* (1776). Smith outlined the major discussion about the effects of industrialism that would persist into the twentieth century. Unlike many of his successors, Smith was a leading advocate of laissez-faire economics and considered the best economic system to be one based on private ownership without government interference. Distribution of goods and economic growth were to result from individuals acting in their own self-interest and competing in a free market.

As mentioned in chapter 1, Smith argued that the education of the worker was necessary to help relate individual interests to the interests of the nation. His specific concern was that "in the progress of the division of labor, far greater part of those who live by labour . . . comes to be confined to a few very simply operations, frequently to one or two." Smith described the results of factory specialization in terms that would be echoed throughout the history of industrialism. Smith warned that modern industrial specialization would make the worker "as stupid and ignorant as it is possible for a human creature to become. The torpor of his mind renders him, not only incapable of relishing or bearing a part in any rational conversation, but of conceiving any generous, noble, or tender sentiment. . . ."[4]

Smith's solution to the effects of industrialism did not involve any major intervention by government or change in the organization of the factory system. His proposal that education could overcome the effects of industrial specialization essentially shifted the argument from the cause of the problem, factory specialization, to another institution, the school. A continuing dilemma for education has been the tendency to use it to solve problems existing in other parts of society because this avoids any real confrontation with the root cause of the problem. This would obviously be Smith's solution because he objected to government involvement in the natural development of the economic system. Government involvement instead would go to partial support of an educational system that would help overcome the evil effects of industrialism.

Karl Marx provided a much more elaborate evaluation of the effects of industrialism in the nineteenth century. Marx's proposals for correcting the evils of the factory system included not only changing the ownership of the means of production but also educational proposals that would influence the development of educational systems in socialist countries in the twentieth century.

Marx was concerned with both the intellectually destructive factors resulting from the factory system and the loss of a sense of self in relationship to the community. Marx believed that in the modern factory the worker became a part of the machinery and a mere appendage to the production process. In 1867 he wrote in *Capital:* "In handcrafts and manufacture, the workman makes use of a tool, in the factory, the machine makes use of him."[5] For Marx, the problem was twofold: specialization and the integration of the worker into the machine process. Both contributed to the deadening of intellectual abilities and the separation of thought from action. The worker provided the action; the intellectual content and planning came from the managers of the factory system. Or, as Marx stated: "The separation of the intellectual powers of production from the manual labour, and the conversion of these powers into the might of capital over labour, is, as we have already shown, finally completed by modern industry erected on the foundation of machinery."[6]

Dealing with the problem of the separation of thought from action has become a major ingredient in socialist plans for education in the twentieth century. There are several levels of concern. First is the argument, advanced by Marx, that the concentration of intellectual activity in the hands of factory owners and the reduction of the worker's role to that of an automation is a means of controlling and in a sense owning the mind of the worker. In a broader context Marx would state this in terms of the social-class division of society. The ruling class develops a set of ideas, an ideology, that justifies its position of control in society.

Another result of the separation of thought from action was the creation within the ruling class of a belief that pure thought could exist separate from practice. Or, put another way, the division between manual and mental labor resulted in a division between ideas and practice. Marx believed that all ideas had a social and historical origin. To act as if ideas had a life of their own was to avoid looking at the social and historical conditions supporting those ideas. This allowed the ruling class to present to the masses ideas like the sanctity of private ownership and the right to property, which justified their position as the ruling class.

Marx's argument was to have a tremendous impact on future socialist educators, who wished to make sure that future socialist leaders maintained an understanding of the relationship between thought and practice. This concern permeated and often dominated socialist educational systems. The concern was not only about the ideas of a ruling class but also about the destructive effect on workers of the separation of thought from action.

Separating thought from action was one reason why workers experienced alienation in modern industrial life. The worker was separated from both the thought that went into planning the object of production and the total product. Because Marx believed that ideas and consciousness were a product of practice and social conditions, he believed that what a worker made contributed to his understanding of self. That is, a person finds out about himself by looking at, and considering, something he has made. The way the individual and others react to a product of labor tells the individual something about himself and contributes to the development of consciousness. Work has meaning to a worker when it reflects his being and is not taken away from him. Marx felt that in the modern factory system work had no meaning for the worker because thought was separate from action and because the capitalist system of ownership took the product away from the worker. The modern worker worked for money and not for the satisfaction of work.

Marx wrote in answer to the question of what constituted the alienation of labor: "First, that the work is external to the worker, that it is not part of his nature; and that consequently, he does not fulfill himself in his work but denies himself, has a feeling of misery rather than well being, does not develop freely his mental and physical energies but is physically exhausted and mentally debased."[7] Marx also believed that the alienation of labor contributed to the destruction of a sense of community, a sense of relationship to others. For it was in the use of the product of one's labor that one related to other people.

Marx referred to the relationship between self and society as one's "species life." Individuals formed a species life by contributing to the building of society. The method of contribution was work. An individual who was alienated from work was alienated from the rest of society. As Marx stated: "The object of labor is, therefore, the objectification of man's species life; for he no longer reproduces himself merely intellectually, as in consciousness, but actively and in a real sense, he sees his own reflection in a world which he has constructed." Alienated labor "takes away his species life, his real objectivity as a species-being. . . ."[8] Marx summed up the issue of alienation thusly: "A direct consequence of the alienation of man from the product of his labor, from his life activity and from his species life is that man is alienated from other men."[9]

Marx's solution to the problems of alienation and other destructive features of the factory system did not hinge on any plan for a system of schooling. He saw the solution in terms of changing the ownership of the means of production from individual capitalists to collectives. Consequently, Marx did not write a great deal about what he envisioned as an ideal system of education. Nevertheless, the few words he did devote to education have provided a central focus for educational debates in socialist countries, particularly the Soviet Union.

In a brief reference to education in *Capital,* Marx wrote what came to be known as the great principle of polytechnical education. Marx argued that one of the crippling effects of specialization was the inability of the worker to adapt to changes in technology after lifelong repetition of a task. Modern industry required, Marx claimed, the replacement of the specialized worker with "the fully developed individual, fit for a variety of labours, ready to face any change of production, and to whom the different social functions he performs, are but so many modes of giving free scope to his own natural and acquired powers."[10] Marx went on to praise the development of technical schools, which combined the study of technology with the practical handling of the implements of work. Referring to the English Factory Act, Marx stated that though it "is limited to combining elementary education with work in the factory, there can be no doubt that when the working class comes into power, as inevitably it must, technical instruction, both theoretical and practical, will take its proper place in the working-class schools."[11]

These rather brief passages would provide the framework for later discussion about the meaning of a socialist education. Although they did not contain any details for the organization of schools or a school curriculum, they did suggest a means of overcoming the problem of the separation of thought from action and the use of education as one facet of ending alienation. Actual work and practice had somehow to be combined with the learning of theory. The student had to be taken into the factory or workplace, or the workplace had partly to be taken into the school. How to accomplish this became a major problem for socialist education.

In the United States, John Dewey expressed concerns similar to those of Marx about the effects of industrialism on the individual. Like Adam Smith, Dewey saw education as having a central role in overcoming the fragmentation of experience and alienation suffered by the worker. Unlike Smith, however, Dewey rejected the idea that self-interest and competition were the best means for operating an economic system. Dewey felt that self-interest and competition fostered economic individualism, which contributed to the alienation of members of society from one another. Rather than competition, Dewey wanted to create a sense of interdependence and community that would result in the cooperative functioning of society. For Dewey, the school was the key to controlling the social consciousness of individuals and achieving an end to alienation and a restoration of the sense of community in American life.

Dewey shared many philosophical premises with Marx but rejected a social analysis based on social class and worker seizure of the means of production. Dewey believed that ideas and institutions were products of particular historical periods and social conditions. To lose sight of the conditions that produced the idea or institution often resulted in the inability to understand that ideas and institutions should change as social conditions change. Ideas and institutions come to be accepted as fixed and eternal parts of history unless one understands that their genesis and growth are dependent on particular social conditions.

The goals of the school, in Dewey's argument, included change in the organization of the institution to meet the needs of changing social conditions and prepare the individual to participate in the continual reconstruction of society. This meant that Dewey's goals for education included an interrelated plan for adapting the school to modern industrial society and training the student to understand the relationship between theory and practice, between history and ideas.

One of Dewey's clearest statements of his idea of the modern school was given as a lecture in 1899 to a group of citizens concerned about activities in Dewey's school. "How many," Dewey told his audience, "of the employed are today mere appendages to the machines which they operated!" Dewey argued that this condition could be a product of the machine and the stress on production, but he added: "It is certainly due in large part to the fact that the worker has had no opportunity to develop his imagination and his sympathetic insight as to the social and scientific values found in his work."[12] For Dewey, the solution was to give workers an understanding of the relationship between their work and the rest of society. Dewey wrote in his most famous book, *Democracy and Education* (1915): "More fundamental is the fact that the great majority of workers have no insight into the social aims of their pursuits and no direct personal interest in them. The results actually achieved are not the ends of their actions, but only of their employers." Dewey went on to express what was becoming a universal concern, that modern industrial organization was destroying all meaning in the work performed by the laborer. Dewey stated: "They do what they do, not freely and intelligently, but for the sake of the wage earned."[13]

The school was to solve this problem by introducing the individual through active work to the history and occupations of society. In addition, the school was to become a miniature community where students through cooperative activity would gain a sense of the interdependence of society. Dewey explained in 1899: "To do this means to make each one of our schools an embryonic community life, active with types of occupations that reflect the life of the larger society, and permeated with the spirit of art, history, and science." Dewey concluded his discussion of the adaptation of the school to modern society with this claim: "When the school introduces and trains each child of society into membership within such a little community . . . providing him with the instruments of effective self-direction, we shall have the deepest and best guarantee of a larger society which is worthy, lovely, and harmonious."[14]

In more concrete terms, the Dewey school attempted to achieve its ends by promoting an education that involved cooperative, active investigation of real-life situations. This could mean anything from cooking to running a play store in the school. Working together, students were to gain a sense of their common purpose and create a community within the school. By studying real-life situations the individual was to learn the interdependence of society. For instance, an investigation of the delivery of milk could lead students to study farming, dairy production, and marketing, as well as all institutions and individuals related to those occupations. In addition, the study of milk could include the study of chemistry, measurement, nutrition, and biology, which are all related to the production or consumption of milk. In this way the student was to see that all knowledge was related to concrete social situations and had its genesis in problems arising from those situations. An education of this kind was to end the separation of thought from action.

For Dewey, concern about the separation between thought and action was a pedagogical issue and a problem related to social reconstruction. As a pedagogical issue, Dewey believed that children learn best when their experiences are related in an active way to what is to be learned. An organized and established curriculum, according to Dewey, was a product of an adult understanding of knowledge. When subjects were taught to the child in a formal and organized manner, it was difficult for the child to understand the principles and purposes of the knowledge. Dewey wanted to create situations where children could actively investigate something they knew about and were interested in studying. Children's own interests were to provide the starting point for education.

By linking knowledge to active social situations, Dewey hoped to teach that all knowledge and institutions developed from real social situations at some point in history. Of children, Dewey stated: "We must be able to carry them back into a social past and see them as the inheritance of previous race activities."[15] It was from this linking of knowledge to history that children were to be prepared to reconstruct society as social conditions changed.

Dewey believed that modern industrial society could end the problems of alienation and stagnation by producing in schools individuals who would understand their work in relation to the work of others, who would have a sense of community and a desire to work for the good of the society, and who would be freed from the shackles of intellectual tradition to experiment with new social forms.

As Karl Marx can be considered the intellectual architect of modern socialism, so John Dewey can be considered the intellectual architect of the modern welfare state. This does not mean that either one of them worked out details of their future economic state. For Marx, it was to be organized around the collective ownership of the means of production. For Dewey, it was to be a cooperative endeavor involving the scientific application of knowledge through government for the solution of social problems. Government was to become positively involved in assuring the welfare of all its members. Society, under government, was to be in the continual process of reconstruction.

This conception of the welfare state resulted in a shift from concern about democracy as a means of increasing individual political control to concern about a society where all members are interested in the welfare of one another. Dewey wrote in *Democracy and Education:* "A democracy is more than a form of government; it is primarily a mode of associated living, of conjoint communicated experience." Dewey went on to argue that democracy allowed the freedom for greater contacts between individuals "who participate in an interest so that each has to refer his own action to that of others. . . ." This Dewey claimed was "equivalent to the breaking down of those barriers of class, race, and national territory which kept men from perceiving the full import of their activity."[16]

What has happened in the twentieth century, and I am not claiming a causal relationship with Dewey, has been an increased demand on government to solve social problems. This has resulted in the rise to power in the welfare state of social scientists with the claimed expertise to solve those problems. As discussed in chapter 1, as the power of the expert and bureaucrat in government increases, the political power of the citizen decreases. The one major flaw in Dewey's thinking may have been that as the individual gains a sense of community and interdependence and participates in the scientific management of society, that individual increasingly gives up political power over the emerging welfare state.

Attempting to Cure the Alienation of the Modern Worker

It is one thing to talk about the fragmentation of experience and the alienation of the worker and another thing to attempt to solve the problem through a system of education. The history of the welfare state and the socialist state in the twentieth century has involved both the failure and the abandonment of attempts to use schooling to solve these problems. In recent times, China and Cuba have launched major attempts to overcome the separation of thought from action and end the alienation of the worker from society and work. The success of these experiments is still to be determined. All we know at this point is that achieving those goals is difficult.

One possible explanation for the difficulty in solving these problems may be that, in reality, the problems do not exist. For all of Marx's and Dewey's claims to being scientific, there was no proof that the modern worker's problems were rooted in a separation of thought from action and the lack of a sense of relationship between specialized labor and the total functioning of society. It would seem correct to say that industrial work can be hard, boring, exploitative, and specialized. This has resulted in the worker gaining more satisfaction out of a paycheck than out of the job and, possibly, has produced a dulling of intellectual life.

It would seem that these are concrete problems that do not require explanations in terms of alienation and the lack of a sense of interdependence. As concrete problems they are rooted in the nature of the industrial system. To solve these problems we must change the organization of factory work so that it is not boring and intellectually deadening. If this is a goal, then the factory system must be organized so that everyone likes his work. Whether or not this is possible is another issue.

In the context of this argument it would seem to be beside the point to argue for a polytechnical education, or to turn the school into a community, if the organization and nature of work remained unchanged. Alienation and a lack of community become no more than useful concepts to justify certain educational practices; they have no meaning in terms of the life of the modern industrial organization. It seems absurd to think of Dewey talking about turning the school into a miniature community to solve those problems inherent in the nature of industrial work. It is hard to imagine any significant difference in the effect of work on a laborer who went to a Dewey-style school and one who did not as they stood shoulder to shoulder in an automobile factory attaching fenders to cars that rolled down the assembly line eight hours a day. Maybe Dewey envisioned the worker who attended his kind of school as whistling and cheerfully performing the repetitive task because the worker felt in harmony with the rest of society and could relate the performance of the task with the interdependence of society. Yet it is hard to imagine this vision finding support in reality.

The same problem exists in Marx's proposal for collective ownership of the means of production and polytechnical education. Collective ownership of the means of production does not directly change the nature of work. To suggest that ownership will end the boring nature of work and its meaninglessness is to miss the point. True, worker ownership might result in greater worker control, which in turn might change the nature and organization of jobs. The counterpart to Dewey's whistling and harmonious worker is the Soviet Union's hero of socialist labor who cheerfully exceeds production quotas because the work is good for the collective.

Another difficulty in attempting to use education to end the effects of industrial organization on the worker has been the pressure for technological development in both socialist and welfare states. A primary need of technology is trained, specialized manpower. As we shall see in the next chapter, the manpower model of education dominates most systems of education in the world. In this model the function of education is to train workers for specific jobs in the economy based on the needs of industry. There is to be a direct link between the schools and the manpower needs of society. The pressure for manpower specialization works against most attempts to end alienation through education.

All these problems can be seen in the evolution of education in the Soviet Union following the revolution of 1917. The period up to the 1930s has often been considered the era of experimentation in the Soviet Union; it eventually gave way to the needs of industrial development. The Soviet Constitution of 1917 called for "free, compulsory general and polytechnical (familiarizing in theory and practice with the main branches of production) education for all children of both sexes up to 16 years of age; close linking of instruction with children's socially productive labor."[17] The institutional mechanism for the introduction of polytechnical education was to be the unified labor school, which would provide a five-year course of study for those between eight and thirteen years of age and a four-year course of study for those aged thirteen to seventeen.

The unified labor school was to combine a general education with active involvement in the study and performance of occupations. It is not surprising that during this period John Dewey had a major influence on the development of Soviet education. The Statute on Unified Labor School described the first stage of teaching as resting "on processes of a more or less handicraft nature, suitable to the weak strength of the children and to their natural bents at that age." In the second stage, modern industrial and agricultural labor was to be studied. All this was to be integrated into a wide range of activities and studies from photography to sculpturing and languages to chemistry. All this was to end the separation of theory from practice and thought from action.[18]

The unified labor school underwent reorganization in the 1920s that produced a primary school of four years and a seven-year and a nine-year secondary school. Each concentration in the school system was related to a particular stage of occupational development. In addition, seven-year factory workshop schools were directly connected to a factory or agricultural collective. This served a dual purpose: to assure that students could participate in productive labor and to train skilled workers rapidly. The factory school was justified in terms of polytechnical education.

In 1931, just before the major rejection of the educational experiments of the 1920s, the Council of the Peoples Commissars of the RSFSR defined polytechnical education as "(a) the combination of education with productive labor; (b) the acquaintance in theory and in practice with the fundamental forms of social production; [and] (c) the scientific knowledge of the fundamental productive processes."[19]

The year 1931 also saw the rise to power of Stalin. Major criticism began of the existing polytechnical school. Newspapers in the Soviet Union argued that relating education to work had resulted in a subordination of general education to the requirements of production. The government charged that the schools were not providing sufficient knowledge in general education to prepare students for higher education and technical training.[20] By the late 1930s, polytechnical education had been almost completely abandoned; it was replaced by a system that put heavy emphasis on academic study. In 1937 the teaching of labor as an independent subject was abolished in all elementary and secondary schools; all school workshops were closed and converted into scientific laboratories; and it was decreed that "all hours freed from teaching of labor to be given to the teaching of the Russian language, literature, mathematics and the Constitution of the U.S.S.R."[21] Polytechnical education raised its head again in the 1950s when Khrushchev instituted ill-fated educational reforms designed to reduce the elitism developing in the Soviet Union.[22]

Essentially the Soviet Union abandoned polytechnical education as a method of ending worker alienation. Of course, collective ownership was to eliminate the alienation of the worker from the product of labor and from fellow workers. In addition, in the 1930s a doctrine of enforced collectivism developed to replace polytechnicalism as a means of creating a sense of interdependence and desire to work for the good of all.

Enforced collectivism was engineered by the famous Soviet educator Anton Makarenko, who is often referred to as the Benjamin Spock of the Soviet Union because of the wide distribution of his book on child rearing, *The Collective Family: A Handbook for Russian Parents*.[23] Makarenko rose to prominence in the 1930s after a period of rejection and criticism of his educational methods a decade earlier. The acceptance of his work reflected the general Soviet rejection of polytechnical education as a means of creating a collective society.

During the 1920s Makarenko organized communities for orphaned and delinquent children. Following World War I, the Soviet Union faced major problems from roving gangs of homeless children left in the wake of the war's destruction. In organizing these communities Makarenko rejected most of the then popular educational reforms in the Soviet Union and thus was looked on with suspicion by fellow educators. With the abandonment of those reforms in the 1930s, the Soviet Union was prepared to accept Makarenko's brand of collectivism.[24]

The most important goal of a socialist education, Makarenko believed, was making the individual part of the collective; the individual was to learn to subordinate his self-interests for the good of the group. Authority was to be lodged in the collective or group. In other words, one's sense of interdependence and relationship to others was to be consciously molded rather than developed through the group activity as proposed by Dewey. In Makarenko's scheme, the concern about alienation was reduced to forcing an individual not to be alienated by subordinating his will to the pressure of the collective.

It is important to understand that Makarenko developed his philosophy while dealing with communities of homeless and delinquent children. In this situation he was forced to develop some means of discipline and control over the group. As part of his method he instituted a military-type organization with uniforms and brigades. The organization permeated the life of the community with bugle calls, salutes, a system of ranks, and industrial shops organized along military lines. The enemy in this military atmosphere became things like underproduction and poor maintenance of the colony. The military commune reflected Makarenko's concept of the collective. Everyone had an assigned place to work for the good of the total organization, and allegiance to the group was a combination of military discipline and the fighting and nationalistic spirit represented by the modern army. Makarenko took a philosophy of education developed in the context of a disadvantaged youth collective and taught it as a universal doctrine.

Makarenko rejected notions of self-discipline and self-organization because he felt they were part of the educational experiments of the 1920s that were products of pure consciousness and not of concrete circumstances. Self-discipline and self-organization belonged to Dewey's style of education in which the individual followed self-interest in learning and worked in groups where there was shared interest. It was this style of group organization and training for collective life that Makarenko rejected. In his most famous book, *The Road to Life*, referring to educational theorists of the 1920s, Makarenko said that they "went even further, deciding that 'conscious discipline' is no good when it is the result of adult influence. This, they maintained, is not conscious discipline, but mere drill. . . ." He went on to state that "they reasoned that any form of organization for children is unnecessary and harmful, excepting 'self-organization,' which is essential."[25]

These concepts, he argued, were without concrete proof and had no meaning because a socialist society knows the kind of individual it wants to produce from the educational system. He wrote: "We all know perfectly well, I reasoned, what sort of human being we should aim at turning out. Every class-conscious worker knows this too. Every Party member knows it well."[26] The problem, Makarenko stated, was not what was to be done but how to do it. In other words, conscious discipline was needed to mold the individual into the ideal socialist.

Makarenko cast the problem in the framework of industrial methods. Makarenko revealed that "the longer I thought about it, the more analogies I discovered between educational processes and ordinary industrial processes. . . ." He went on to state, in a passage that reflects a major shift from self-organized interdependence and community to disciplined collectivism: "At any rate it was clear to me that many details of human personality and behaviour could be made from dies, simply stamped out en masse, although of course the dies themselves had to be of the finest description, demanding scrupulous care and precision."[27]

The conscious disciplining of collective existence was the hallmark of Makarenko's thinking. In his popular handbook for parents he made the distinction between children treated as flowers and children treated as fruit trees. Those treated as flowers were admired and allowed to bloom in any manner. Those treated as fruit trees required that one "dig, water, get rid of the caterpillars, prune out the dead branches." He reminded his readers of Stalin's words: "People should be reared with care and attention as a gardener rears his chosen fruit tree." Makarenko told parents that the family must function as a collective unit preparing the child to participate in the greater collective of society: "The decisive factor in successful family upbringing lies in the constant, active, and conscious fulfullment by parents of their civic duty toward Soviet society."[28]

The disciplined collectivism of Makarenko was much like the education for nationalism discussed in chapter 1. The difference is that in one situation the person is educated to place the good of the nation above self, whereas in the other he is educated to put the good of society above self. It could be argued in the case of the Soviet Union that this is logical because, with collective ownership of production, the society does not represent the interests of any particular group of owners but of all people. The major problem with this argument is that even with common ownership, some one or some group must manage the economy. The danger exists that those who manage the economy can use collective discipline as a means of getting the people to act in the managers' interest and not in their self-interest.

The most intensive attempt to overcome the separation of thought from action, eliminate alienation, and create a collective society through education has taken place in the People's Republic of China in the last thirty years. After the triumph of the Chinese Communists in 1949, a major effort was launched to create an educational system that would have a central role in uniting the people. The ideological direction for this educational system was provided by Mao Tse-tung.

Mao accepted the Marxist position that ideas and institutions originated from material conditions and had to be understood in the context of those conditions. The ideas that were to guide communism had to emerge from social practice in relationship to the economic organization of society and the struggle of the people to overcome the social class of the owners of production. In other words, the ideas that were to be accepted and guide action must be products of the conditions that would make communism possible. Mao wrote: "Where do correct ideas come from? Do they drop from the skies? No. Are they innate in the mind? No. They come from social practice and from it alone; they come from three kinds of social practice, the struggle for production, the class struggle, and scientific experiment."[29]

The attempt to ensure the link between ideas and social practice in China meant the introduction of workshops in schools and the involvement of students in agricultural and industrial production. This aspect of Chinese education is not that much different from the polytechnical education in the early days of the Soviet Union and the group work advocated by John Dewey. What is different is the extreme concern with assuring that learning does not produce an intellectual class separate from the masses. Marx argued that the ability of the owner class to dominate the worker was in part based on that class's having a monopoly on knowledge and learning. Thus, separation of thought from action was not only a problem related to ideas originating from social practice but of class struggle.

The Chinese have attempted to overcome this problem by requiring intellectuals and university students to spend part of their time working in factories or agricultural communes. In addition, the Chinese instituted a policy in the 1960s by which university admissions depended on selection by the workers. This policy was started during the Cultural Revolution when it was felt that China was being sidetracked from its purpose of creating a revolutionary society and instead was creating a bureaucratic and intellectual ruling class. To counter this situation a unified nine-year primary and secondary school was instituted, which was to be followed by a two-year work moratorium before a student could apply for higher education.[30] Mao stated in 1968: "We must still run physics and engineering colleges, but the period of schooling ought to be shortened, the education revolutionized. . . . Students must be selected from workers and peasants with practical experience, and after their study at school for several years they should return to practical production."[31]

"Red and expert" best describes the social goals of Chinese education and the effort to create social unity. Individualism, the "expert" part of the term, means the specialized or individual contribution a person can make for the good of all people. In other words, individualism is not conceived as a pursuit of self-interest or economic gain, or as something apart from the total social organization. To be an expert is to do what one does best for the good of other people. Alienation is overcome by being able to see the direct contribution of individual social actions to the well-being of other people. To be "red" is to be selfless and serve others.

The major educational problem is linking the expert to social service. The creation of a sense of service, or being "red," begins in the early years of schooling and continues through the school system; it provides some justification for having intellectuals participate in work. Preschoolers begin to learn to serve the people through school plays, musicals, and games. A recent visitor to China has described how in games, the competitive spirit between teams has been changed from a desire to win to an emphasis on friendship. The role of the winner in any contest is to help the loser improve. Service and helpfulness permeate the social values stressed in the school.[32]

One method used to persuade and mold the person to think in terms of the good of all people is criticism and self-criticism. Throughout the school system, and throughout Chinese society, a constant process of criticism goes on within a group about the individual's relationship and service to the people. In school this involves students criticizing other students and the teacher; the teacher undergoes self-criticism and criticizes students. Mao believed that the process of criticism was essential for the progress of communism. He argued: "The mistakes of the past must be exposed without sparing anyone's sensibilities; it is necessary to analyze and criticize what was bad in the past with a scientific attitude so that work in the future will be done more carefully and done better."[33] Self-criticism before the group was necessary for the improvement of the individual. The individual was to receive the help of the group in solving problems. For this to be possible, the group had to know the nature of the problem. Mao likened this to a patient telling a doctor about medical problems so that the doctor could begin treatment. Mao wrote: "So long as a person who has made mistakes does not hide his sickness for fear of treatment or persist in his mistakes until he is beyond cure, so long as he honestly and sincerely wishes to be cured and to mend his ways, we should welcome him and cure his sickness so that he can become a good comrade."[34]

Group criticism and moralizing through group activities and lessons have made attempts to create unity in Chinese society somewhat different from those of John Dewey and the disciplined collectivism of Makarenko. Dewey saw unity emerging from a participation in the community and not from criticism of the group or from games and plays designed to inculcate social service. Makarenko's disciplined collectivism is much more rigid and imposing in its drive to create the collective.

The Chinese concern about unity and service approaches a religion. For unity is to grow out of dedication to the good of all, which means the sacrifice of self for others. Mao wrote: "Our point of departure is to serve the people whole-heartedly and never for a moment divorce ourselves from the masses, to proceed in all cases from the interests of the people and not from one's self-interest or from the interest of a small group. . . ."[35]

The religious overtones of this concept of service were best expressed when Mao discussed service in relationship to death: "All men must die, but death can vary in its significance. The ancient

Chinese writer Szuma Chien said, 'Though death befalls all men alike, it may be weightier than Mount Tai or lighter than a feather.' To die for the people is weightier than Mount Tai, but to work for the fascists and die for the exploiters and oppressors is lighter than a feather."[36]

In 1975 the Chinese educational system began to receive heavy internal criticism for its attempts to end the separation of thought from action and assure that intellectual training was continually linked to the social processes of the masses. The major reason for this criticism was precisely that which had occurred in the Soviet Union. A desire for economic growth resulted in a greater demand for trained, specialized workers who could fulfill the manpower needs of the economy. Like the Soviet Union, the Chinese gradually began to succumb to the need for schools to stress academic knowledge.

The stimulus for the reappraisal of educational policy, particularly higher educational policy, came in the form of a report on the work of the government in 1975 that outlined long-range economic goals including the building of "an independent and relatively comprehensive industrial and economic system in fifteen years. . . ."[37] It was almost immediately argued that the admission of students to universities on the basis of selection by workers in factories and agricultural groups would reduce the intellectual quality and preparation of students to a level that would make it difficult for universities to produce technicians and engineers needed to fulfill economic plans. In addition, it was argued that the requirement of two years of labor before entering the university was a waste of time that could be better spent in study. The attempt to bridge the gap between learning in the university and actual working conditions came under criticism for producing students who could solve industrial problems but not do advanced research and development.

The tension between the political demands of communism and the desire for economic growth will probably continue in China. One thing it highlights is the almost universal tug-of-war between the desire to use education as a means of easing the effects of industrialism and at the same time to use education as a means of economic growth. The issue of the relationship between education and economic growth is more fully explored in the next chapter. What is important to realize here is that continuing conflict will exist between these two educational goals, particularly in socialist countries.

In welfare states like the United States, the desire to overcome alienation and create social unity succumbed by the middle of the twentieth century to an educational policy geared toward economic growth and manpower needs. This is best exemplified in the evolution of the American high school in the twentieth century. The doctrine that permeated the development of the high school in the early part of the century has been called "social efficiency." Edward Krug, the great historian of the American high school, described social efficiency as a call for training the individual for social service and a sense of unity with the rest of society.[38] In practice, this meant gearing the curriculum for the future social destination of the individual through the use of vocational guidance, testing, and tracking. "Tracking" refers to directing students into college preparatory, general, or vocational curriculums. The social life of the school provides the sense of unity and social service. High school sports, clubs, assemblies, and other extracurricular activities are all justified in terms of their training the individual to work for others and feel united with the rest of society. The student transfers the unity created in participation in the life of the school to a unity of feeling with the rest of society.[39]

The document that gave the fullest expression to these goals in a democracy was the report entitled *Cardinal Principles of Secondary Education* put out by the National Education Association in 1918. This report defined and gave national guidance to the development of the American comprehensive high school. The report rejected separate high schools such as college preparatory and vocational schools and instead endorsed a comprehensive high school that would house all students under one roof as a means of promoting social unity. Students, although separated into different curriculums, would meet in common extracurricular activities . . . such as athletic games, social activities, and the government of the school."[40]

The report defined democracy primarily as a social organization that allowed everyone to do what he or she was best able to do. Education was to fit the individual for a social position that would allow for maximum contribution to society. The report argued that "education in a democracy . . . should develop in each individual the knowledge, interests, ideals, habits, and powers whereby he will find his place and use that place to shape both himself and society toward ever nobler ends." Unification was that part of the ideal of democracy that brought men together and gave them "common ideas, common ideals, and common modes of thought, feeling, and action that made for cooperation, social cohesion, and social solidarity."

Some obvious parallels can be drawn between this concern about social service and the concern expressed in the Soviet Union and China. In the United States, a major revolution in thinking claimed that modern industrialism could not operate under a system of individual economic competition. What was required was cooperation and individual specialization within the economic system. The concern, which John Dewey influenced, was that too much economic competition would result in alienation of the individual from the economic system and an increase in social conflict. In this regard, the desire to use education to promote economic and social unity was similar to attempts made in socialist countries.[41]

What was different was that social unity in the United States was not linked to a common ownership of the means of production or the elmination of a hierarchical social structure. This meant that no attempt was made to prevent the development of a distinct intellectual group separate from the workers. Unlike students in China, students in the United States were not sent into the factories and agricultural fields to overcome the segregation of knowledge. Nor was social unity to end the hierarchical social structure. Social unity was to be a product primarily of the social activities of the school.

With the aid of hindsight we can argue that it was naive to believe that social unity could be produced by extracurricular activities in the American high school. In fact, the whole idea seems absurd. There is also the question of unity for whose benefit. Socialist countries could at least claim that unity was for the benefit of all because all owned the means of production. In the United States it was never made clear how all people would benefit from a sense of unity. Attempting to use the social dedication of the individual to protect special interests that claimed to represent society seems to have been a greater danger in the United States than in socialist countries. But this discussion is academic because there is no evidence that extracurricular activities in the American high school created any sense of social service and unity.

By the 1950s concern about social unity and service was pushed into the background as the American school system geared up to fill the manpower needs of the technological race during the cold war. The structure of extracurricular activities remained with the high school as a legacy from the past but without the ideology of social efficiency. As we shall see in the next chapter, the United States, China, and the Soviet Union began to emphasize education for economic growth and manpower needs. Interestingly enough, it was the cold-war competition with the Soviet Union that resulted in the American striving to relate education to the needs of the economy. Many Americans cited what they viewed as the superior academic training of Soviet schools to call for a heavier emphasis on academic subjects in U.S. schools and a deemphasis on social training. In the 1960s and '70s schools were more directly geared to economic goals as attempts were made to use schools to end poverty by expanding vocational and career education.[42]

In socialist countries like Cuba, there is an ongoing attempt to use education to overcome the effects of industrialism. A Cuban report to UNESCO in 1962 stated, ". . . we see two basic aims of socialist education the linking of education with productive labor as a means of developing men in every aspect."[43] Cuba's goal is to create the "new socialist man"; a collective consciousness will eliminate the alienation of person from person and the separation of thought from action by combining work and school. In the late 1960s, after the Cuban government decided to emphasize agricultural development rather than industrial development, schools began to move to the coun-tryside, where work and study could be combined. Again, as in the case of the Soviet Union, China, and the United States, complaints are being voiced about the effect on the quality of education and the costs to the economic system of trying to produce the "new socialist man" through education. Only the future will tell if Cubans are able to overcome the tension between economic goals and using the school system to overcome the social and psychological effects of modern society.

Conclusions

A major theme of this chapter has been the failure or abandonment by the economic state of plans to use education to overcome the social and psychological effects of modern industrial society. It is important to understand that the term "economic state" refers to the shift in concern in the twentieth century from government as a means of equalizing political control to government as a means of sharing the economic benefits of modern industrialism. This means that government actively intervenes in the economic system. Whether that intervention results in an equalization of the economic benefits of modern society is debatable. Under socialism this economic intervention means common ownership of production; under the welfare state it means the government attempts to share economic benefits through social programs for health, education, income assistance, retirement, and unemployment.

The abandonment by the economic state of attempts to overcome the personal effects of industrialism has been accompanied by a direct linking of the school to the needs of the economic system. The school is considered as the supplier of trained human resources needed for economic growth. (This point is explored in detail in the next chapter.)

Several reasons have been suggested for the demise of educational programs designed to overcome worker alienation and the separation of thought from action. One of the major reasons has been the conflict between the need for trained and educated human resources and the lack of strong academic training that results from attempts to combine theory and practice in the school. Placing students in factories or bringing industry into the school is time-consuming and expensive. Such practices also have been criticized for causing a lack of academic rigor in the schools.

This chapter has also suggested that no proof exists of the psychological effects of industrialism described by John Dewey and Karl Marx. It seems correct to say that modern industrialism has resulted in the creation of work that is meaningless, lacks social content, and discourages the worker. It is absurd to argue that common ownership or training workers in Dewey-style schools will solve these problems without changes in the organization of work.

The ideas of social service and unity that have prevailed in educational systems in the United States and socialist countries carry with them the same problems as the nineteenth-century patriotism described in chapter 1. The concepts place the good of society above the desires of the individual. Although this sounds humanitarian and altruistic, the concepts tend to lose meaning when questions are asked about who or what defines the good of society. Is the good of society to be defined by the government, by leading economic concerns, by political groups, by bureaucrats, by public-spirited professionals, or by socialist organizations? It would certainly be difficult to locate a group or organization one would feel comfortable acknowledging as able to express the needs of society in general. This is particularly true of American government since the corruption of the Nixon administration. In socialist countries, common ownership of production does not guarantee that the state represents the good of all people because the state mechanism is operated by bureaucrats and professionals with their own interests.

A major danger in using education to promote social unity and service has been the possibility of a group or government claiming to represent the interests of the people and demanding that everyone give allegiance to its interests. Used in this manner, education for service and unity can become a mechanism for domination and control of the population.

3

EDUCATION
AND THE
WELFARE STATE

IN THE WELFARE STATE, EDUCATION HAS BEEN LINKED to the economic goals of
full employment and growth. As the welfare state has developed,
there has been increasing concern with providing economic justice and
efficiency. This has resulted in a lessened concern about education
fulfilling the political functions debated in the nineteenth century.
Schools in the welfare state have become more involved with helping
the student toward a job and efficient functioning in the economic
system than with the student's place in the political system. The
United States in the 1970s has focused on career education, or the
study of occupations.

By "the welfare state" I mean a political and economic system that
maintains some form of representative government in which the
government takes an active role in the economic system. This
represents the abandonment of the concept of an economy governed
by the free interplay of competition in which employment and prices
are functions of supply and demand. The welfare state does maintain a
system of private ownership of production. Ideally, in the welfare
state, government, business, and labor unions work cooperatively to
assure economic growth, justice, and efficiency.[1]

The welfare state's government intervenes by regulating the
wage-price system and by providing public monies to solve economic

problems. Welfare includes all public expenditures for health, education, unemployment insurance, social security, housing, community development, and income maintenance. Government expenditures in these areas have increased rapidly in the twentieth century. In the United States during the Great Depression of the 1930s, welfare expenditures amounted to 10 percent of the gross national product. This figure dropped to 4.4 percent during World War II and increased to 15.3 percent by 1970. In 1970, the Federal Republic of West Germany spent 19.5 percent of its gross national product on welfare; and in France the figure was 20.9 percent.[2]

One important thing to understand about the welfare state is that it has not resulted in any significant redistribution of income. There is an assumption that state intervention in the economy will result in greater economic growth, which in turn will create a better standard of living for all people; but this does not necessarily mean that those at the bottom of the economic ladder will receive a larger percentage of the national income.[3]

Even a concern about economic justice does not necessarily mean a goal of income redistribution. What economic justice has meant has been to give everyone an equal chance to compete for jobs and find employment, and to provide some income for those unable to work because of age, physical disability, or some other problem. This does not mean that workers will receive a larger share of the economic pie but that they will be assured of employment and care if they are unable to work.

This concept of economic justice is important when we consider the role of education in the welfare state. Education is meant to provide the individual with the knowledge and skills necessary to compete on equal terms with others for existing jobs. This competition will result in some members of society moving up the economic ladder and some moving down the economic ladder. Again, this does not mean that those at the bottom receive any greater share of the national income; it means only that they have a chance to compete. Education in the welfare state is not meant to result in a redistribution of income but is supposed to permit increased mobility up (and down) the social scale.

Education in the welfare state also contributes to economic growth by making efficient use of human resources and providing training. Efficient use of human resources means giving individuals equal opportunities to find places in society best suited for their talents and interests without regard for their social and economic backgrounds. The school provides equal opportunity by offering an education related to individual needs and abilities. In this manner, natural abilities will not be lost to the system because of inferior social conditions. It is argued that this makes the economic system more efficient because it allows for the more efficient use of human resources. In addition, training received by individuals in the welfare state's educational system aims at improving their ability to perform on the job, which is supposed to increase productivity and spur economic growth.

Economic growth in the welfare state is directly linked to economic justice. As increased education results in increased economic growth, this should result in an increased standard of living for everyone. In addition, the poor are supposed to be given a better chance to compete for employment through special educational programs. In the United States in the 1960s the so-called war on poverty directed a major part of its effort at helping children of the poor by providing them with an early childhood education (Head Start) that would prepare them to compete in school on equal terms with children from other parts of society. Once in school, poor children were to receive additional help through compensatory education.

Related to the welfare state's concepts of employment and efficient use of human resources has been manpower planning. Full employment is a major goal of the welfare state. In terms of manpower planning this means that enough workers will be available to industry. An oversupply of workers trained in one field could lead to unemployment; an undersupply could hinder efficient production.

One goal of education and manpower planning has been to adapt school programs to the needs of the labor market. Under this plan, students entering the educational system would be sorted according to interests and abilities and put into educational programs that would lead to occupations that have a shortage of workers. Manpower planning would thus contribute to the welfare of society by aiding in full employment by making efficient use of human resources resulting in economic growth.

Manpower planning fits neatly into arguments for equality of opportunity and social mobility. In fact, they are essential if manpower planning is to be effective. Individual talent, in this framework, must not be restricted to social circumstances. Manpower planning calls for maximum social mobility. The gifted child of the laborer should be able to make it as an engineer. The limited-ability child of the engineer should replace the laborer on the occupational ladder. It should be remembered that manpower planning and social mobility do not involve changing the occupational structure but redistributing individuals entering the occupational structure.

The reader is by now aware that the welfare state has not been able to achieve its goals of full employment, growth, and economic justice. This means, of course, that the role of education in the welfare system has met with the same failures. Schooling has not solved the problems of unemployment and unequal opportunity. And questions are being asked about the extent to which education can contribute to economic growth. Part of the problem lies in the assumptions made about the role of education in the welfare system.

To provide an understanding of the role of education in the welfare state, the remainder of this chapter explores education's role in economic growth, providing for economic justice, and providing for full employment.

Human Capital and Education

The concept of human capital has been important in supporting arguments for increased investment in education in the welfare state. Keep in mind, however, that the notion of investment in human capital as a means of increasing economic productivity has not been the only justification for the welfare state. The idea of human capital considers human beings as objects to be improved, like machinery, for the more efficient operation of the industrial system. To view the welfare system in this manner can obscure the fact that a strong humanitarian impulse exists that feels society has an obligation to take care of its members. There is also an authoritarian impulse that views the welfare system as a means of strengthening the state by creating a dependent population.

Although the concept of human capital has been extremely important for the expansion of education under a welfare system, the concept has not played that important a role in justifying other aspects of the welfare system. Before we explore the meaning of human capital as it relates to education, we must gain perspective on the variety of arguments given to justify a welfare system.

One argument for the expansion of welfare has been to create a dependent population that will support the government because it has a stake in the system. This argument was advanced by Bismarck in Germany in the late nineteenth century to justify the creation of national health, accident, and old-age insurance. Bismarck "wanted the worker as a loyal and obedient ally, and to accomplish this the worker's interests had to be closely tied to the state. . . . Bismarck aimed at the dual objective of lessening worker discontent and of increasing their stake in the stability of the existing order." Workers and socialists in Germany supported the expansion of the state welfare system as a means of improving their condition in society. There is also an argument that government-sponsored welfare programs represent basic human rights. This was an important justification for the expanded welfare system in England following World War II. The "social rights" thesis argues that the individual has a right to be protected from starvation and economic deprivation and receive basic health care.[4]

The human capital argument views the welfare system as a means of improving the condition of the work force and therefore increasing economic productivity. Increased productivity, it is claimed, will result in economic growth and raise the general standard of living. Investment in human capital means providing an educational system that will enhance individual skills and provide living conditions that will free the worker from health problems and hunger. Improved physical condition and training of the worker will result in a more efficient and competent worker on the job.

There is a general and an individual aspect to the human capital argument. On one hand, it can be viewed on a societal basis: Society invests in human capital to increase economic growth. On the other hand, it can be viewed on an individual basis: The individual invests in education to increase personal income. An object of concern for economists is determining the rate of return on investment for both society and the individual.

Concern about investment in human capital began in the early part of the twentieth century and was particularly associated with the development of vocational education. Its importance did not reach major proportions until the 1960s when economists began to devise improved techniques for determining rates of return on investment in human resources. The concept was quickly swept up into plans for the development of Third World countries. It was used to justify the expansion of educational systems in order to promote economic growth in underdeveloped countries. By the late 1970s, investment in education as a means of improving human capital had come under severe attack as personal rates of return on investment in education began to decrease and educational inflation began to occur.

An example of the interest in developing human capital through education can be found in reports of the Committee on Industrial Education of the National Association of Manufacturers in the United States in 1905 and 1912. In 1905 the committee argued that "technical and trade education for youth is a national necessity, and the nation that wins success in competition with other nations must train its youth in the arts of production and distribution." In its 1912 report, titled *Our Human Capital,* the committee placed the training of youth in the context of a general concept of capital. The report argued that there were two forms of capital: One form consisted of land, machinery, buildings, and money; the other form consisted of the character, brains, and muscle of the people. The value of these human resources, or capital, was estimated at $250 billion. "This capital," the committee report argued, "we have not developed; we have overlooked the whole question of its complete and efficient development. Yet its value in every efficient nation, is five times in money the total value of all other resources combined." The report recommended vocational education as a mechanism for increasing human capital.[5]

Two important points in this early argument would haunt economists later in the century. First, it treats human beings as objects in the industrial system that must be trained and molded for the most efficient functioning of the system. This is a technological model for society in which the individual is molded to meet the needs of technology; the system is not altered to meet the desires of the individual. Second, education is treated as investment and not as consumption. That is, education is considered not in terms of personal enjoyment and appreciation but in terms of economic gain. In the human capital framework, one goes to school to get a better job and higher income, not for the inherent joy of learning and gaining knowledge to enhance the enjoyment of life.

Theodore Schultz, one of the leading economists to develop the human capital concept in the 1960s and '70s, stated that the general neglect of the human capital argument after its early beginnings in the twentieth century resulted from its conceptualization of the human as industrial object and education as investment. Schultz wrote: "Free men are first and foremost the end to be served by economic endeavor; they are not property or marketable assets. . . . Our values and beliefs inhibit us from looking upon human beings as capital goods, except in slavery, and this we harbor." Schultz did not deny these values but argued that they should not stop the individual or society from the investment aspects of human capital. In fact, without the use of the concept, he argued, we fail to understand that "laborers have become capitalists not from a diffusion of the ownership of corporation stocks, as folklore would have it, but from the acquisition of knowledge and skill that have economic value."[6]

In the 1960s and '70s the definition and measurement of human capital was fully developed. Theodore Schultz defined human capital as that form of capital which is an integral part of a person and enhances the capabilities of individuals to produce. As a form of capital it lends itself to investment. The five major forms of investment in human capital, according to Schultz, are health facilities and services, on-the-job training, formally organized education, study programs for adults, and the migration of individuals to adjust to changing job opportunities. All these elements play important roles in improving human capital. Improvement in health services should result in a stronger and more energetic population. On-the-job training can provide the worker with additional skills to improve task performance. Adult study programs should result in an increase in productivity and the migration of individuals to areas where their skills can be used more efficiently to increase production.[7]

All these forms of investment in human capital result in different methodological problems when measuring rates of return. For instance, how much money invested in health services or on-the-job training will result in how much economic growth? How do you isolate the factor of improved health care from other factors affecting economic growth? And, in the case of health care, does it mean that one limits investment in health services to a level beyond which there would be no contribution to economic growth?

These questions are central to the idea of education as investment in human capital. It was Theodore Schultz who launched the major investigation into the relationship between education and economic growth. Schultz argued that if one compared increases in the amount of labor and capital invested in the economy in the United States between 1919 and 1957 with amount of economic growth during that period, 2.1 percent per annum economic growth could not be explained by inputs from the quantity of labor and capital. In other words, whereas the number of man-hours and capital increased each year by 1 percent, the output of the system increased by 3.1 percent. To Schultz, part of the unexplained annual increase of 2.1 percent was the result of improvement in human capital, which in turn was a consequence of increased levels of education.[8]

To measure the effect of increased education on economic growth, Schultz developed a method to determine the "stock," or amount, of education held by the labor force and compared that to increases in income. According to Schultz, the stock—the millions of school years held by the entire U.S. labor force over the age of fourteen years— increased from 116 in 1900 to 740 in 1967. Part of this increase reflects the growth of the size of the labor force, but part of it indicates the increase in the number of years of schooling attained by individual members of the labor force.

The amount of education held by the labor force can be given a monetary value in terms of the cost of schooling. How much did each year of schooling in the labor force cost? And what is the total cost of the schooling attained by the labor force? This cost factor represents the amounted invested in education.

Schultz considered the cost of schooling as earnings foregone by students while they attended school plus direct school costs. Earnings foregone by students were calculated in terms of the amount of money individuals could have been earning if they had not been attending school. Schultz found this a very significant item in the total costs of schooling. It was a more significant factor in secondary education than in college, and has decreased in significance in the United States as the century has progressed. Schultz stated in his original study: "Earnings foregone while attending high school were well over half of the total costs in each of the years; they were 73 percent in 1900 and 60 percent in 1956; the two low years were 1930 and 1940, when they fell to 57 and 58 percent of total costs."[9] The costs of earnings foregone were added to such school costs as buildings and teachers salaries to arrive at a total cost for schooling.

The economic value of the educational stock of the labor force is calculated by taking the total number of years of schooling possessed by the labor force and the cost of those years of schooling. Schultz estimated that between 1929 and 1935, the educational stock of the U.S. labor force rose by $355 billion (in 1956 prices). Of that amount, $69 billion was a result of the growth of the size of the labor force, while $286 billion resulted from increases in levels of education reached by each worker. During this same period, real income increased from $150 billion to $302 billion (in 1956 prices).

The question for Schultz was how much this increase in income was the result of increases in the stock of education. Using three different estimates, he concluded that "the increase in the education per person of the labor force that occurred between 1929 and 1957 explains between 36 and 70 percent of the otherwise unexplained increase in earnings per laborer, depending on which of the estimates of the rate of return that is applied."[10] Even at the lower figure of 36 percent, education made a significant contribution to increasing national income.

According to Schultz's conclusions, the welfare state had nothing to lose and everything to gain by pouring money into education. Schultz's optimism about the importance of education in economic development continued into the 1970s when he stated: "Education has become a major source of economic growth in winning the abundance that is to be had by developing a modern agriculture and industry. It simply would not be possible to have this abundance if people were predominantly illiterate and unskilled."[11] Other studies seemed to confirm Schultz's conclusions. Economist Edward Denison stated that education accounted for one fifth of the increase in national income in the United States between 1929 and 1957. Studies of underdeveloped countries seemed to confirm that investment in education resulted in economic growth.[12]

Another aspect of this argument is the rate of return for the individual's investment in education. This gives a slightly different slant to the issue. Instead of a national investment in human resources, it considers the economics of the individual decision to attend school to increase future individual income. Individual investment is calculated by determining income foregone while the individual attends school plus school costs.

The pioneer study of individual rates of return was done by the economist Gary Becker in the 1960s. Becker estimated that the private rate of return on a college education in 1949 was close to 13 percent; for high school students, it was around 18 percent. These figures suggest that investment in more schooling was a shrewd decision.[13]

In making his calculations Becker was aware of several important issues that could affect these figures in future years. In some ways, a close reading of his study could have led to better predictions about one of the current questions in education: How much does the rate of return depend on the supply of educated people? Does schooling lose its economic value when it stops being a scarce commodity? The other issue, and the one we shall deal with first, is whether actual attendance at school or individual ability as reflected in more years of school attendance is the more important contributor to rate of return.

One can immediately see the difficulty of determining whether higher rates of return were a result of people with higher abilities receiving more years of schooling. If this were true, it would mean that the investment decision in education really depended on individual ability; increased investment in education for the general population would not result in high rates of return for everyone.

Investigating this issue, Becker compared rates of return between college and high school graduates. He also considered differential ability through rank in class, IQ, father's education and occupation, and personality traits. Were these factors more important in determining rates of return than actual graduation from college? Becker concluded that all evidence suggested "that college education itself explains most of the unadjusted earnings differential between college and high school graduates." He went on to claim that "even after adjustment for differential ability, the private rate of return to a typical white male college graduate would be considered, say, certainly more than 10 percent."[14]

Becker's conclusions added another spark of optimism that investment in education would result not only in national economic growth but in increased individual income. In the welfare state this seemed like an ideal means of eliminating poverty without forcing a redistribution of income or changing individual ownership of the means of production. Invest money in education, and the economic system would make everyone richer.

The problem of a possible surplus of educated people still existed. Could a point be reached where the market would be saturated with educated people, thus causing a decline in rates of return on education and a reduction of the contribution of education to national growth? Would the value of education, like other commodities, depend on supply and demand?

Working with historical data in the 1960s, Becker estimated that rates of return on college and high school educations declined significantly between 1900 and 1940 but increased after 1940. Becker questioned the reliability of these data, but there was an element of doubt about the economic limits of investment in education. His conclusion suggested that the economic value of education depended on other forces in the economy.[15]

Becker argued that the reason for the increase in rate of return for education after 1940 was industrial and technological expansion. The 1940s was a decade of a war economy following a long period of depression. The 1950s was a period of technological expansion as a result of the cold war with the Soviet Union. This expansion after 1940 was large enough to absorb the increase in school graduates. Becker stated that "advances in technology and other forces increasing the demand for educated persons must have offset the increase in college graduates and more than offset the increase in high-school graduates."[16] But Becker still did not answer one question: What would happen when the economy stopped growing?

One result of the optimistic conclusions by human capital economists in the 1960s was the inclusion of education in plans for economic development. This was particularly important for under-developed countries in Asia, Africa, and South America. The economists were essentially saying that investment in education was a vital part of economic growth. During this period, a younger breed of economist was being trained who would reverse the argument of its elders and claim that education was not used primarily as a means of promoting economic growth in developed countries but was used as a means of domination and maintenance of the class structure of society.

In 1964, Martin Carnoy completed his doctoral dissertation in economics at the University of Chicago, "The Cost and Return to Schooling in Mexico"; and in the 1970s he published a book on how education was used as a means of international domination.[17] Following the same pattern, Samuel Bowles completed his dissertation at Harvard in 1965, "The Efficient Allocation of Resources in Education: A Planning Model with Applications to Northern Nigeria." In the 1970s he co-authored with economist Herbert Gintis a widely read book that claimed educational systems were used to maintain the class structure of society.[18]

In addition to these rumblings from the 1960s, a sharp reaction was to develop in the late 1970s as the optimism of human capital economists exploded in the face of worldwide crises in human capital and education. The belief in the economic power of education that preceded this period was best expressed by Theodore Schultz in the early 1970s when he went beyond his data and asserted: "A strong welfare goal of our community is to reduce the unequal distribution of personal income among individuals and families." He recognized that in the past the welfare state had attempted to do this through "progressive income and inheritance taxation." He went on: "Given public revenue from these sources, it may well be true that public investment entering into schooling, elementary and secondary, is an effective and efficient set of expenditures for attaining this goal."[19] While there might have been some hard evidence that education contributed to economic growth, there was no proof that it reduced the unequal distribution of income. This was a statement of belief in the power of education and not a conclusion based on strong data.

The Crises in Human Capital and Education

A major educational crisis of the late 1970s was the increasingly high educational level of the unemployed. The better educated began to encounter economies with slow rates of growth and expansion. The supply of educated people began to exceed demand. Rates of return on investment in education began to decline, and education seemed to be impeding rather than increasing economic growth. This was happening in underdeveloped countries where large amounts of money were poured into education that could have been used in other sectors of the economy to spur growth.

The term "educational inflation" was coined during this period to describe the declining economic value of education. Jobs that in the past required only a secondary diploma now might require two years of college or a college degree. This would occur without any basic change in the nature of the job. In other words, with educational inflation a diploma could not gain its possessor employment as good, or income as high, as in the past.

In an introduction to an article for the United Nation's International Institute for Educational Planning in 1977, the economist Martin Carnoy noted that "non-industrialized countries are faced by an apparent 'excess' of highly schooled labour; the average level of schooling in the labour force has increased but so has the average level of schooling in the unemployed labour force."[20]

This condition was accompanied by expansion and increasing costs for education. This raised the specter of reversing the situation where education contributed to economic growth to one where education absorbed such a large part of the gross national product that it actually depressed economic growth. In this context the issue would become one of balancing investment in education with the requirements of growth and recognizing the potential limits of the contribution of education to increased national productivity.

These educational problems were signaled in the late 1960s in a book by Philip H. Coombs called *The World Educational Crisis*. His analysis of the crisis that was unfolding fairly accurately described conditions that would exist by the end of the 1970s. Understanding his analysis is an important steppingstone to understanding the present crises in education and human capital.

Coombs analyzed the world educational crisis as an increasing social demand for education confronting increasing educational costs and unemployment for school graduates. Coombs defined three major reasons for the heightened social demand for education. First, the increasing educational aspirations of parents and children sparked a belief that more schooling would lead to a better job and a higher income. The second reason for the expansion was the new stress on education as part of a public policy designed for national development. This was the argument of the human capital economists being heard in national policy. And third, a factor contributing to a general rise in educational demand was an increase in the world's population.[21]

Coombs' prediction of an increasing social demand for education was borne out by events in the 1970s. One factor that Coombs had not originally recognized as a future contributor to social demand was the pressure for more education resulting from the increasing unemployment of school graduates. By the late 1970s, as unemployment among school graduates increased, those graduates began to demand higher levels of education in order to increase their possibilities of employment. For instance, as unemployment of secondary school graduates increased and educational inflation increased the number of years of schooling required for a job, secondary school graduates began to demand an expansion of and access to higher education. As Ronald Dore stated: "The paradox of the situation is that the worse the educated unemployment situation gets and the more useless educational certificates become, the stronger grows the pressure for an expansion of educational facilities."[22]

This situation ecame known in the 1970s as "qualification escalation," which simply resulted from the apparent situation that the higher one's educational qualification, the better chance one has of getting some job. As Dore put it, ". . . if you find that your junior secondary certificate does not get you one [a job], there is nothing to be done except to press on and try to get a senior secondary certificate, and if that doesn't work to press on to the university."[23]

Coombs argued in the late 1960s that the increasing social demand for education was encountering difficulties because of the increasing costs of education and the increasing percentage of national budgets being devoted to education. Coombs saw that education was a rising-cost industry with real costs per pupil constantly increasing. The effects of this increase were multiplied by increasing enrollments. The result, if countries were to keep pace with social demands, was an increasing share of the national budget being devoted to education.

Coombs' figures showed the steady increase in the share of the national economy being consumed by schooling. Considered as a percentage of the gross national product, the educational share between 1955 and 1965 had risen in the United States from a little over 4 percent to close to 6.5 percent, in Sweden from a little over 4 percent to over 5 percent, and in France from a little below 3 percent to a little over 4 percent. As a percentage between 1955 and 1964, costs rose in France from 9.6 percent to 16.9 percent, in Belgium from 10.8 percent to 17.1 percent, and in The Netherlands from 11.3 percent to 20.7 percent.[24]

In developing countries the cost of education was taking even larger segments of the public budget. UNESCO reported that in many underdeveloped countries education was taking between 10 and 15 percent of government expenditures in 1960 and 20 to 25 percent by the 1970s. In 1960 the average developing country spent 2.4 percent of its gross national product on education; by 1970, it was spending 3.4 percent.[25]

Coombs warned that "education cannot continue to command a

rapidly increasing share of available resources without producing serious stresses and distortions in the whole society and economy. This is not a question of philosophy or viewpoint; it is a matter of elementary arithmetic."[26]

Added to the problems of increasing demand and costs was the decreasing ability of labor markets to absorb an increasingly educated labor force. In underdeveloped countries in the 1970s, school enrollments grew faster than job opportunities.[27] Coombs recognized the serious potential problem in the late 1960s. By the middle and late 1970s this situation became a reality in underdeveloped countries and resulted in the previously discussed rise in demand for more education and educational inflation.

One factor that aggravated the situation of school graduates unable to find jobs appropriate to their level of training was the high rate of general unemployment. Even without the problem of educational inflation, high unemployment rates would have created difficulties. Carnoy was to write in the late 1970s: "Furthermore, unemployment shows no sign of diminishing even though the unemployed—on average—are in theory more adequately prepared to participate in the growth of the economy."[28]

In the economics of human capital the condition of educational inflation or underemployment of the educated and increasing investment in education suggests both a decrease in personal rates of return on education and a decrease in education's contribution to economic growth. In the language of supply and demand, this would mean that as the supply of educated people has outstripped demand, the economic value of an education has decreased.

One of the most extensive economic analyses of this situation in the United States was conducted by the economist Richard Freeman in the mid-1970s. Freeman analyzed the problem of the educated unemployed in terms of supply and demand. Put in this framework, an individual decision to attend college was an economic decision based on prospects of future earnings.

Freeman arrived at his conclusion by comparing variations in the proportion of young men going to college with the availability of jobs and income between 1951 and 1974 in the United States. He claimed: "Formal statistical analysis indicates that 95 percent of the variation in the fraction of young men in college over the 1951-1974 period can be attributed to two simple measures of the economic incentive to enroll: the income of graduates relative to other workers and relative employment opportunities."[29] The actual figures presented by Freeman showed a decline by the 1970s of job opportunities for college graduates and rates of return for investment in education. His figures on rates of return on a college education showed a marked change from the figures presented by previous economists, which had given hope that education could raise everyone's income. Freeman used two methods of calculating rates of return. The first method assumed exceptional future income gains for college graduates. This method showed a decline of 2.5 percent (from 12.5 to 11 percent) between 1968 and 1973. The second method assumed that future income gains of college graduates would equal those of similar age groups during the 1963 to 1973 period. This more realistic calculation found that rates of return had declined by 3.5 percent (from 11 to 7.5 percent) between 1968 and 1973.[30]

The decline in rates of return came about because the supply of college graduates increased at a more rapid rate than did job opportunities. Freeman produced a variety of figures to support his position. One way of assessing the problem of job opportunities for college graduates was to take the proportion of professional and managerial employment and relate it to total jobs in the economy. The number of professional jobs is one of the best measures of the availability of high-level employment for college graduates. Between the late nineteenth century and the early 1970s, the proportion of these jobs, compared with the total number of jobs in the economy, steadily increased. Then the growth leveled off; in fact, between 1970 and 1972, these jobs actually declined as a fraction of total jobs. Because the number of college graduates continued to increase, there was a decrease in the number of professional and managerial jobs available for each college graduate.[31]

One of Freeman's important findings was that student educational and career aspirations could not shift fast enough to match changes in job opportunities and future earnings. Students did change their aspirations because of fluctuations in the market, but the time lag between beginning an educational program and graduation made it difficult to maintain a balance between the market and graduation. For instance, students in the United States changed their educational and occupational aspirations between 1966 and 1974. Among freshman male college students, there was a decline of those choosing careers as college professors from 2.1 percent to .7 percent, as engineers from 16.3 percent to 8.5 percent, and as scientists from 4.9 percent to 2.7 percent. Interestingly, a different pattern existed for women in some occupations, but this reflects the general increase in job opportunities for females. There was an increase in the number of freshman women who chose as careers business (from 3.3 to 8.5 percent) and medicine (from 1.7 to 3.5 percent).[32]

What is more important, these shifts in educational and career aspirations could not keep pace with market conditions. This is what Freeman calls the "cobweb effect." Essentially it works in the following manner. Many students are attracted to a field when salaries are high, employment opportunities are good, and there is an existing shortage of graduates entering the occupation. Thus, in about four years, the length of time required to gain an education to enter the occupation, a large graduating class is prepared to enter the occupation. This causes a depression in salaries in the occupation, a weakening of employment opportunities, and a surplus of graduates. These conditions in turn influence fewer members of the next generation of college students to enter the occupation, thus resulting in a future shortage of graduates and a repeat of the cycle.

The cobweb effect oversimplifies the actual functioning of the college job market. There are a number of intervening factors. An expansion of the economic system that results in continuing increases in job opportunities can offset the cobweb effect. In the United States, one factor that has influenced the number of jobs available to college graduates has been the decline in the percentage of the gross national product devoted to defense and research and development. These are what are called "college-manpower-intensive activities," and they have had an effect on the job market that is independent of the cobweb effect.

What is important about the cobweb effect is that it has reduced the optimism displayed by economists in the 1960s that an expansion of educational systems would result in a reduction of poverty and unemployment and a general increase in incomes. As we discovered in the 1970s, this argument has to be considered in the light of the actual job market. A no-growth or slow-growth economy can result in major reductions in rates of return on education and in educational inflation. The cobweb effect suggests that education can create its own unemployment by attracting large numbers of students to a particular field of study, thus causing a future surplus of graduates in that field and unemployment in terms of students' qualifications.

Education and Economic Growth

One of the major unanswered questions is, at what point can investment in education actually cause a decrease in economic growth and expansion of the job market? In the 1960s economists felt that continual investment and expansion in education would contribute to continual economic growth. It does seem true that education can produce more productive workers who will contribute to economic growth. The problem discovered in the 1970s was that there are limits to what investment in education can accomplish. At some point of investment in education, all that is accomplished is increasing the educational level of the unemployed.

It is possible that the amount invested in education may become so large that it can reduce economic growth by making less funds available to the rest of the economy. To state this in the form of a question: At what point does the amount of the gross national product consumed by education become so large that it retards future increases in the gross national product? This situation, of course, would mean a retarding of the growth of the job market.

There have been no direct answers to these questions. Most solutions to the human capital problems of the 1970s have been directed at reducing educational systems and changing curriculums, but never with any sense that in so doing, one can actually determine the balance between investment in education and economic growth. Some proposals have called for a decrease in the number of university graduates in the labor force either by shifting the cost from the government to parents or by making admissions examinations more difficult.[33]

One interesting proposal has been that of reducing the rates of return on education as a means of discouraging school attendance. This could be accomplished by having government change its wage structure so that college graduates earned less money, which would have a direct effect on rates of return. This solution might be particularly effective in underdeveloped countries where governments are the principal employers of labor. Other proposals have called for changing the curriculum so that there is a direct link between educational training and employment opportunities.

But these solutions involve additional manipulation of the educational system and the job market by economists and educational planners. What might be at the heart of the problem is the economic system itself. An economist like Martin Carnoy would argue that the issue is one of changing the economic system that produces unemployment and using strong government action to assure full employment. For Carnoy, the problem is not the educational system but the economic system. He calls for government intervention for job protection in the face of plant closings, as well as for retraining and relocation guarantees. He also proposes that governments provide a direct subsidy to firms for workers employed and reorganize the Social Security System.[34]

Carnoy would certainly shift the responsibility for improvement of the economic and social systems from education, but he also calls for further expansion of other parts of the welfare state. As these functions of the welfare state expand, the problem of their effect on economic growth remains. It has been estimated that a 3 percent growth rate is necessary to produce the economic surplus required to maintain the social programs of the welfare state. In the 1970s, growth rates in the United States, the Federal Republic of Germany, Italy, and Great Britain all fell below this level.[35] This raised serious doubts about arguments that investment in human capital through welfare programs would result in enough economic growth to provide an economic surplus to support those programs.

The crisis in human capital has also raised important questions about the ability of education in the welfare state to provide equality of opportunity and social mobility. These two issues are seen in a different perspective when educational inflation sets in and rates of return on education decline. As there are limits to education's ability to contribute to economic growth, there also seems to be limits to the ability of education to provide equality of opportunity and social mobility. This theme is explored in the next chapter.

4

SOCIAL MOBILITY
AND THE
BUREAUCRATIC SOCIETY

INDUSTRIAL AND POLITICAL CHANGES IN THE NINETEENTH AND twentieth centuries have resulted in major occupational shifts between generations. Most notable has been the decline of agricultural occupations in industrialized countries and the expansion of white-collar and industrial jobs. By this shift in the occupational structure of society, successive generations have been able to improve their social and economic conditions compared with the previous generation.[1]

As a result, stress is often placed on the possibility of social mobility between generations. Parents hope that their children will live in better social and economic conditions than those in which they were raised. In addition, those who advocate a more efficient use of human resources believe that maximizing the opportunity for social mobility will result in individuals who are more able to achieve success in occupations that match their talents.

Formal education has come to play an increasing role in mobility patterns with the development of large-scale corporations, government bureaucracies, and social organizations. These developments have resulted in what has been called a "new middle class" of office workers, supervisors, managers, technicians, scientists, and service providers.[2] The new middle class makes its claims for social prestige on the basis of the educational and cultural characteristics of its work.

Formal education often defines class roles in modern organizations, and their social importance. Consequently, formal education becomes the primary route for movement into this new middle class.[3]

The stress on formal education as a means of social mobility must be viewed as something different from upward mobility achieved as a result of entrepreneurial skill. In the Horatio Alger tradition, the young person with luck and pluck rose from rags to riches and built an industrial empire. This dream of social mobility set no career pattern for the young person. Advancement and economic gain resulted from taking advantage of unique situations and adapting quickly to opportunities.

Mobility into and within the new middle class has become institutionalized; career patterns have become formalized so that a certain number of years of education is expected to lead to a degree, which in turn will result in employment in a particular organization with its own formal pattern of advancement. Competition, once confined to the marketplace, now takes place in school examinations and in overcoming hurdles within corporate organizations. In the entrepreneurial model, the talented rose in society as a result of free competition between individuals in the economic marketplace. In the career model, competition occurs in formal educational institutions and bureaucratic organizations.[4]

One result of this institutionalization of mobility in educational organizations has been an endless debate about whether schools hinder individual competition by discriminating or being biased against any race, ethnic group, or social class. Can schools be impartial places for competition for social mobility?

The latter part of the twentieth century has also seen an increased concern about the monopolistic nature of many new career routes and the control they exert over the rest of society. Many middle-class occupations have become professions that control entrance into their ranks by formal educational requirements and through government licensing control of the market for their services. The expert training that provides these occupations with social status also results in their power to claim a monopoly over the market for their services.

Social Mobility, the Professions, and Bureaucratic Organization

The expansion of the professions has produced occupations to which individuals can aspire for purposes of social mobility and has provided for collective mobility. What I mean by "collective mobility" is the increase in status of an entire occupation through professionalization. For instance, medical doctors in the United States in the nineteenth century had low social status and low income relative to their counterparts in the twentieth century. In both status and income medical doctors tended to rank below engineers and lawyers. The professionalization of medicine early in the twentieth century raised the status and income of all doctors; it provided for collective mobility.

Professionalization has not been limited to doctors and lawyers but has extended to many occupations. It has resulted in collective mobility and the use of the educational system as gatekeeper to the occupation. Entrance into many middle-class occupations has depended on passage through educational programs that are prescribed and controlled by the profession.

Early occupations to professionalize were dentists, doctors, engineers, pharmacists, teachers, architects, veterinarians, social workers, librarians, lawyers, accountants, nurses, and opticians. What I mean by "professionalize" is that in these occupations, a monopoly is granted by the state to provide a particular service. Usually this monopoly takes the form of licensing, which depends on completing a particular course of study in an educational institution and, generally, passing a professional examination. Monopoly situations are usually justified as providing a particular body of expert knowledge required for the performance of the occupation.[5]

The existence of a profession runs counter to a free enterprise economy where the value and use of service is determined in the marketplace without the interference of government. By granting a monopoly, the state restricts the number of individuals who can perform an occupational role. For medicine in the United States, this has meant a decline in the number of doctors in relation to the population and a resulting increase in doctors' incomes and prestige. Teaching is restricted by licensing laws, but teachers' salaries and prestige have not increased to the extent of most other professions.

The state's role is crucial in the rise of professions. In *The Rise of Professionalism*, Magali Larson writes that "only the state, as the supreme legitimizing and enforcing institution, could sanction the modern professions' monopolistic claims of superiority for their 'commodities.' The attitude of the state toward education and toward monopolies of competence is thus a crucial variable in the development of the professional project."[6]

In addition, Larson argues that professions have been able to claim a monopoly of practice and superior rewards without any serious challenge from the general public because entrance into the professions is through educational institutions linked to universal systems of education. These systems hold out the possibility of entrance into the profession to all members of society. Says Larson: "The rise of modern educational systems brings an ideological resolution to the tension between universalistic principles and exclusive privilege embodied in the notion of expertise. Mass access to the lower echelons of the public school system allows the higher levels of the educational hierarchy to claim meritocratic legitimations of their selection of entrants."[7]

What this means is that educational institutions not only allow for the control and monopoly of a profession over a service, based on expert knowledge, but also defuse resentment of that monopoly by holding out the promise of equal access or social mobility into the profession.

Modern corporate political and social organizations have expanded the idea of a monopoly of expertise to several areas. For example, organizations claim that expert managerial skills are attained through special training. Larson states: "Hospital administrators, 'professional' business administrators, management analysts, school superintendents, college presidents and the like illustrate this type."[8] The expansion of government services has resulted in a set of "expert" occupations dealing with education, welfare, and regulatory matters.

The modern bureaucratic structures of business and government have created numerous occupations that claim a certain expertise and consequently are accessible only through formal education institutions. And, like the traditional professions, the claim of expertise and special training enhances the status of the occupation within the bureaucratic organization. A presumption of expertise can provide collective mobility for the entire occupation and at the same time channel mobility into the occupation through educational institutions.

This discussion of professions and bureaucratic roles highlights one of the problems in concentrating access to an occupation in education institutions. A monopoly situation can be created in which only those with training sanctioned by the profession or educational institution are allowed into the occupation. The ideology used to justify this situation is that the educational institutions providing the training are open to all on the basis of merit. This becomes the doctrine of equality of opportunity. Simply stated, it means that it is all right to concentrate access to occupations in educational institutions if everyone has an equal chance within those institutions.

Equality of Opportunity and Social Mobility

In discussing equality of opportunity as it relates to schooling, it is important to make a distinction between equality of opportunity in the school and equality of opportunity in the marketplace. For instance, if the school were to prepare students for equal opportunity to compete in the marketplace for occupations, it might provide everyone with the same knowledge and skills so that when competition began, all would start at the same point. The most extreme example of this was a proposal by the New York Workingman's party in the nineteenth century to remove all children from their families and place them in state boarding schools (a day school was considered insufficient to offset cultural inequalities). There they would all wear the same clothes, receive the same instruction, and have the same cultural opportunities. All children would leave school with equal advantages and training to compete in the marketplace. The status and occupation achieved by the individual would be a product of competition in society.[9]

But, as noted earlier in the chapter, in modern industrial society competition in the marketplace has tended to be replaced by competition in the educational institution. Children leave school with different skills and knowledge geared to different occupations. Modern schools provide unequal opportunities to compete in the marketplace. An individual who graduates from a vocational school with a major in cosmetology has an unequal opportunity to compete with an individual graduating from a college preparatory program.

Equality of opportunity has become difficult to define. Equality of opportunity can mean that everyone has an equal opportunity to attend school. In the United States this has been called "equality of educational opportunity" and has been the major issue in school desegregation and finance cases.[10] The courts have ruled that children attending segregated schools or schools with lower financial support than other schools in the district are receiving an unequal educational opportunity.

Equality of educational opportunity does not mean that everyone receives an equal education. The child placed in a lower-ability group in school does not receive the same education as a child in a higher-ability group, although one can argue that individuals receive an equal education according to their abilities. Also, individuals who eventually enter vocational programs graduate with unequal opportunities to attend college compared with graduates of college preparatory courses. Equality of educational opportunity tends to be limited in meaning to equality of initial access to educational institutions. Once those institutions separate children according to their abilities and future social destinations, equality of educational opportunity becomes reduced in meaning to an equal chance to receive an unequal education.

Let us assume that all children have equal educational opportunity to enter equal educational institutions. It could be argued that equality of opportunity for future occupations in this case means an equal opportunity to compete within educational institutions. But what happens to the child who comes from a home that offers few educational advantages? For instance, one child may have illiterate parents and be without reading material in the home; another child may have a large collection of books on hand and spend a great deal of time reading. The latter child would seem to have a better opportunity to compete in school because of the reading advantage.

During the 1960s in the United States, situations like the one just described became a central concern of the war on poverty. Several educational programs were launched to provide the disadvantaged child with an equal opportunity to compete in school. One popular program was Head Start, which was designed to provide a preschool program for children designated as disadvantaged. As the name of the program implies, it was designed to give these children a head start in formal education so that when they entered primary grades, they could compete on equal terms with children from more advantaged homes. Compensatory education programs were instituted in schools to provide extra help for children labeled as disadvantaged so that they could compete equally with their peers.[11]

The unequal opportunity of the so-called disadvantaged child to compete in school highlights a fundamental problem of internalizing competition for occupations, and consequently social mobility, in educational institutions. What factor or factors causes one child to succeed in educational activities and another child to succeed in other activities? If children are given an equal opportunity to compete in school, why does one child end up in a vocational program and another in a college preparatory program? Are some children born with more native intelligence and ability and when given an equal opportunity to compete in the school, does this natural ability determine their place in the competition? Or is competition in educational institutions determined by family background, translating family advantages into educational advantages? Or is it a matter of personality; are certain behavioral traits rewarded by the school?

This is the fundamental problem when one faces competition for careers in educational institutions: *What determines the outcome of the competition?* The variety of answers and arguments given in the twentieth century demonstrates the uncertainty and confusion that has accompanied the internalization of social mobility in educational institutions.

Certainly the most controversial answer to this problem is the one that stresses native intelligence. It argues that all people are born with a natural level of intelligence, or IQ. The most efficient society matches the level of intelligence to the intellectual requirements of the occupation. Maximum social mobility is important if individuals are to have opportunities to enter occupations suited to their native abilities. An important goal should be to create a social environment in which native intelligence, not family background or economic advantages, is the prime determiner of success. Early proponents of the importance of native intelligence believed that schools should be institutions where individuals were given an equal opportunity to exercise their native abilities.

The developers of IQ tests in the early part of the twentieth century envisioned an ordered society in which these tests, combined with universal schooling, would sort people into their proper occupations. Political and social leaders were also to be determined in this manner. Plato's dream of philosopher-kings ruling the world was to be actualized with universal IQ tests. Edward Thorndike, one of the early developers of the tests, when asked why he believed those with high IQs were most suited to rule, replied that those who scored highest on IQ tests were the most just and humane.[12]

Any discussion of native intelligence brings up a most explosive issue. Native intelligence implies something biological and therefore something than can be passed down from generation to generation. Some of those people who believe in the existence of native intelligence believe that there are differences in intelligence between racial groups. IQ tests given during World War I purported to show that not only did whites have higher average IQs then other racial groups but also that Nordic whites had higher average native intelligence than whites labeled "Alpine" and "Mediterranean."[13]

A belief in the inheritance of native intelligence led many early developers of IQ tests to become involved in eugenics and become advocates of the planned breeding of humans. In recent years, psychologist Arthur Jensen has argued that inherited levels of intelligence are measurable and that certain racial groups tend to have higher average intelligence than other racial groups. On this basis he has stated that compensatory education cannot succeed because ability is determined by inheritance and not by environment. All that can be done is to provide an environment that will maximize the opportunity for the development of inherited intelligence.[14]

It is not possible in this book to discuss all the criticisms of theories on intelligence and IQ tests. It should be mentioned, however, that two key arguments against IQ testing are that no adequate test has been developed that can measure native intelligence apart from other cultural factors. Thus, an adequate definition or description of intelligence does not exist. IQ tests are also challenged as culturally biased. The definition of intelligence has become simply that intelligence is what intelligence tests measure, a hopelessly circular definition at best.[15]

The prime concern of this chapter is that the argument for the existence and possible measuring of native intelligence has been used to justify the use of educational institutions as the central mechanism for sorting the population. Now, if the existence of native intelligence is undiscoverable, still another argument can be used to justify the school as the main source of social mobility. This is the argument that the school is somehow fairer than the marketplace in allowing for competition for occupations. By "fairer" is usually meant that the school pays less attention to family background and economic advantage than does open competition in the marketplace.

Several problems arise when we try to determine whether educational institutions are fairer than the marketplace in terms of social mobility and whether education increases the amount of social mobility. Most literature on mobility assumes that the amount of mobility is related to fairness of competition in the mobility process. For instance, a great deal of change in social class between generations is assumed to mean that greater opportunity exists for individuals to achieve a different social position from their parents. More movement up (and down) the social scale in a society is viewed as evidence of increased equality of opportunity.

Most mobility studies also assume that the important issue is social movement up an occupational scale. For instance, a traditional Marxist would argue that crossing social-class lines primarily means movement between social groups who own the means of production and those who do not own the means of production. Most mobility studies concerned about schooling consider mobility in terms of hierarchy of occupations where position is determined by income and status. In this conceptualization of mobility, intergenerational mobility would occur if the individual had an occupation that was better (or worse) in income and prestige than that of his mother or father. An obvious example of this mobility would be the son of a mechanic becoming a doctor.

Defining mobility in terms of movement up or down a scale of occupations fits into the concept of a professionalized and bureaucratic society. It also represents an acceptance of a hierarchical society where rewards or income are distributed not on the basis of how hard a person works but on the prestige of the occupation. The hierarchy of occupational rewards is often linked to the amount of education required for the job and the claim to expertise. A construction worker may work harder in terms of time and effort but not receive anywhere near the income received by a corporate lawyer.

An example of the acceptance of this hierarchy of occupations is a major study of mobility by Seymour Lipset and Reinhard Bendix called *Social Mobility in Industrial Society.* The authors begin their book with this statement: "In every complex society there is a division of labor and hierarchy of prestige. Positions of leadership and social responsibility are usually ranked at the top, and positions requiring long training and superior intelligence are ranked just below." The authors describe society as a pyramid with few at the top and many at the bottom. The majority at the bottom are "persons in the lower strata who perform manual and routine work of every sort and who command scant rewards and little prestige." Social mobility is defined as movement up or down this pyramid. The authors state: "It is possible to conceive of the result of this process as a distribution of talent and training such that privileges and perquisites accrue to each position in proportion to its difficulty and responsibility."[16] Here is the ideal model of the bureaucratic society where location in the hierarchical pyramid is determined by talent (in this case undefined), and the reward system matches the hierarchical structure.

In their classic study Lipset and Bendix were interested in comparing rates of mobility between industrial societies and the means of individual mobility. One of their major conclusions was that there was little difference in rates of social mobility between manual and nonmanual occupations in industrial societies. What this meant was that mobility was primarily a result of economic expansion, which creates new jobs and destroys old jobs. Changes in the occupational structure result in sons or daughters having jobs different from those of former generations. As mentioned at the beginning of this chapter, one cause of social mobility in the twentieth century in industrial society has been the decline of agricultural occupations and the rise of white-collar jobs.

Of importance to our discussion was the finding by Lipset and Bendix that variations between countries in rates of mobility in the professions and government bureaucracies was related to the amount of educational opportunity available in a society. Whereas the degree of educational opportunity did not seem to affect mobility in other occupational categories, it did in those occupations specifically requiring formal training in an educational institution or related to high-ranking positions in government civil service. This reflects the increasing reliance of these occupations on formal educational institutions.[17]

In addition, Lipset and Bendix argued that the growth of the large corporation with its bureaucratic structure had increased the possibilities of mobility into the American business elite. They found, contrary to what they claimed was popular myth, that the great majority of those who entered the American business elite in the nineteenth century came from privileged social and economic backgrounds. Only 10 to 20 percent of the American business elite came "from families in which the father was a worker, craftsman, small entrepreneur, lower-white-collar employee, or small farmer." Their overall finding was "that the recruitment of the American business elite has remained remarkably stable."[18]

This stability of recruitment, they argued, has been declining in the twentieth century because the American business elite has been unable to protect positions for their children from "the inroads that bureaucratization of business and industry has made upon family influence, especially in the largest corporation." They used the ideology of equality of opportunity to justify the bureaucratic society in their conclusion that "bureaucratization of economic enterprise also serves in some measure to facilitate the upward social mobility of the individual and thus to reinforce the social base of American ideological equalitarianism."[19]

Another major study of mobility patterns concerned with equality of opportunity was Peter Blau and Otis Duncan's *The American Occupational Structure*. On the first page of their book they directly link mobility studies to social and educational policy. In other words, they see as one benefit of studying mobility patterns the implementation of social policy to stimulate increased mobility. They do not spell out the practical implications of their work, but they "repeatedly indicate whether the inferior occupational chances of some groups compared to those of others are primarily due to the former's educational attainments or to other factors."[20]

Blau and Duncan formulated their study in the same conceptual framework of a hierarchy of occupations used by Lipset and Bendix. Blau and Duncan write that the "hierarchy of occupational strata reveals the relationship between the social contributions men make by furnishing various services and the rewards they receive in return. . . ."[21] They argue that Marx's division of classes on the basis of ownership or nonownership of the means of production is "no longer adequate for differentiating men in control of the large capitalistic enterprises from those subject to their control, because the controlling managers of the largest concerns today are themselves employees of corporations."[22]

Blau and Duncan believed that three major historical reasons could be cited for increasing rates of social mobility. The first reason was change in the occupational structure caused by technological progress. Second, in the United States, immigration and differential fertility contributed to increased mobility rates. Immigration contributed to mobility rates by providing a steady flow of workers into the lower ranks of the occupational hierarchy and freeing children of parents in the lower strata to move up to higher occupational levels. Differential fertility refers to the differing birthrates associated with individuals in different parts of the occupational structure. Blau and Duncan argued that "relatively low birth rates of the white-collar class, finally, opened up additional opportunities for upward mobility." A third aspect, linked to both technological progress and differential fertility, was the expansion of the professional group at the top. This reflected a change in the occupational structure, and differences in birthrate meant that many children of families that were low on the occupational scale were able to fill these positions. "For example," they wrote, "the number of professional, technical, and kindred workers was less than one-tenth the number working on farms in 1900; today the first group outnumbers the second nearly two to one."[23]

It is important to comment on the role of education in the historical conditions described by Blau and Duncan. Here, schooling is not a cause but a means for movement through the occupational structure. The career route for those who moved from families in the lower strata of the occupational structure to white-collar and professional occupations was often through educational institutions. These institutions did not create the occupations, but they made it possible for people to move into those occupations. It is possible for those who made this climb up the occupational scale to confuse the means with the cause and create and perpetuate the myth that education is the key for getting ahead. This is the same issue discussed in chapter 3 on human resource development. Education can be a means for reaching an occupational goal only if there is room in the occupation.

Blau and Duncan, in dealing with the role of education in social mobility, put the issue in the framework of a question: "What determines an individual's chances of achieving upward mobility?" Their answer: social origin, education, and career beginnings. They conclude from their study: "A man's social origins exert a considerable influence on his chances of occupational success, but his own training and early experience exert a more profound influence on his success status."[24] All these factors, the authors admit, are interrelated, but they still conclude that education has the strongest direct effect on occupational achievement.

This conclusion, which seems to ascribe central importance to education, is tempered by their finding that social origin, education, and career beginnings explain only half the variations between individuals in terms of occupational success. This leaves a large area of unexplained causes for occupational success and individual social mobility. Blau and Duncan can explain the causes of general social mobility (e.g., differential fertility and technological change), but they are unable to explain all the factors involved in individual mobility at the time these general social conditions occurred.

Blau and Duncan's study is important not only because it is the major study of social mobility in the occupational structure but also because it provides a lucid statement and support of the ideology of equality of opportunity. The term "ideology" is used here because Blau and Duncan discuss equality of opportunity as a system of ideas that maintains the political and social structure of society. In other words, they present equality of opportunity as a political and social doctrine.

The ideology of equality of opportunity, they argue, provides for social efficiency, social stability, and social solidarity. Social efficiency refers to the human resource argument that maximum social mobility will allow for human talent to find its best place in the occupational structure. In their words: "The great potential of society's human resources can be more fully exploited in a fluid class structure with a high degree of mobility than a rigid class structure."[25]

Equality of opportunity will provide for social solidarity by promoting what they call "universalism." Universalism refers to individual attachment to the entire society rather than to particular groups or families. Social mobility moves individuals in both a real and a figurative sense from their families and original friendships and community groups. Loyalty to particular groups is replaced with loyalty to the social system and a feeling for the interdependence of society. Blau and Duncan argue that the individual's loyalty is directed toward his place in the occupational structure: "The achieved status of a man, what he has accomplished in terms of some objective criteria, becomes more important than his ascribed status, who he is in the sense of what family he comes from."[26]

In this argument, the ideology of equality of opportunity and social mobility becomes the means of wedding the individual to the bureaucratic structure of society. One's life has meaning primarily through the occupation and success one achieves in the organizational structure of the economic and political system. Family, friendships, and any group contacts that are separate from the occupation take on secondary meaning.

Social stability is achieved through equality of opportunity because social dissatisfaction is channeled into competition for jobs in the occupational structure. If a person is dissatisfied with his current economic or social condition, rather than stage a revolution to overthrow the system he should work harder to move up the occupational ladder. What is important to note about this argument is that it does not require the actual existence of high rates of social mobility. All it requires is that people believe that equality of opportunity exists and that they have a chance to get ahead. The role of the school in this case could be either to provide for real social mobility or to convince people that it exists.

Other studies of the role of educational institutions in providing equality of opportunity have come to the same limited conclusions as did Blau and Duncan. For instance, Christopher Jencks concluded in his massive study of *Inequality* in American society: "Men's occupational statuses turned out to be quite closely tied to their educational attainment. Yet there was a great deal of variation in the status of men with exactly the same amount of education, and this variation did not seem to be explained by any other readily identified characteristic."[27]

This conclusion points out the obvious fact that in the twentieth century, access to many occupations depends on educational credentials, but just because one has the credentials does not guarantee access to status occupations. In other words, education is a necessary but not sufficient requirement for occupational mobility.

One of Jencks' more interesting findings concerned individual income. An assumption of the model of an occupational hierarchy is that rewards are distributed according to one's place in the occupational structure. In fact, for the individual interested in moving up the ladder of success, the primary concern is probably not status (though this certainly is a motivating factor) but increased income. Jencks found that "variation in men's incomes proved even harder to explain than variation in their occupational statuses. Educational credentials influence the occupations men enter, but credentials do not have much effect on earnings within any given occupation, so their overall effect on income is moderate."[28]

The literature on mobility confirms the lack of proof about schools providing equality of opportunity and also contains many studies claiming that schools hinder equality of opportunity and maintain social status. The central point of most arguments is that family background is the most important determinant of success in school and number of years of schooling obtained, and consequently family background is the most important factor in determining an individual's place in the occupational structure.

These findings have resulted in heavy criticism of the school as a mechanism for perpetuating social differences. It is argued that the school translates the social and economic advantages of the child into educational achievement. The child from a poor family does not do as well in school or receive as many years of schooling as does the child from a more economically advantaged background. For example, Ivan Illich has argued that the spread of universal schooling has resulted in economic differences being translated into educational differences. These differences are supported by a doctrine of equality of opportunity that tells individuals they were given an equal chance to compete in school and their failure to achieve or receive a large number of years of schooling is their own failure. They then blame themselves and not social and economic conditions for their poverty.[29]

Another way of viewing this issue is to say that the school reflects the dominant interests of society. In these terms, the school will continue to perpetuate class differences as long as elites are in control of the major economic institutions in society. The ideology of equality of opportunity is only a cover for the perpetuation of class differences.[30]

The problem with the above argument is that attempts to achieve equality of opportunity through educational institutions seem to be in as much difficulty in socialist countries as in capitalist countries. A perplexing problem in the Soviet Union has been the link between education and family background. Richard Dobson writes that "the studies conducted by Soviet sociologists demonstrate that the educational attainment process in the USSR is in many ways similar to that observed in Western countries. A young person's educational attainment is largely a function of parents' socio-occupational status and educational level, family per capita income, and place of residence. . . ."[31] In the 1950s Premier Khrushchev tried to correct this situation after it was discovered that only 30 to 40 percent of students in Moscow's universities came from farm and working-class families. But by the late 1960s the dilemma continued to plague the Soviet educational system.[32]

The problems faced in the Soviet Union give a different meaning to the charge that schools in capitalist societies are a means of class domination in the Marxist sense. It is not a matter of the social class that owns the means of production perpetuating its power through the school; it is that the hierarchy of professional and bureaucratic positions transmit their advantages to their children through the school. A study conducted in Leningrad in 1968 found that the percentage of eighth-grade pupils continuing into ninth grade paralleled occupational status. In terms of parents' occupation the percentages for those continuing were 86 percent professional, 70 percent semiprofessional, 52 percent skilled workers, and 25 percent manual and nonmanual workers. The same pattern of differences between children with parents of different occupational statuses continued through the higher grades.[33]

The Conflict Between Equality of Educational Opportunity and Social Mobility

It is important at this point to summarize some of the main conclusions in this chapter. First, no study of social mobility has been able to demonstrate conclusively that the school is fairer than the marketplace in the competition for occupations. In other words, there is no proof that the internalization of competition in the school for places in the social hierarchy has increased equality of opportunity. None of the studies has found that education increases rates of mobility. Rates of mobility depend on changes in the occupational structure and population.

Why, one might ask, do so many people believe that education will provide equality of opportunity for social mobility when there is no demonstrated proof of this phenomenon? Part of the answer might lie in the fact that education provides a means for movement up the occupational hierarchy *when population and occupational changes occur.* This is the example given earlier of those who in the early part of the twentieth century gained access to professional and white-collar occupations.

Education as a means for intergenerational mobility when changes occur in the occupational structure and population has probably been reinforced by the fact that educational institutions are the means of gaining access to more and more jobs in modern society. It may be necessary to go to school to enter an occupation that in previous generations did not require schooling. This is part of the phenomenon of educational inflation discussed in chapter 3. The economic value of an education decreases as more people go to school and receive more education. If everyone has a college degree, a college degree is less likely to be a means of upward social mobility.

This situation results in individuals having to attend school to get a job but not necessarily a job that will result in social mobility. A child of a factory worker might have to get more years of schooling than his father just to be able to compete for the same job held by his father. The child might end up with the same occupational status as his father but with more years of schooling. Lester C. Thurow summarizes the situation in these words: "Education becomes a good investment, not because it would raise people's incomes above what they would have been if no one had increased his education, but rather because it raises their income above what it will be if others acquire an education and they do not."[34]

Thurow argues that in modern industrial society education had become a "defensive expenditure necessary to protect one's 'market share.'" In other words, education is no longer primarily a means of upward mobility but a means of avoiding downward mobility. This is directly related to educational inflation. In reference to education as a defense against downward mobility, Thurow writes: "The larger the class of educated labor and the more rapidly it grows, the more such defensive expenditures become imperative."[35]

Education as a defensive expenditure against downward mobility highlights the conflict between equality of educational opportunity and the value of education in promoting increased rates of social mobility. As expansion of equality of educational opportunity occurs, there is an increase in the number of years of education held by larger numbers of the population. This results in educational inflation, which results in decreasing the value of education for upward social mobility. In other words, education is of more value to the poor individual in getting a job higher up in the occupational hierarchy when not many other poor people are getting an education. Increased educational opportunity for poor people decreases education's value for upward mobility.

A one-sentence paragraph might summarize the situation in the following manner: Education is no longer a means for getting ahead, but it is a means for staying in the same place.

The above statement is supported by a study of the effects of the rise of the welfare state after World War II in England. Sociologist A. H. Halsey found that the increase in educational opportunity resulting from welfare state programs increased the importance of educational certification for entering the job market but did not decrease the importance of family background in determining entry-level occupation.

It is important to understand the meaning of this conclusion. Education not only has decreased in value for social mobility but also has not provided equality of opportunity. In terms of Illich's argument, given earlier, social background is translated into educational differences. Halsey describes the situation in England's welfare state: "The direct effect of the class hierarchy of families on educational opportunity and certification has risen since the war. And at the same time the articulation of education to the first entry into the labor market has been tightening." He concludes: "Thus education is increasingly the mediator of the transmission of status between generations."[36]

Thus all that has been accomplished in the attempt to use educational institutions as a means of providing equality of opportunity has been to tighten the relationship between educational certification and the occupational structure. Expansion of educational institutions and equality of educational opportunity have not resulted in increased rates of upward mobility, equality of opportunity, or equality of income.

The major thing that the rhetoric of equality of opportunity through schooling has accomplished has been to convince society that the monopoly of expertise created by the relationship between the professions and bureaucratic occupations, educational institutions, and the state was not undemocratic or monopolistic because all people had equality of opportunity to enter these occupations through educational institutions. Thus, educational institutions have been used to both establish and protect the monopoly of expertise and to gain social acceptance of the monopoly.

There is another aspect to the internalization of competition in the school rather than the marketplace for occupations and for tightening the relationship between educational certification and jobs. Not only do schools protect and promote the prestige of professions but they also become objects of professional control. Competition in the schoolhouse has become an object of professional control and planning. Schools protect and promote professional occupations and at the same time have their own professional and bureaucratic hierarchy. The next chapter deals with the professionalization and bureaucratization of educational institutions.

5

PROFESSIONALISM
AND BUREAUCRACY
IN EDUCATION

THE PREVIOUS CHAPTER DISCUSSED SOCIAL MOBILITY AND EQUALITY of opportunity in the context of the rise of a bureaucratic and professional society. It was argued that both equal opportunity and the rise of professionalism are heavily dependent on the development of mass public schooling in modern societies. Modern societies have tended to shift the competitive arena for occupations from the marketplace to the school and have justified this with the claim that schools can provide a fairer arena for competition. The rise and expansion of professionalism has been based on claims of expert knowledge that justify a monopoly of services through government licensing. The attempt to resolve the apparent contradiction between a claim of monopoly over services and a society based on economic competition lies in the doctrine that all people are given a fair chance to compete in schooling.

An interesting thing about this discussion is that it centers on the school, which is itself a professional and bureaucratic organization. If the school is the central institution for producing a professional and bureaucratic society, then an investigation of the nature of professionalism and bureaucracy within the institution has important implications for understanding the nature of these phenomena in the rest of society. I am not saying that there is a direct correspondence between the professional and bureaucratic nature of schooling and the rest of society but that the school socializes the individual into early models of professionalism and bureaucracy. How effective and lasting this socialization is on the individual is not known.

This chapter first investigates the professionalization of teaching and then the science of school administration and bureaucracy in education. The concluding section of the chapter relates these investigations to the broader issues of equality of opportunity and the development of a professional and bureaucratic society. The meaning of professionalism and bureaucracy are discussed in this context.

Teachers and Professionalism

For the purposes of this chapter, the term "professionalism" will be used to characterize an occupation for which graduation from an educational institution or an examination is required and there is a claim to expert knowledge that justifies a monopoly of services granted by government licensing. In the teaching profession, this usually means graduation from a college or university with a claim to expert knowledge based on courses taken in departments or colleges of education. Teacher licenses are usually granted by the government on the basis of fulfilling certain educational requirements. In addition, the concept of professionalism contains an ideology of service; the professional is viewed as an individual who puts client interest before self-interest. In the teaching profession, this has meant an orientation toward serving the student and the community.[1]

This is an ideal definition of professionalism and takes on a different meaning when one looks at the reality. For instance, the expert knowledge gained by teachers in education courses is not highly regarded by teachers, university faculty members not associated with departments of education, or the community. Teaching has a low status compared with other professions.

As an example of this attitude, consider the remarks of sociologist Dan Lortie in his recent investigation of teachers in the United States. "Teachers are inclined to talk about their training as easy ('mickey mouse'); I have yet to hear a teacher complain that education courses were too difficult or demanded too much effort." Lortie found that teachers did not feel that preparation in education courses provided a feeling of special training. As a result, Lortie wrote that "teachers do not consider training the key to their legitimation as teachers."[2]

A number of historical and social reasons can be cited for the low status of teacher education. During the early years of its development, teacher training was primarily related to preparation for teaching in elementary schools and teaching children from the lower classes. Education courses and specific teacher training became associated with lower-status educational institutions and lower-status clients. As one went up the prestige scale of educational institutions, fewer courses in education were (and are) required for teaching. Secondary schools required less special training in education than elementary schools, and universities usually required no special preparation for teaching.[3]

The low status of teacher education is best exemplified by teacher-training institutions in Germany, which provided an early model for normal schools in the United States. In early-nineteenth-century Prussia, entrance into normal school was at age thirteen or fourteen after graduation from a folk, or middle, school. Graduation from the normal school took place at age nineteen, from whence the individual returned to teach in the middle schools. Because students from middle schools came primarily from working-class families, a self-perpetuating cycle developed: Children of working-class families taught children of other workers. This gave a low-social-class status to the normal school.[4]

This model was introduced in the United States without the social-class stigma but with the emphasis on training for elementary school teaching. In the nineteenth century the route to normal school was much like that of Germany. Most normal school students went directly from elementary school to normal school. Even as late as 1900, high school graduation was not a requirement for entrance into normal school.[5]

In England, too, low-social-class status and low educational prestige were associated with teacher training. The first major organized teacher training was begun by Joseph Lancaster to provide "monitors" for his system of education, which was specifically designed to provide mass education for the lower classes. The whole atmosphere of early-nineteenth-century English normal schools was to produce elementary teachers who, as one author has stated, "were to be missionaries to the poor; inspired by 'Christian charity.' . . ."[6]

These early normal schools created a status system in education based on the amount of educational training: the more specialized the training in teaching, the lower the status of the teacher. In most countries this created a major division between secondary and elementary school teachers. Secondary school teachers usually were graduates of secondary schools and attended universities or colleges; most elementary teachers experienced only elementary and normal schools.

In the United States this created an interesting split between teachers and the developers of educational policy. The more educational training an individual had, the more likely that he or she would not assume a leadership role in education. Historian Merle Borrowman wrote: "The first national organization of men who were professionally concerned with the making of policy for the public schools was the National Association of School Superintendents which first met in 1866. Most of these men were probably trained in the liberal arts colleges and had received no formal education in a professional sequence." Borrowman concluded that this situation resulted in a dualistic system where the "graduates of the normal school did not at first assume policy-making responsibility; those who did were educated in the liberal arts colleges."[7]

In France and England, the same situation has prevailed. The more prestigious the status in education institutions, the fewer the education courses that have been required to achieve that status. Sociologists James Lynch and H. Dudley Plunkett write: "In both England and France it has been quite common for secondary teachers, particularly the more prestigious, to receive no training as teachers." Since 1890 in England, an individual can enter secondary school teaching by giving evidence of knowledge of an academic field and receiving a postgraduate certificate of education after completing a university degree course. In France, the elite among secondary school teachers are required only to undergo four weeks of teacher training.[8]

Since World War II, most normal schools in the United States have expanded into four-year colleges or universities with an upgrading of elementary teacher requirements to include graduation from a secondary school and college. The same phenomenon has occurred in England with the faculties of teacher-education institutions expanding from one thousand just before World War II to ten thousand by 1969. In 1971, 50 percent of the students in these institutions were being trained for secondary schools. In West Germany, teachers are trained in colleges of education, and many of them are university-equivalent institutions.[9]

The upgrading of elementary education requirements has lessened the status difference between elementary and secondary teachers, but it has not affected actual courses in teacher training. Most of the upgrading of normal schools has resulted from adding more academic courses.

Another problem is the lowly status of the education professoriate compared with other members of college and university faculties. This situation has serious consequences for teachers' feelings about their training. Not only tradition but the regard of the rest of the academic community shape their view of the worth and status of teacher training. Taking courses in a college or department of education on a university campus is often viewed as intellectual slumming.

One irony of the expansion of normal schools into colleges and the addition of colleges of education to universities has been the creation of the low-status professor of education. Theodore Sizer and Arthur Powell, at the time dean and associate dean of the Harvard School of Education, portray the professor of education as a "gentle, unintellectual, saccharine, and well-meaning . . . bumbling doctor of undiagnosable ills, harmless if morosely defensive. He is either a mechanic . . . or he is the flatulent promoter of irrelevant trivia."[10]

Sizer and Powell feel the lowly status of the education professoriate in part results from the faculty recruiting required when education faculties expanded rapidly in the twentieth century. Most of the new positions were filled by people who had been trained in different occupations in education. Colleges and departments of education became staffed with former school administrators and teachers who primarily taught and wrote about their experiences. Rather than the study of education having been grounded in theory, like other academic areas, it has often reflected personal experience. Rather than having been viewed as intellectuals, education faculties have often been viewed as antiintellectuals.[11]

In addition, the organization of the study of education tended to be around occupations rather than around areas of knowledge. Colleges of education divided into departments of school administration, vocational education, secondary education, elementary education, special education, and counselor education. Dividing the study of education into occupations almost guaranteed that a unified academic discipline in education would never exist. Study in colleges of education became primarily the study of occupational roles.[12]

Sizer and Powell suggest that faculties of education are too oriented toward supplying people to the public schools and not geared to the study of the general social and psychological processes of education and learning, of which public schooling is one element. The latter approach might upgrade the status of the education professoriate and at the same time increase the status and quality of the professional training of teachers.

The history, status, and content of training in education tends to lower the overall professional status of teaching. The status of a profession in part depends on a claim to expert knowledge. In the teaching profession this claim is seriously weakened by the low status of faculties that teach education courses, a history that has associated education courses with low-status educational institutions, and a field of knowledge primarily determined by the occupational roles in existing public schools. An increase in the professional status of teaching will require a significant change in the content and curriculum of teacher-training institutions.

Another factor contributing to the difficulty of legitimating the professional status of teachers by claiming expert knowledge has been the lack of relationship between educational training and the perception of the teacher's role in the community. As mentioned, a distinctive feature of professionalism is that it places client interest before self-interest. In the teaching profession, meeting client needs and interests could be considered in terms of the expert knowledge of method and subject matter of the educator. The teacher's responsibility could be to use the best methods to teach the client. This would represent a close relationship between expert knowledge and client interest.

The problem has been that the teacher's relationship to the client has not been defined within the narrow limits of expert knowledge of method and subject matter. In the nineteenth and twentieth centuries, the teacher has been perceived as a moral and social agent whose responsibility to the client has been to shape moral and social values and end a host of social problems ranging from crime and poverty to alcoholism and drug addiction. This role of the teacher has not always been legitimated in terms of expert knowledge and training. What has been used is screening and control.

For instance, it was once hoped that the moral power of the teacher would eliminate crime and train generations of moral and loyal citizens. This did not mean making teachers moral experts; it meant controlling their moral behavior. In the United States, character qualifications were considered of great importance for teacher certification. Teachers were expected to have exemplary moral and social habits. Even their manner of dress was considered of prime importance for teaching. The fourth annual report of the Boston Board of Education in 1841 stated that if the "manners of the teacher are to be imitated by the pupils,—if he is the glass, at which they 'do dress themselves,' how strong is the necessity, that he should understand those nameless and innumerable practices, in regard to deportment, dress, conversation, and all personal habits, that constitute the difference between a gentleman and a clown." The report went on to make clear the exemplary character expected of teachers. "We can bear some oddity," the report declared, "or eccentricity in a friend whom we admire for his talents, or revere for his virtues; but it becomes quite a different thing, when the oddity, or the eccentricity, is to be a pattern or model, from which fifty or a hundred children are to form their manners."[13]

Teachers lived like goldfish in a bowl. All their actions were open to public scrutiny and judgment. The use of alcohol or tobacco was often grounds for dismissal, gambling was forbidden, church attendance was expected, and a teacher's relationship to a member of the opposite sex had to fall strictly within the boundaries of propriety. The teacher as moral agent often resulted in the teacher as second-class citizen.[14]

Similar situations existed in Germany and England. The emphasis was on the teacher as a character model for the rest of society. Again it must be emphasized that this model was not based on expert knowledge of moral and social values but on the control and screening of those values. One sociologist has written about France, England, and Germany that the teachers' "public image of social conformity and teachers' own self-images have been important factors in the quantitative and qualitative development of education to this day."[15]

That this social role was based on conformity and control seriously undermined the professional nature of teaching. This role could not be legitimated in terms of expert knowledge, as it could be for the ministry. Ministers could be moral leaders and still protect their professionalism by claiming expert training in theology and philosophy. For teachers, the claim to moral leadership meant only social conformity and second-class citizenship.

In the twentieth century some attempt has been made to provide an expert-knowledge base for the continually expanding social role of the teacher. The problem has been that demands on teachers have far outpaced developments in training teachers. In fact, it may be impossible to train any human being to accomplish the tasks assigned to the teaching role. Can anyone be an expert in teaching methods and subject matter and at the same time solve the social and psychological problems of students, reform their families, and end poverty in modern society?

This expanded perception of the social role of the teacher occurred in the United States in the early part of the twentieth century when "the whole child came to school." What this meant in practice was that the teacher was to assume responsibility for the psychological state of the student and all social factors affecting the child's life. Sociologists began to claim that the family and church were collapsing in modern society and that the school had to expand its role to pick up the pieces.

The school became a social agency; it assumed responsibility for health care, cleanliness, and social and psychological problems, and provided a center for community activity. Teachers' activities expanded into extracurricular events and involvement in the family life of students and their social environment.[16]

This expanded role for teachers occurred as new subject matter was being added to teacher-training curriculums. The study of educational psychology, human development, and the sociology of education was designed to improve methods of instruction and extend the teachers' expertise to deal with broad social issues. The teacher was introduced to the scientific study of the child and society as it relates to education. But the brief exposure to these courses could hardly be considered an expert preparation for the problems teachers were being asked to handle.[17]

These changes in the role of the teacher did not take place in Europe to any significant degree until after World War II with the expansion of equality of educational opportunity. The attempt to create universal systems of education in Europe occurred when human capitalist economists were beginning to argue that education could be a means of eliminating poverty. In both the United States and Europe in the 1960s, the teacher became a warrior against poverty.[18]

These changes in the social functions of schooling are reflected in changes in the curriculum of teacher-training institutions. The social science base of the curriculum was broadened with emphasis on special help to the "disadvantaged" child. In the United States this training went under the name "urban education," which was a special field of study in some teacher-training institutions and an additional topic in traditional courses elsewhere. The training was never adequate to prepare teachers to eliminate poverty in the United States or deal with children who were victims of poverty. It was just another subject in the already confused curriculum of teacher education.[19]

In Europe the same shift toward a social science curriculum took place. Sociologist James Lynch and H. Dudley Plunkett directly link these changes to the expansion of equality of educational opportunity: "The traditional courses in pedagogical or educational theory are giving way in a number of colleges to more interrelated behavioural studies in education and in socially related fields." In England there is the same concern with providing special training for dealing with the children of the poor. Lynch and Plunkett write that this "found expression in the educational priority areas where colleges of education have established annexes in inner-city areas to afford their students continued close experience of the complex of social disadvantages common to large numbers of inner-city areas."[20]

On the surface, additions to, and in some cases changes in, teacher training to deal with the "disadvantaged" seemed laudable. But considering the goals already placed on educational institutions and teachers, these changes were overwhelming. By the late 1970s education had not ended the problem of poverty, and that goal seemed unattainable in view of the workload in educational institutions.

As the teacher-training curriculum became more diffuse, the content in courses on methods of instruction came into conflict with the professional values and independence of teachers. One of the attempts since the early part of the twentieth century has been to reduce classroom teaching to a series of technical steps governed by something called the "science of education."

In the early part of the twentieth century this movement was led by Edward Thorndike, who primarily saw teaching in terms of sequentially reinforcing learning by what he considered scientific laws.[21] In the 1940s and '50s this view was elaborated by psychologist B. F. Skinner, who believed that all human behavior could be explained and controlled by planned reinforcement. Skinner hoped to revolutionize teaching by the introduction of programmed learning, teaching machines, and a methodology based on the science of human behavior.[22]

One aspect of this revolution in teaching was greater control over the actions of the classroom teacher. In a sense the teacher was to become a technician implementing the methodology devised by instructional experts. During the 1950s this was part of an attempt to devise "teacherproof" materials. What this meant was that an instructional package of audiovisual materials, programmed learning devices, and other instructional aids would be provided to teachers; no matter how bad the teacher, the student would learn.[23]

In the 1960s and '70s, control over teacher behavior became part of the movement for competency-based education. Ideally, competencies are defined in terms of specific behavioral objectives, where the teacher presents organized material to help the student achieve those objectives and then measures the outcome. Both the specific behavioral objectives and the measurement of achievement of those objectives became devices for controlling teacher behavior. If the curriculum was uniform throughout the school system, the teacher became a technician who implemented centrally determined objectives; measurement of student achievement became the method of evaluating teacher performance.

The behavioral method of instruction has created a dilemma regarding the professional status of teachers. On one hand, it lends an air of expertise that can be used to legitimize the professional nature of teaching. Teachers can claim to have learned a scientific methodology that gives them special tools to help students learn. Like the medical examining room or the laboratory, the classroom can be filled with equipment and methods that are mysterious and awesome to the general public. The teacher is a keeper of special knowledge.

On the other hand, the methodology is a means of controlling teacher behavior and threatens the professional independence of teaching. It becomes difficult for teachers to claim professional independence in their classrooms when they are forced to teach and measure in terms of specific behavioral objectives defined by some external source. In this situation the teacher is a technician implementing a centralized plan.

This issue becomes more important as school systems become more centralized. In the twentieth century teachers have not had the independence of doctors and lawyers. Teachers are employed primarily in institutions run by government. Few teachers or groups of teachers have formed their own schools, though this has happened with the expansion of Montessori education in the United States. The professional independence of teachers has centered on the autonomy of the classroom. This autonomy is threatened by the behavioral model of instruction.

Sociologist Dan Lortie touches on this dilemma and on increasing bureaucratic centralization when he warns teachers that they "will stand a better chance of winning autonomy within a state-dominated system if they can persuade decision-makers that they are a 'professionalizing' occupation." What they must do, he argues, is convince these decision makers that teaching requires highly technical preparation. "But," he writes, "the axes of professionalization . . . run against the ethos of the occupation. . . ."[24]

Many problems await attempts to legitimate the profession of teaching by claims to expert knowledge. History and the social structure of education have helped to give a low-status image to teacher education. In addition, the education professoriate has low status within the academic community. The broad social goals of education have made claims on teacher-training institutions that have diffused the curriculum and created a training program that will give mastery of methods of teaching and subject matter, and the ability to solve a wide range of social and psychological problems.

Also, the autonomy of the teacher has traditionally been limited. The role of teacher as moral agent was not formed on the basis of expert knowledge but on demands for social and moral conformity.

The present behavioral methods of instruction can require a similar conformity. This issue reflects the tension that exists between professionalism and a bureaucratic structure.

Teaching in a Bureaucracy

A characteristic feature of the school in the twentieth century has been a continually expanding bureaucratic structure. As a result, the proportion of classroom teachers to total school staff has been steadily declining. What this means in terms of a teacher's identity in the school organization is not clear. But bureaucratic theory suggests a possible alienation of the individual in expanding organizations.

The most dramatic representations of the growth of the bureaucratic structure in education in the United States are the historical changes in the proportion of supervisors and principals to teachers and current figures on the total noninstructional staff of schools. According to the 1976 *Digest of Education Statistics* in public elementary and secondary schools in the United States, in 1919–20 there was 1 supervisor or principal for every 31 teachers, librarians, and other nonsupervisory instructional staff. As we shall see later in the chapter, the 1920s was an important period for the professionalization of educational administration and the expansion of school management systems. In any event, by 1929–30 the ratio had changed so that there was 1 principal or supervisor for every 22 teachers, librarians, and other nonsupervisory instructional staff. The depression of the 1930s seemed to restrict the expansion of administrative personnel; the ratio shifted slightly in favor of instructional staff (to 1 per 23) in 1939–40. After World War II there was a steady increase in the number of principals and supervisors in proportion to instructional staff. In 1949–50 the ratio was 1 to 19, in 1959–60 it was 1 to 17, in 1969–70 it was 1 to 17, and in 1973–74 it was 1 to 16.[25]

It is important to understand that these changes have not been at the expense of the proportion of instructional staff to students. These changes parallel the expansion of supervisors and principals. In 1919–20 the ratio of teachers, librarians, and other supervisory staff to students was approximately 1 to 33; and in 1973–74 it was approximately 1 to 20. One thing that should be noted is that the ratio of administrators to instructional staff is better than the ratio of instructional staff to students.[26]

The differences in ratios are highlighted when one isolates the classroom teacher from the total instructional staff and looks at the administrator to classroom teacher ratio compared with the classroom teacher to pupil ratio. In 1973–74 public elementary and secondary schools in the United States had approximately 1 classroom teacher for every 21 students, and there was 1 supervisor or principal for every 15.5 teachers.[27]

Another reflection of the expanding bureaucratic structure in education is the continuing consolidation of school districts. The actual number of school districts has declined rapidly since the 1940s. At the end of World War II there were 101,000 school districts in the United States. By 1975–76 this number had been reduced to 16,300 districts. This is a dramatic reduction of 83.8 percent in thirty years.[28]

The most rapid period of consolidation of school districts occurred between 1947 and 1959 when the number dropped from 94,900 to 40,500. During the 1960s the rate of decline was 2,000 a year, leaving 19,200 districts at the end of the decade. By the late 1970s the rate of decline had slowed to about 250 per year.[29] Of course this slower rate of decline reflects fewer numbers of school districts that can consolidate. Future consolidation will be affected by the growth of metropolitan desegregation plans and the centralization of school finances. The issue of school finances is discussed in more detail in a later chapter, but it should point to the possibility of larger and more centralized school systems.

Paralleling the decline in numbers of school districts has been the increased size of educational systems. In 1949–50 there were about 25 million students in elementary and secondary public schools in the United States. By 1973–74 this figure had increased to 45 million. During the same period the number of principals and supervisors had increased from 48,000 to 138,000, and the instructional staff had increased from 914,000 to 2,287,000.[30]

The combination of consolidation with increases in staff and students meant that teachers witnessed a rapid growth of distance between themselves and the leadership of local school districts. The consolidation of school districts resulted in superintendents and their staffs serving a larger geographical area and a larger staff. The possibility of direct contact between a classroom teacher and the administrative leadership of a school district became more difficult under these circumstances. The superintendent was a remote figure whom the classroom teacher might see only in newspapers or on local television.

As school districts have consolidated and grown and the proportion of administrators to teachers has increased, a vast administrative layer has developed between the classroom teacher and the leadership of the school district. This structure is usually hierarchical with the individual classroom teacher faced with a chain of command that leads through a head teacher or assistant principal to a building principal to a district superintendent to a network of administrators in the central office of the school district. The administrative structure creates a wall that blocks any access by the individual teacher.

Several potential effects on teachers stem from the growth of these seemingly monolithic structures. One effect can be a sense of alienation from the organizational structure and a decline in a sense of personal worth. The distance between the teacher and the leadership, and the consequent inability of the teacher to influence policy, may create a sense of powerlessness that did not exist in earlier and smaller school districts where personal contact between the teacher and superintendent was possible. The present situation may be one reason for the growing militancy of teacher organizations and the rapid development of collective bargaining. Teachers' unions have provided a mechanism to bypass the hierarchical structure and directly confront the leadership of local school districts in collective bargaining sessions. Of course, this is through an organized group of teachers and not because an individual teacher influences policy.

Bureaucratic theory has approached the issue of alienation and sense of powerlessness from several perspectives. In this chapter, bureaucracy will be defined as an organization with the following characteristics: (1) job specialization, (2) hierarchical authority structure, (3) impersonality of relationships between members of the organization, (4) recruitment to membership in the organization on the basis of expert knowledge and training, and (5) control within the organization based on rational rules. This is what sociologists call an "ideal definition." In other words, it might not describe how organizations actually function, but it does provide a definition for the purposes of discussion.[31]

Classical sociological theory has stressed the crippling effect of this kind of organization on its membership. Rational regulation and hierarchical authority, it has been argued, tend to stunt creativity and force the individual to act within a narrowly specialized role. As suggested earlier in the chapter, this is one of the problems currently facing teachers. Behavioral methodology and centralization of control are threatening teacher autonomy and creativity in the classroom.[32]

Bureaucrats have been pictured as so bound by organizational rules that they develop a fear of assuming responsibility and a lack of initiative. The rules of the organization motivate and define the limits of action. Alienation in a bureaucratic structure occurs when the individual loses sight of his actions as they relate to the goals of the total organization. For the individual, the most important thing becomes obedience to rules. For instance, in education this could mean that an administrator or teacher becomes obsessively concerned with the procedures and rules of the school system at the expense of the general goal of educating students.

This concept of the bureaucratic structure portrays its individual members as having an increasing sense of powerlessness as they become cogs in the organizational machine. A real powerlessness occurs through the person's ignorance of the operation of the total organization as he or she becomes more confined to a specialized role. In other words, a person trained to fulfill a specialized function as an expert acts out this role within a system of apparent rational rules. But the overspecialization of training can lead to a lack of knowledge and understanding of the political process within the organization and the general goals of the organization. Through the ignorance caused by overspecialization, the individual can be manipulated and controlled by the organization.[33]

An example of this in education might be a teacher who is highly trained in teaching methodology but has never been introduced to the study of the politics of education or the social and economic purposes of education. Because of this generalized ignorance of the organization, the teacher becomes manipulated by rules established by the hierarchical bureaucratic structure without understanding why or how these rules came into existence.

Bureaucratic behavior is also described in classical sociological literature as being directed toward self-aggrandizement. Bureaucrats continually seek to expand their roles and increase the importance of their positions. This occurs independently of the general goals of the organization and in some cases at the expense of those goals. In other words, a school administrator in charge of a program like career education will tend, according to bureaucratic theory, to work to increase the amount of money and staff allocated to career education and increase the share of student time occupied by that program in relation to other programs.[34]

The above is a brief theoretical description of bureaucratic organizations and does not necessarily describe existing educational institutions. In fact, I now argue that a major tension in education systems is caused by the tendency toward bureaucratic organization and the classroom autonomy of teachers. At this time, teachers' actions in the classroom are not carefully prescribed by rules. Their training contains many subjects that can provide an understanding of the general political and social goals of organizations.

According to our previous discussion of bureaucracy, as educational institutions become more bureaucratic there will be a tendency to control more actions of classroom teachers through specific rules. In addition, there will be a tendency to make teacher education more specialized and technical and reduce teachers' exposure to general academic subjects. Generalized ignorance with specialized knowledge can allow for bureaucratic manipulation.

The tension between the autonomy and the professionalism of teachers and the bureaucratic nature of schooling is reflected in the changes that have occurred in teacher organizations. Of major importance to the process has been the professionalization of school administrators. This professionalization has contributed to the bureaucratization of schooling, which in turn has helped spark the militant nature of teacher organizations.

Teacher Organizations and the Bureaucratic Structure of Education

An interesting thing about the rise of teacher militancy in the United States is that it occurred during the period in which school systems were consolidating and there was a significant increase in the ratio of school administrator to teacher. There is no proof that a causal relationship exists between these two sets of events. What can be said is that as the bureaucratic structure of education increased, and it became difficult for individual teachers to gain access to local educational leaders, collective bargaining by teacher organizations made it possible for teachers to gain access to local educational leadership and influence policy at state and national levels.

It is interesting that the two major teacher organizations in the United States began with disparate backgrounds but ended up with similar organizations. The oldest and largest organization of teachers in the United States is the National Education Association (NEA), founded in 1857. Its history reflects the changing status of teachers. During its early years it was dominated by college professors and educational administrators and excluded females from membership. Through the first half of the twentieth century the NEA served as an important forum for the development of educational policy. Its reports and policy statements provided the means for nationalizing American education by creating some uniformity in educational structures and organizations. Its work provided national standardization for elementary and secondary schools and teacher-training institutions.[35]

During the 1960s the NEA underwent dramatic transformations in organization and purpose. In 1962 the NEA launched a program for local organizations to rewrite their contracts for collective bargaining. Until then, many local education associations had been controlled by local administrators who tended to use the organization to convey policies determined by local school boards and administrators. Collective bargaining reversed this situation and turned the local affiliates into organizations that told boards and administrators what teachers wanted.

Members of the American Federation of Teachers (AFT) often claim that the NEA's acceptance of collective bargaining resulted from successes of the AFT. The AFT traces its early days to the formation of the Chicago Federation of Teachers in 1897 by elementary grade teachers to fight for an adequate pension law in Illinois. Unlike the NEA, the AFT was from its beginnings primarily an organization concerned with teacher welfare issues like pensions, salaries, and academic freedom. The AFT also saw itself as representing the interests of organized labor in the public schools. This was symbolized in 1916 when the AFT was accepted into the American Federation of Labor. The close association between the AFT and organized labor has been the trademark of the organization and represents one of its major differences with the NEA.

Even with its association with the American Federation of Labor, the AFT followed a no-strike policy until actions by local affiliates forced the national organization to reverse its policies. The first collective bargaining contract was signed in Cicero, Illinois, in 1944; the contract followed the lines of a regular labor-union settlement. In 1946 the AFT began to seriously study collective bargaining and material from organized labor on the education of shop stewards and union practices. In 1947 the Buffalo Teachers Federation went on strike for higher salaries and created the worst teacher work stoppage in the history of the country. Even with this event, the national AFT maintained a no-strike policy.

The event that has come to symbolize teacher militancy in the United States was the organization in the early 1960s of a New York City local of the AFT under the leadership of Albert Shanker, who in the 1970s became president of the AFT. The New York City local, the United Federation of Teachers (UFT), in 1961 won a major strike and became one of the largest and most influential locals in the AFT.

By the late 1970s collective bargaining by locals of the NEA or AFT provided a means for organized teachers to directly confront the educational leadership in local school districts. Collective bargaining took place between members of local teacher organizations and representatives of the local school board and central administration. This bargaining bypassed existing layers of administrative organization. By being strongly organized, teachers could exert power over an expanding bureaucracy and a hierarchical authority structure.

It is important to understand that teacher organizations are not solely concerned with welfare issues but direct their efforts toward shaping general educational policy. In the late 1970s the NEA was concerned about civil rights enforcement, minority rights, desegregation and integration, antiracism and antisexism, and student rights and teacher responsibility. In addition, the NEA created a great deal of controversy by calling for an end to standardized testing in the schools until testing organizations could police the tests. The AFT supported lifelong learning through the expansion of adult and continuing education.[36]

Attempts by the two teacher organizations to improve the welfare of teachers and influence educational policy are not limited to the bargaining table at the local level. Both organizations support lobbyists at state and national levels. They attempt to influence legislation and the policies of state and federal government administrators. In 1976 both organizations became actively involved in the presidential campaign in the hope of influencing the educational policy of the national administration.

The growth of teachers' unions has had some important effects on the expanding educational bureaucracy. First, as mentioned, unions have enabled teachers to gain power against an increasingly hierarchical authority structure. Second, even though unions have provided power against an expanding bureaucracy, they have contributed to the continuance and possible growth of that bureaucracy by their reliance on collective bargaining. Third, unions have created their own bureaucratic organization and their own hierarchical structure.

The argument that collective bargaining can lead to the continuance and expansion of the existing educational bureaucracy is based on one of the traditional arguments of organized labor. Since the beginning of the twentieth century, the American Federation of Labor has viewed collective bargaining as being between organized labor and organized business. In fact, Samuel Gompers, founder of the American Federation of Labor, consistently argued that large business trusts were essential for the development of the American economy and for the growth of collective bargaining. He saw the future economy as one shared by big business and big labor.[37]

This acceptance of large organized corporations was based on some practical considerations. It is much easier to bargain with several large businesses than with a large number of small companies. More workers can be represented in a single bargaining session with one big company than with a small company. It is also much easier to conduct a strike against an industry dominated by a few companies than against an industry shared by large numbers of small businesses. Each strike requires separate organization and tactics and a separate contract. In addition, once a union has reached a satisfactory contract with a corporation, it has an economic stake in the continuing existence of that corporation.

All of the above comments are applicable to teachers' unions. For instance, past history has shown that teachers' unions are not in favor of decentralized control or shifting control from existing administrative structures to community or parental groups. This is best illustrated by the community-control issue in New York City in the late 1960s. In this situation, control of the schools was returned to local community groups in response to complaints about the centralization of administration and the bureaucratic structure of education. When community control led to attempts to control who would teach in a local school, the New York teachers' union was swift to call a strike and demand an end to the experiment.[38]

Several obvious threats to teachers' unions are involved in decentralization and community control. Assuming that a collective bargaining contract exists, as it did in New York, decentralization or community control can throw out the existing union contract and require new negotiations with smaller educational units. This does not necessarily happen with decentralization because it is possible to have a single teacher contract for a large school district and decentralize just the administrative operations. But it is impossible to have community control and have a single contract for large districts. Effective community control requires bargaining with teachers at the community level about salary, working conditions, and general educational policy.

Community control is also a threat to union leadership. By reducing the size of the bargaining unit, the power of the union leader, which depends on the existence of the larger district, is greatly reduced. For instance, at the time of the community-control issue in New York City the head of the New York teachers' union was Albert Shanker. His power and leadership were based on the single contract and union structure supporting that contract for the entire city. Community control might have changed the course of events and destroyed the base of power that later made it possible for Shanker to become president of the American Federation of Teachers.

One of the best illustrations of union dependency on the existing structure of education is the tremendous effort made by both the NEA and AFT to stop legislation for tuition tax credits in 1978.[39] The tax credits, which many people seem to have forgotten could have been used for both public and private schools, were considered a direct threat to public schools. There were many other claims, for example, that tax credits would aid only the rich and would promote segregation. Answers to these charges from supporters of tax credits were that the majority of children who attended private schools came from families with incomes below the national average, and the proposed credits of $250 to $500 were not large enough to be significant to the rich. On the segregation issue, it was admitted that some private schools had developed to resist integration but that private schools had a better record of integration than public schools. For instance, Catholic schools have been better integrated than public schools in most northern cities. In addition, the Congress on Racial Equality supported tax credits because it believed that minority children and children of poor parents should be given an opportunity to choose between public and private schooling. Supporters of tax credits also charged opponents with religious bigotry.[40]

Although they recognized the existence of these other issues regarding tax credits, the central issue for teachers' unions was the threat to public schooling. Parents could gain partial control over public spending for education. This could threaten the existing monopoly of public schools over government spending on education and possibly expand the private sector in education.

Why should teachers' unions feel threatened by the possible expansion of the private sector in education? Other unions bargain with privately owned companies. In fact, the ideology of American unionism is the recognition of private ownership with the right of labor to organize and bargain. Given this situation, it is not inconceivable that teachers' unions, like any union, could bargain with private schools. The problem arose because a shift from a public to a private bargaining unit would create the same threat to the existing structure of the unions and their leadership as did the issue of community control.

One could hypothesize from the previous discussion that teachers' unions are developing conservative tendencies based on the protection of the existing bureaucratic structure of the union and the desire by its leadership to maintain power. "Conservative" in this case means the desire to conserve existing institutional relationships. One student of teachers' unions has written: "Teacher unions, once having achieved a modicum of influence, have not revealed any great interest in questioning the ideological and political foundations of the educational power structure. . . . Teacher unionism does not question the hierarchical governing arrangements of school systems."[41]

In fact, what seems to be happening is the development of a hierarchical structure in the union to match the hierarchical structure of education. Unions provide new career routes for teachers. At the local level teachers can become union staff leaders or board negotiators. From the local level they can advance to positions within state organizations of the unions and eventually to national offices. Each level of the local union matches each level in the educational power structure.

All this has created a rather ironic situation where teachers' unions have rapidly developed to increase the power of teachers against an increasingly bureaucratic structure and in the process have developed into hierarchical organizations that tend to conserve the bureaucracy against which they were organized. A new teacher is now faced with an expanded and hierarchical educational structure and a hierarchical union organization. There is now administrative leadership and union leadership, and administrative control and union control.

Professionalism and Scientific Management

The tension between the professionalism and autonomy of the teacher and the bureaucratic organization of education has been heightened by the professionalization that has occurred among the ranks of school administrators. Consider for a moment the options available for the professionalization of school administration. According to the definition of professionalism used in this chapter, a claim to expert knowledge is legitimized by special training in an educational institution. It is conceivable, therefore, that school administrators could have chosen as the route to professionalization the acquiring of doctoral degrees in academic fields of study like philosophy or history. Or they might have based their claim to expertise on a study of the philosophy of education or curriculum and instruction. Any of these options could have served as the basis for providing educational leadership in a school or school district.

What is important is that none of these options became the major means for the professionalization of school administrators. What happened is that school administrators became professionals by claiming expertise in scientific management and administration. Rather than having become leaders in subject matter and the organization of subject matter, school administrators have become experts in how to administrate and control organizations. Rather then the philosopher having been the model for the school administrator, the business executive was the model.

The professionalization of school administrators occurred in the early part of the twentieth century when scientific management was becoming an important part of American business. The main features of the early development of organizational science involved the scientific study of methods of organization to produce maximum productivity and the control of workers' actions on the basis of this scientific knowledge. This last point is important because it directly relates to the issue of teacher autonomy. In industry, scientific management meant that the worker would no longer solve operative problems encountered during work, for managers would train the individual how best to perform the work. This meant a separation between planning and performance. Management would do the planning, and workers would be trained to fulfill the plans of management.[42]

Colleges of education in the early part of the twentieth century began to train future school administrators in principles of scientific management as applied to educational institutions. The professionalization of school administration took place in this context. Administrators claimed expertise in the management and control of educational institutions. In other words, the object of professionalization became the control of teachers and staff.

In his classic history of public school administration in the United States, Raymond Callahan wrote: "Schoolmen adopted the business and industrial procedures . . . largely to demonstrate efficiency and to maintain themselves thereby. . . ." One of the keys to this process became university training so that claims could be made to expert knowledge in administrative technique. Callahan said that "university work . . . was useful in establishing the fact and reinforcing the claim that they were experts. Such expertness, they were told, was becoming a prerequisite for obtaining a position in educational administration and for subsequent success on the job."[43]

The pattern of the professionalization of public school administrators was reflected in course offerings at colleges of education. At the beginning of the twentieth century, major training centers like Columbia's Teachers College, Harvard, and the University of Chicago typically offered only two courses in educational administration. By the 1920s this situation had changed dramatically. As mentioned, this was the period when a rapid change began to take place with schools increasing the number of administrators per teacher. At Teachers College in 1924 the number of courses in educational administration went from the original two to twenty-nine. At the University of Chicago two courses were offered in 1915 and fifteen in 1917. By 1927 the catalogue at Harvard described the superintendent of schools "as the professional 'general manager of the entire school system,' claiming that the job compared with the best in the older professions and in business and industry."[44]

The content of the training of school administrators reflected this business and industrial orientation. One study of eighteen textbooks in administration found that four fifths of the pages were devoted to executive, organizational, and administrative aspects of education without any discussion of the educational and social implications of these topics. An analysis of doctoral dissertations in educational administration found them to be mainly concerned with fiscal, business, legal, and personnel problems; many of them dealt with trivial topics like plumbing, janitors, insurance, and cafeterias.[45]

Administrative training changed over time, primarily as changes took place in business management. Later developments in organizational theory and a human relations approach to organizations had an impact on courses in educational administration. The important point for our purposes is that the professionalization of educational administrators was related to professional business training and not to other possible areas such as educational philosophy, sociology, or theories of learning.

The other important point about the professionalization of educational administrators is that the science of industrial management is the direct counterpart of human capital economics and the argument for equality of opportunity. David Noble has shown in his study *America by Design* that the industrial leaders who were concerned about the proper classification and use of human resources in industry were the same group of individuals to develop a science for managing those human resources.[46]

These industrial leaders, who were primarily engineers by training, promoted the use of testing, personnel management, and sorting in the schools as a means of matching the abilities of human resources with industrial needs. They promoted the manpower model of education described in previous chapters. They worked closely with psychologists during World War I to develop intelligence tests for the proper classification of labor. They had the same vision of a meritocracy of talent in which the ideology of equality of opportunity would allow for the free flow of talent in the social system. Equality of opportunity, in their thinking, meant giving everyone an equal chance to exercise his or her talents so that human resources could find their best place in the occupational structure.[47]

These same industrial leaders were responsible for the development and introduction of scientific management or, as they often referred to it, the science of human engineering. Once human resources had been properly sorted and selected, they had to be trained and scientifically managed on the job. As mentioned, this meant management would plan, and workers would be trained to fulfill those plans. This concept of management fit well with the hierarchical social system involved in meritocracy and equality of opportunity. It was assumed, and this was reflected in the role that intelligence tests were to perform in this system, that those with the most intelligence would occupy managerial positions and would apply their intelligence to managing people with lesser degrees of intelligence. Here was the model for the efficient society. Proper selection of human resources followed by proper management and control.[48]

When this model was applied to educational institutions, it made the school administrator a scientific manager of an institution whose primary responsibilities were the promotion of equality of opportunity and the sorting of human resources. Thus students became commodities to be channeled through the educational system into the labor market, and teachers were trained workers who had to be managed to achieve the ends of the institution. The professional ability of teachers was recognized in their classroom teaching, but general management and planning of educational policy were in the hands of school administrators. Within the hierarchical structure involved in this model, it was assumed that administrators had talent superior to that of most teachers, and that superiority, combined with their training and decision-making ability, should give them greater rewards in the form of higher salaries. As mentioned in chapter 4, there is an assumed justice to having the hierarchy of rewards match the hierarchy of occupations.

The professionalization of school administrators has created a situation where dialogue between administrators and teachers is primarily about managerial problems and not about subject matter or the content of teaching. In reality, for many school administrators this has meant supervising cafeterias, parking areas, and school discipline. It has also created a professional hierarchy in which the professionalization of school administration has been used to justify a superior position over the increasing professionalization of teachers.

The Professionalization of Education and the Professional Society

As stated at the beginning of this chapter, the investigation of the professional and bureaucratic nature of schooling was important to understand both the educational process and the growing professional and bureaucratic nature of society. In this sense the school could be viewed as one model of this more general social phenomenon. It was also hoped that this investigation would give some additional meaning to the ideology of equality of opportunity.

In this regard, consider the following major points of the chapter. The increasing professionalization of teachers has been based on an educational training with low status both in terms of content and the educational professoriate. Expert training has not been the means for teachers to claim increasing professional autonomy; rather, it has perpetuated the lowly status of teachers in the face of an expanding educational bureaucracy. To counteract the powerlessness of teachers in a bureaucracy, teachers' unions have become increasingly militant. But the organization of these unions tends to conserve the bureaucratic structure against which they bargain. In addition, the professionalization of school administrators has been in terms of business management, which establishes a hierarchical bureaucratic structure in the schools. The administrator and teacher face each other as manager and worker.

What is interesting about this pattern of professionalization in education is that it demonstrates how professionalization can be a means of subordination rather than independence and autonomy. The nature of professional training can teach people their place in the educational hierarchy. The lowly status of the professional training of teachers makes it difficult to claim high status in the bureaucratic structure of education. Imagine if teacher training had the same status as training for law or medicine! On the other hand, the business content of the professionalization of educational administrators has been a means of increasing their status in the educational hierarchy through its association with managers of industry.

What this suggests is that as society becomes more professionalized, that is, as entry into an occupation depends on expert training in an educational institution, the status of the occupation will depend on the status of the training. The future status of child-care workers trained in junior or community colleges may reflect the status of those institutions. The same thing may be true in occupations such as health care, auto mechanics, and clerical work, as they become professionalized. Rather than an educational training that increases the status of the occupation, it may define the status of the occupation.

When status is considered in the ideology of equality of opportunity, we are presented with a picture of educational institutions sorting individuals for different occupations and giving status to those occupations on the basis of the status of the required training. Justified in this process is a hierarchical occupational and bureaucratic structure and a hierarchical reward system to match that structure.

All these considerations are important in terms of political power. As society has become more professionalized, political power has become increasingly concentrated in the bureaucratic structure of government. This is an important issue in education because education has a completely professionalized bureaucracy. The next chapter looks at this issue in the context of the political control of schooling.

6

THE
CONTROL
OF SCHOOLING

THE PREVIOUS CHAPTER ARGUED THAT SCHOOLING HAS BECOME dominated by a professional bureaucratic structure. There is a relationship between the nature of this control and the dominant twentieth-century ideology of schooling. You will recall that this ideology has emphasized the school's role in providing equality of opportunity to create a more efficient economic and social structure. This gives the school a positive interventionist role in the social process. In fact, as has been noted, the school becomes the central arena for attempts to provide equality of opportunity because competition has been internalized in the structure of schooling. Students receive unequal educations based on school decisions about their abilities and future vocational destinations. Consequently, the stress is on providing equality of opportunity in schools with students graduating with different kinds of training.

This social role of the school is directly related to a society governed by bureaucratic professionals. Within the model of equality of opportunity, student entrance into the hierarchical structure of occupations is based on the sorting function of the school and expert training. At present, a completely professionalized society does not exist. In its extreme form it would mean that entrance into all occupations would be based on expert training in educational institutions; these institutions would decide which occupations would be most suitable for individual talents.

This model of society places the expert at the center of the governing process. Government decision making, like other occupations, requires expert training and proper recruitment. This is particularly true when the decisions being made are of a highly technical nature. This is precisely the model, as we shall see, that has come to dominate the decision-making process in education. Most educational decisions, or so it is claimed by educational professionals, require highly technical and expert knowledge. Consequently, major public participation in the governance of education is not appropriate and should be limited. The majority of decision making should be in the hands of professionals with expert training and knowledge.

One can see how in this model the ideology of equality of opportunity justifies the idea of the professional governing education and at the same time defines the central mission of the institution being governed. The goal of the institution becomes supportive of the justifications used to support the manner in which the institution is governed. If society were completely professionalized, the decisions made by professionals governing education would be central to the whole social process.

In the extreme case of the total professionalization of society, the ideology of equality of opportunity serves to justify the right of professionals to govern education, makes the school the central institution for distribution of human resources, and consequently gives the professional decision maker in education a central role in the governance of the society.

What this suggests is a possible material base for the ideology of equality of opportunity. You will recall from chapters 4 and 5 that there is no proof that the school is any fairer than the marketplace in providing equality of opportunity. Since the ideology is not supported by any overwhelming evidence, one might look for material support in the structure of education. It is, after all, this ideology that gives schools a central role in modern society and, consequently, gives professionals involved in education an increased status in the social process. In other words, the ideology of equality of opportunity may receive support because it can enhance the status, power, and material rewards of the professionals governing education. This is not to suggest a crude model in which educators consciously act in their own self-interest to accept the ideology of equality of opportunity, but to suggest that no conflict exists between the material interests of educators and the ideology. There is no proof, and it would be difficult to prove or disprove, that the material interests of educators cause them to adopt a particular ideology. All that can be said is that the material base for supporting the ideology is located in the bureaucratic structure of education.

If a model of ideology as a product of self-interest were used, that is, if people supported or accepted systems of ideas because those ideas enhanced their material and social status, then one would have to look at a linkage between the institutions and the people who produce ideas and the governing structure. In education this would primarily mean colleges of education, research and development centers in education, and the kinds of research funded by government and foundations. With individuals, this would include researchers and consultants to educational institutions. A professor of education who derives a certain amount of his salary from consulting work in, say, school desegregation or school finance develops a material interest in those areas. An educational researcher who specializes in research related to issues involving equality of opportunity develops a material interest in that area.

I am not arguing that a clear relationship exists between self-interest, action, and ideology, or that the actions of educational consultants and researchers can be entirely explained by self-interest. All I can say is that material self-interest does exist, that in the case of education it receives support from an ideology of equality of opportunity, but that there is no proof of a causal relationship.

Related to these issues is the social production of knowledge. When professional experts make decisions about institutions like schools, they usually consider particular sets of ideas. These ideas provide a framework for the decision-making process. For instance, one might ask an administrator who is deciding between two different curriculums how he plans to make the decision and where the ideas involved in the two curriculums originated. In this case, concern with the social production of knowledge is related to the origin of the two curriculums and not how the administrator makes a decision.

In education, identifiable institutions are engaged in the production of ideas about education. As mentioned, these include universities and research centers. Sometimes decisions about which ideas should be investigated or produced are made on the basis of research that the government and private foundations support. There is clearly a politics of research that involves what and how ideas should be produced.

The politics of the social production of knowledge is related to ideology and the governing process in education. The social production of ideas contributes to creating the framework for decision making in education. Part of understanding how education is controlled is understanding how ideas are produced in education.

This chapter begins an investigation of these issues by tracing the rise of professional control of education and the justification of that control in terms of what I call "administrative elitism." In the process it is necessary to clearly define this phenomenon in terms of general political theory. The reader should be reminded that the definitions of bureaucracy and professionalism used in this chapter are the same definitions used in chapter 5.

The Control of Schooling and Theories of Democratic Elitism

The United States is a good example of how the evolution of control by a bureaucratic structure was premised on the desirability of elite control. The basic premise is that decisions about something like education cannot be left to popular control. Involved in this is a profound distrust of the actions of the average citizen. Political scientist Peter Bachrach writes that "all elite theories are founded on two basic assumptions: first, that the masses are inherently incompetent, and second, that they are, at best, pliable, inert stuff or, at worst, aroused, unruly creatures possessing an insatiable proclivity to undermine both culture and liberty."[1]

Bachrach's description of theories of democratic elitism provide an understanding of the evolution of the control of schooling. One of the basic models for describing modern democratic societies is a polyarchy.[2] A polyarchy is a society governed by competing political elites who are accountable to the public at periodic elections. These political elites make decisions about what is good for the rest of society. Because of the size and complexity of modern society, mass participation in the decision-making process is considered to be impossible. It is also assumed that mass participation will result in "illiberal" decisions, such as the destruction of the Bill of Rights or extreme censorship. Implicit in the idea of polyarchy is that political elites protect the people from destroying their own liberties. In other words, the public interest, or what is best for society, can best be decided by political elites and not by the average citizen.

Polyarchical theory does not deny individual participation in government but encourages it in terms of choosing between elites. Citizenship, in this context, means voting for political rulers and not direct participation in the decision-making process. Bachrach writes: "In this view elites become the core of . . . polyarchical theory. To be sure, the ordinary man still plays a role in the system since he has the freedom to vote, to bring pressure upon political elites, and to attempt himself to rise to an elite position."[3] But, Bachrach emphasizes, citizenship is not an active process within this model. As he states: "But by and large he does, and is expected to, remain relatively passive—in fact the health of the system depends upon it. For if he becomes too active, too aroused in politics, awakening the alienated, the apathetic masses . . . political equilibrium is thrown out of balance. . . ."[4]

Within the context of polyarchical theory, equality of opportunity takes on a special meaning. It is recognized that equality of power over government decisions is impossible because of differences among citizens in income, status, and education. Because actual decisions are made in the arena of competitive elites, there cannot in reality be any equality of power among citizens to influence decision making. Equality of opportunity to gain influence will not produce equality of influence. Recognizing these limitations, in the theory of polyarchy equality of opportunity becomes having an equal opportunity to be recruited into political elites and having "an equal and indefinitely enduring opportunity to exercise as much power over key governmental decisions as any other citizen exercises."[5]

The first part of this definition complements our earlier discussions of equality of opportunity with regard to economics and social mobility. In political terms, equality of opportunity becomes the means for all citizens to join ruling elites. It is assumed that if equality of opportunity is maintained, then political elitism will be acceptable. If the school and other social agencies along with the political system work to maximize movement in and out of the ruling groups, then modern democratic processes are maintained. It is also assumed, as part of a general theory of equality of opportunity, that competition for admission into the political elites will result in the best people, in terms of qualifications, becoming the key decision makers in society.

The second part of the definition of equality of opportunity, in terms of the exercise of power, gives emphasis to the passive role of the citizen. The exercise of power is not in making decisions but in selecting elites and trying to influence elites. Mechanisms for exercising this power are voting, gaining the attention of decision makers, and influencing criteria for selection into political elites.

The importance of the above discussion of polyarchy is that it precisely describes the justifications given for the present mechanisms of political control of American public schools and accurately describes the passive role of the citizen and parent in that political control. For instance, the present organization of school boards in the United States is a direct product of political reforms in the early part of the twentieth century that emphasized distrust of the average citizen in school affairs and the importance of gaining elite control.

Specific school board reforms in the early part of the twentieth century were designed to limit access to board positions to "successful" members of the community. These reforms in urban areas included the replacement of local ward control of the schools with a centralized school board, creation of nonpartisan elections, and citywide election of board members. The best people to make decisions about schools, it was argued, were successful people with high levels of education. This meant primarily professionals and successful businessmen in the community.[6]

The proposed political reforms were to accomplish these ends by making it difficult for the average citizen to run for the board. When school control is located in a small district, it is easier and less costly for the average citizen to be elected to the school board. It is more difficult for the average citizen to gain a place on a centralized school board with citywide elections because of the cost and difficulty of conducting a citywide campaign. The citizen must find the money and the organization to gain citywide recognition and inform voters of his or her position on school issues. In addition, the machinery of political parties is effectively eliminated as an organizational tool for the candidate because of nonpartisan school board elections.

The elite nature of these political reforms and the actors in the reform movement was best summarized by historian David Tyack. Tyack wrote that the membership of this reform movement was "composed mostly of business and professional elites, including university people and the new school managers. At the turn of the twentieth century, they planned a basic shift in the control of urban education which would vest political power in a small committee composed of 'successful men.'"[7]

The purpose of this reform was not only to gain elite control of the board of education but also to increase the power of the superintendent. Essentially the vision was that of an elite board of education standing between the average citizen and the expert administration of the schools. Tyack quoted the leaders of this reform movement: "Effective political reform, said one of their leaders, might require 'the imposition of limitations upon the common suffrage.' They ridiculed 'the exceedingly democratic idea that all are equal' and urged that schooling be adapted to social stratification."[8]

Political reforms in school board elections were part of a general reform in municipal politics that sought to centralize control in democratic elites and expert managers. For instance, in 1911

Pittsburgh switched from elections based on a ward system to citywide elections. When elections were based on wards, there were 387 elected officials. With the switch to citywide elections, the number of elected officials was reduced to 9 city council members and 15 school board members. These changes had a dramatic effect on the social composition of the elected organizations. Under the ward system 67 percent were "small businessmen-grocers, saloonkeepers, livery-stable proprietors, owners of small hotels, druggists, white-collar workers such as clerks and bookkeepers, and skilled and unskilled workmen."[9] With citywide elections, there were no elected officials who were small businessmen or white-collar workers. On either basis, only one person might be called a representative of the working class.

The important point about this example is that not only was the intention to exclude a majority of social groups from elected office but that the goal was achieved. The elitist attitude was explicitly stated during the 1911 election by the Voters League, the organization that spearheaded the reform campaign. Their pamphlet deplored the fact that school boards contained only a small number of "men prominent throughout the city in business life . . . in professional occupations . . . holding positions as managers, secretaries, auditors, superintendents and foreman." The pamphlet argued that a person's occupation was a strong indication of his qualifications for the school board. Elitism was evident in the statement that "employment as ordinary laborer and in the lowest class of mill work would naturally lead to the conclusion that such men did not have sufficient education or business training to act as school directors."[10]

The pattern established in the early twentieth century was for school board members to be drawn primarily from leaders of the professional and business communities in each school district. Studies of the social composition of boards of education since that time have shown a disproportionate number of business and professional members in relationship to the total population. The governing groups at both state and local levels have higher incomes, more education, and more male representation than the rest of the population. This is true of local boards of education and state boards of education.[11]

The most recent study of the social composition of boards of education found that 90 percent of school board members in the United States were white males, whereas only 48 percent of the general public were males. Other comparisons of board members with the general population found that 36 percent of the board members were in the highest income category of $20,000 or more, whereas only 6 percent of the general population were in that group. As for education, 72 percent of board members had one or more years of college with 25 percent having attended graduate or professional school, whereas only 27 percent of the general public had one or more years of college and only 4 percent had attended graduate or professional school. An occupational comparison revealed that 66 percent of school board members are in professional, technical, managerial, official or proprietary categories, whereas only 30 percent of the general public can be included in those groups. The majority of the general public (57 percent) is categorized as clerical, sales, craft, operative, service, and laboring workers; only 21 percent of school board members are in these occupations.[12]

These figures raise a number of questions about representation. "Representation" does not necessarily mean that a governing body represents the general public by reflecting its social and economic composition. Certainly the intention of school board reformers in the early part of the century was to create elite governing groups, which they felt could better represent the interests of the people through superior knowledge and life experiences. The argument for representation by democratically selected elites assumes the existence of a public interest that can be known and understood only by certain members of the public.

To understand this argument one must consider theories of representation as they relate to arguments for democratic elitism. These issues take us back to the discussion of representative government and the existence of a general will or public interest in chapter 1. That discussion now needs to be elaborated in terms of the governing of education.

How can representatives know the public interest? has been a central question for representative government. The *Federalist Papers,* which provided much of the theoretical argument for the support of a representative government in the United States, argued that a distinction had to be made between momentary and immediate interests and the general welfare or the public interest. It was argued that elected representatives, by being one step removed from the immediate and particular interests of individual citizens, would be better able to discern the public interest. Not only was representative government preferable to direct democracy because it was impractical to call all citizens together to decide on issues, but also direct democracy could become an expression of immediate and particular interests at the expense of the long-range public interest. Representatives would filter out particular interests for the general interest. Although federalists admitted that this filtering might distort the public interest by eliminating desirable parts of it, they argued that any factionalism that might result between representatives would balance out in a national forum. Hanna Pitkin summarized the viewpoint of the *Federalist Papers* as "the task of representative government is thus, in a sense, to bring the major social forces into the legislature and keep them there until time passes."[13] Time would allow immediate interests and factionalism to be replaced with the public interest.

English utilitarians in the nineteenth century emphasized the responsiveness of representatives to their constituencies as an expression of the public interest. In this model, every citizen, including the representative, is guided by self-interest. It was argued that "no one who knows what is for your interest, so well as yourself."[14] Given these conditions, the representative would work for the public interest because as a citizen of the community his or her individual interests were related to the welfare of the general community. Representatives were viewed as citizens who must live with the laws they helped establish. In addition, if all people voted, then representatives must please the interests of all people or the public interest. Pitkin described this argument as "representation makes it to the interest of the ruler to act in the interest of the subjects—not to give in to their passing whims, but to act in their true interest. For if he gives in to their passing whims, they will not really be pleased. . . ." Stated another way: "The representative promotes the people's true interests, the people cannot fail to support him. . . ."[15]

Theories of democratic elitism are not contradictory to the above ideas about the workings of representative government. In both considerations of the workings of representative government there is no argument that the social and economic characteristics of the representatives have to match the social and economic characteristics of the population. This is not considered a necessary condition for the expression of the public interest. In federalist theory, the public interest will emerge from particular interests by the distance between representatives and the public and the balance of social forces in the representative assembly. In utilitarian theory, representatives will give expression to the public interest because they depend on public support for election.

Consider the above statements in terms of the democratic elitism in the political structure of American education. It can be argued, and was argued during the reform period of the early part of the twentieth century, that citywide nonpartisan elections would remove school board members from factionalism and immediate personal interests.

Some communities even eliminated elections and substituted school board selection by the mayor, the city council, or judges, thus removing school board members further from the pressures of particular interests and political factionalism. This also meant a rejection of the utilitarian idea that representatives of the people can be forced to act in the public interest because of the requirement of elections. In fact, whether school boards are elected or appointed, there seems to be a rejection of the idea that individuals, including representatives, act out of self-interest. The model of the American school board is of an altruistic group of representatives acting in the interests of all people.

The major question remains unanswered: How does an elite group know the public interest? In both the federalist and utilitarian models there was an assumption of an invisible hand at work, which produced the public interest. Federalists saw the invisible hand balancing factions in representative assemblies to produce the public good; in utilitarian theory, the invisible hand was at work in elections where the representative, responding to the whole public, came to represent the public good. But there is no assumption of an invisible hand at work in American school boards in producing the public interest by balancing or adding up factions and interests. In fact, in both theory and practice, American school boards have been free of significant controversy and factionalism.

The answer to the central question is that school board members are to gain their knowledge about the public interest from the professional experts and managers of the school system. Historically, school board reform was accompanied by a belief that professional experts should assume major control of the school system in the public interest. Currently, most political studies of the control of education in the United States find that the primary locus of control is in the hands of the professional educator and administrator.

The intentional political restructuring of school boards to assure control by elites was accompanied by changes in the educational bureaucracy, which increased the power of the administrative staff. It is important to understand that these changes did not mean the creation of a bureaucracy—one already existed—but the profes-sionalization of the bureaucracy.

The reader should remember from the previous chapter that during the early part of the twentieth century there was an expansion of degree programs in educational administration in colleges and departments of education with a modeling of educational administra-tion after that of business administration. The professional education administrator was to take charge of the school system as political reform resulted in elite control of boards of education.

The key figure in this professionalization process was the superintendent of schools. The model became that of the business manager acting in the name of a board of directors. Of course, the business manager, like the superintendent, could be dismissed by the board, but while he was in charge the superintendent was to make most of the basic decisions based on expert knowledge. One concrete power the superintendent of schools gained during this reform period was control over the hiring of school personnel. A complaint about previous boards of education centered on their direct role in the hiring of teachers, janitors, and other school staff. Under this system, it was charged, many people were appointed for political reasons and not because of merit. Under the reform system, the hiring initiative was given to the superintendent with the superintendent recommending appointments to the board and the board giving approval.[16]

Historian David Tyack quotes a professor of government at Harvard, a member of the Boston school board, as stating that it helped to have a school board "to act as a buffer between the professional force and the public—a body that sanctions the acts of the experts and assumes the responsibility for them."[17] This quote certainly does not represent the attitude of all board members, but it does portray one of the tensions that came to exist between professional school administrators and boards of education. School boards tended to view administrators as their managers, whereas administrators sometimes viewed the actions of boards as public interference in professional matters. As educational administrators gained control and increased their professionalization, a belief developed that public interference in schools should end and complete control should be given to the experts.

This attitude was most strongly expressed by Charles Judd, director of the Department of Education at the University of Chicago in the 1930s. Judd argued that school boards blocked important educational reforms and were often tools of political bosses. He suggested that "a movement to abolish school boards is in order and should be supported by all who believe in the simplification of government and in reliance on experts."[18] Judd's colleague at the University of Chicago, political science professor Charles Merriam, supported Judd's approach to government with the argument that the professionalization of all administrative services of government would create a new era of political competence.[19]

Judd's proposal to abolish school boards and replace them with complete professional control created a storm of protest that became one of the major controversies about the politics of education in the United States. School board members and other members of the public began to complain that control of the schools had passed from elected representatives to professionals. This argument was prevalent during the 1950s when professionals educators were accused of making schools antiintellectual and weakening America's defense in the cold war against the Soviet Union by not producing enough scientists and engineers. Federal intervention in education in the late 1950s, in the form of the National Defense Education Act and the creation of new curriculums by the National Science Foundation, was designed to correct errors believed to have been caused by the control of professional educators.[20] By the 1970s school boards were not only complaining about professional control but also that most of their power had eroded to government and other organizations.

School boards felt almost powerless as courts became involved in education because of desegregation and school finance suits, increased collective bargaining by teachers' unions, and increased control by state and federal government. These changes meant increased layers of professional involvement and control of education.

Administrative Elitism and Professional Control of Education

Like elite control of school boards, professional control of education was not a historical accident but was to a certain extent planned. What was not intended was the possible conflict between elite control and professional control. This situation again raises the issue of representation. Do professional experts represent the public interest better than elite school board members do? Some educators, like Charles Judd in the 1930s, have answered this question in the affirmative. This raises a number of questions about the meaning of politics in a democratic society, because it suggests that the farther removed the judgment is from political pressures, the more likely it is that the decision will be in the public interest.

I will call this argument "administrative elitism," as opposed to democratic elitism. Democratic elitism gives the voter the role of selecting between elites to represent the public interest. Administrative elitism gives the voter the role of selecting between elites who will in turn select administrative experts who will make the actual decisions about what is in the public interest. In administrative elitism, it is argued that by creating the greatest distance between the public and the decision-making process, actual decisions will be made in the public interest because there will be a lessened pressure from particular interests and immediate concerns. Also the public interest will be protected because decisions will be made by professional experts who will primarily be making decisions on the basis of knowledge and not political pressures.

Administrative elitism does not completely exclude the public from the decision-making process. An important element of modern administrative technique is public participation through advisory councils or other organizations. These groups help the professional administrator determine what the public wants and needs. An important point about this method, which also includes social science surveys and opinion polls, is that this form of public participation does not involve the exercise of direct political power through mechanisms like voting. What is involved is the supplying of information so that the expert can make a decision about what the public wants and needs. In the most extreme form of administrative elitism, voting as a means of conveying information would be replaced by teams of social scientists who would manage participation and conduct opinion surveys about the desires of the public. The professional expert would in this manner determine the true public interest.

Before dealing directly with the issue of administrative or professional representation of the public interest, it would be in order to give a description of the nature of professional control of education in the United States. The most extensive study at the local level in the 1970s is Zeigler and Jennings' *Governing American Schools*.[21] Through close observation of the workings of school boards and school administrators the authors found specific methods used by school administrators to control educational policy. One such method was gatekeeping, or the control of information received by the board. School administrators are in an ideal position to select the information they want the board to hear. In addition, school administrators can convince boards that most issues require technical expertise and should be decided on the basis of advice from the school staff.

Zeigler and Jennings measured the degree of gatekeeping exercised by the school administrator by determining the control of agenda setting at board meetings. The agenda essentially defines the range of topics and items that will be considered by the school board. It is an important political tool because it can be used to control discussion and the kinds of information that will be presented to board members. In their national survey, Zeigler and Jennings found that in 70 percent of the school districts in the United States, superintendents had the primary responsibility for setting the agenda; in two thirds of all districts, they were solely responsible for agenda setting.

Zeigler and Jennings located other important sources of administrative power in the supplying of information to board members, contact hours between administrators and board members, and the indoctrination of new board members. The model of action in most school districts is for the administrative staff to propose policies to the board and recommend action and for the board to concur with that recommendation. This does not mean that there is never any conflict, but in most cases administrative control of information and policy making dominates board action.[22]

When we move from the local to the state level of educational decision making, we again find professional experts holding key positions. A majority of educational decisions at the state level are made in state departments of education. This occurs for a variety of reasons including the weak role of state boards of education. Like local boards of education, state boards are primarily composed of elite members of the population. This is true whether the board is elected or appointed by the governor. In states with elected boards, the elections are considered almost nonevents. There is little public interest in them, and over half the elected state board members do not campaign. State boards of education are even less active than local boards of education. State boards primarily legitimate policies initiated and developed by experts in state departments of education. The weak role of state boards of education results in a strong role for the professional experts, who run state departments of education.[23]

Weaknesses in state legislatures also contribute to the heightened role of state bureaucrats. State legislatures are faced with low salaries, rapid turnover of members, and a shortage of professional staff. Unlike members of Congress, state legislators do not have large staffs that provide them with information and investigate legislative items under consideration. All these factors contribute to a general lack of expertise and an inability to formulate public policy. Consequently, state legislators must rely heavily on lobbying groups and state administrative agencies for information and policy proposals. State departments of education are a major source of information and policy development regarding educational legislation.[24]

The weakness of state legislatures also contributes to the important role of educational lobbying groups in supplying information and formulating policy. Educational lobbying groups are not necessarily in opposition to state departments of education. A common situation is a close working relationship among the state affiliate of the National Education Association, the state department of education, and the state legislative committee handling educational legislation. In fact, members of the state departments of education are often members of the NEA or some other professional educational association.[25]

In states where educational associations and the state department of education work together to formulate educational policy, they have a virtual monopoly over information about education received by the state legislature. Usually when this working relationship is established, it is dominated by school administrators who rely on university experts to formulate policy.[26]

In states where this monolithic structure does not exist, the important influence of the educational professional can still be seen. In some states there is a close working relationship between state legislators and local school administrators. When this is the case, statewide lobbying groups do not have as much power. In some states, educational lobbying groups are not united, and there is a great deal of conflict. This situation can occur when lobbying groups that primarily represent teachers conflict with lobbying groups for school administrators, or when the state affiliates of the two major teacher organizations (the NEA and the AFT) are in conflict. Even in these situations, however, the debate is often between professional educators and does not include members of the public.[27]

In recent years, the control and influence of state departments of education has been enhanced by federal education programs and court cases dealing with school finance. Beginning in the 1960s, the federal government provided funds for increasing the size and effectivenss of state departments of education. This was done to offset the charge that increased federal involvement in education was resulting in the destruction of local control over education, and to provide a mechanism for the implementation of federal programs.[28] State departments of education now play a major role in monitoring educational programs from the federal level and consequently have increased their control over education at the local level.

Recent court decisions have required a restructuring of educational financing in some states to assure that all students receive equal educational opportunity. The basic issue is that large differences exist among local school districts in some states in the amount of money spent per student for public schooling. The requirement of the courts has been that the state provide some means for the equalization of spending. Details of these court cases and their potential consequences are discussed in chapter 8 on the economics of education. What is important to understand in this chapter is that these court decisions have resulted in an expanded role for state departments of education in developing financing plans and ensuring that equality of educational opportunity is provided in the state. This has tended to give bureaucrats in state departments of education a major role in monitoring the actions of local school districts.[29]

There is a certain irony in the expansion of the federal educational bureaucracy. As mentioned, the increased involvement of the federal government in education beginning in the 1950s in part resulted from concern about professional educators controlling American education. At that time, a major criticism of schools was their lack of academic rigor in mathematics and the sciences. The 1958 National Defense Education Act was designed to correct this situation by providing money for expanding programs in science, mathematics, and foreign languages and developing new curriculums in those areas. Although attempting to correct what were viewed as the evils of professional control over education, the legislation resulted in an expansion of the federal Office of Education.

In the 1960s the Office of Education was transformed from a sleepy little bureaucracy that primarily collected statistics to an active agency responsible for monitoring programs and policing local schools. The police function was a result of the 1964 Civil Rights Act, which stated that no person, because of race, color, or national origin, could be excluded from or denied the benefits of any program receiving federal financial assistance.[30] In the 1970s this act was expanded to include discrimination on the basis of sex. The Office of Education had the responsibility to police local school districts to assure that civil rights were not violated in any district receiving federal money. Since 1965, with the passage of the Elementary and Secondary Education Act, this has included practically every school district in the United States.

At present, professionals in the Office of Education have a major role in interpreting educational legislation passed by Congress and drafting regulations that will govern the implementation of the legislation. The Office of Education works closely with professional organizations like the National Education Association and the Chief State School Officers to gain information about the impact and response to federal programs. The Office of Education also uses these groups as a means of conveying information about federal programs and how to apply for benefits from federal legislation.[31]

National professional organizations thus have a number of mechanisms for influencing federal action in education. They can lobby in Congress by supplying information and applying political pressure. They can influence the meaning and implementation of legislation by working closely with the Office of Education, which gave added recognition to the important role of professional organizations in policy making and implementation in the 1970s when it organized a national forum for leaders of educational organizations. This group has a membership restricted to actual leaders of educational organizations and meets annually to discuss national educational policy.[32]

Professionals exert tremendous influence over educational decisions at the federal level, but their power is even greater at the state level. Members of the House of Representatives and the Senate have large staffs and can conduct their own research into educational matters. They do not have to rely as much on information supplied by the professional education lobby as state legislators do. In fact, a certain anti-educator feeling persists in Congress. This was evidenced by the strong protests against the inclusion of Head Start and school nutrition programs in a proposed federal Department of Education. The feeling was that such programs should be kept out of the hands of professional educators.[33]

Samuel Halperin, former deputy assistant secretary of the Department of Health, Education, and Welfare and former assistant commissioner of the Office of Education, argues: "It is clear that there are powerful elites—particularly in the Congress and its staffs—whose views on educational policy usually prevail." From his perspective, the control by these elites is justified because the majority of their educational policies have been directed at benefiting the poor and minority groups in the United States. Halperin writes: "In sum, the federal decision-making process in education has little to apologize for in one important respect: The power structure that operates it is elitist only in composition, not in performance."[34]

The federal level, therefore, contains elements of both elite and professional control of education. These elements are present throughout the decision-making structure from the local to the national level. What is not clear is the degree of conflict that may exist between various elite groups and the professional expert in the bureaucratic structure. It was mentioned previously that some federal policy in education has emerged as a result of conflict between two sets of actors. But it is difficult to determine how much congruence actually exists between them. It should be noted, too, that the term "sets of actors" is used here to avoid giving the impression that what is being described are monolithic groups that share common opinions. There is no proof that elites in the United States share common political and economic objectives or that professionals in the administrative bureaucracy share common goals.

The difficulty in matching, in ideological terms, members of the elite with the professionals in the bureaucracy makes it difficult to talk about a congruence of opinion. An important question must be asked: Has the control by professionals increased because the professionals reflect the ideology of elected elites? For instance, at the local level, have the superintendent and central office staff been given increased decision-making power because their decisions are similar to what the elected elites would have decided? Is this why state school boards have given major control to state departments of education? At this point, answers to these questions are not available, but one thing is clear. Fewer and fewer decisions about public education are being made by parents and the general public, and more and more decisions are being made outside public control and within an administrative bureaucracy.

The issue of the control of education by professional decision makers is sharpened when the experience in the United States is compared with that of a country like England. A good study has been done by George Male, *The Struggle for Power: Who Controls the Schools in England and the United States.*[35] What impresses a reader of this study is not the differences that exist between the two countries but the similarities in trends and issues regarding education since the 1940s. Obviously, the different histories of the two countries have given different meanings to these trends.

The major similarity between the countries has been the increasing control of education by a bureaucratic structure with similar social and educational objectives. More specifically, in England education has come under greater control by the national government and its bureaucratic structure as the social policy of the schools has been directed toward providing equality of educational opportunity and equality of opportunity.

Since the 1960s, English schools have been experiencing an integration of social classes in schools similar to the experience of the United States in racial desegregation. Social-class integration in England has centered on the establishment of comprehensive high schools. Until the early 1960s, the top 20 percent academically of English school students were assigned at age eleven to high-prestige academic schools; 3 percent were placed in secondary technical schools; 6 percent were entered in private schools; and the rest were assigned to secondary modern schools. In social-class terms, the children of the middle class mainly attended academic secondary schools; working-class children primarily went to secondary modern schools. In 1965 the national government applied pressure on local educational authorities, requiring them to submit plans for establishing comprehensive schools.[36] This occurred in the same period that the federal government in the United States was applying pressure on southern schools to desegregate. In England, the establishment of comprehensive schools was greeted with opposition from middle-class parents that was similar to the opposition by southern racists in the United States.

The British move to establish comprehensive high schools has to be understood in the context of the general acceptance of the role of the school as one of providing equality of opportunity as part of the general policy of the welfare state discussed in chapter 3. As in the United States, this has resulted in greater national control over local educational policies.

The Education Act of 1944 in England set the stage for increased national control and the expansion of equality of educational opportunity in secondary education. The act established a minister of education with specific powers "to secure the effective execution by local authorities, under his control and direction, of the national policy for providing a varied and comprehensive educational service in every area."[37] In the 1960s , the title "Minister of Education" was changed to "Secretary of the Department of Education and Science." The bureaucratic structure within the Department of Education and Science has exerted increasing control over local education authorities since the Education Act of 1944.

Currently, the national government in England not only has power to mandate major educational reforms like the establishment of comprehensive secondary schools but also decides standards for school buildings, whether a new school building proposed by local governments will be constructed, and details like whether or not teachers will supervise lunch periods. Beginning in the 1950s, the government has established quotas on the number of teachers each local educational authority can hire. This was done originally because of a teacher shortage in the 1950s; when the shortage turned to a surplus in the 1970s, quotas were made minimums rather than maximums.[38]

What is more important in terms of the actual content of education is that the minister of education established a Curriculum Study Group in 1960 because it was felt that local government and teachers were not capable of coping with the rapid changes that needed to be made in a changing society. In 1963 the Curriculum Study Group was absorbed into a Schools Council for the Curriculum and Examinations, which was to be a private national association funded by the government with a majority of the membership held by teachers.[39]

The Schools Council is a model of professional control of education; noneducators are not represented, and control is in the hands of dominant groups in education. Membership includes teacher organizations, the Department of Education and Science, and education committees of local education authorities. The Schools Council does not have direct control over the national curriculum but is an important center for the development and dissemination of ideas about changes in the curriculum. As we shall see in the next chapter, this involves the social production of knowledge that often provides the framework for ideas that spark educational change. Direct political control is not necessary. What is controlled is the production of ideas about educational change.

For instance, the work of the Schools Council was the primary stimulus for the development of teacher centers in England in the late 1960s.[40] Indeed, the effectiveness of the Schools Council in promoting teacher centers as places for professional control of inservice training is evidenced by the spread of the idea to the United States in the 1970s. In England, teacher centers have functioned not only for inservice training but also as places for research and curriculum development.

In terms of a model of professional control of education, teacher centers have the potential to become places where teachers can gain control over curricular change. Here is the interesting phenomenon of a private group, supported by the government and controlled by professional educators, creating new institutional structures—teacher centers—that will allow for even greater professional control of the curriculum.

It should be noted that the Schools Council has been criticized as being dominated by the major English teachers' union, the National Union of Teachers (NUT). In 1972, NUT members amounted to about one fourth of the membership on the Schools Council; the rest of the membership was dispersed over other educational organizations. The importance of NUT extends beyond the Schools Council. It is the largest teachers' union in England; its rival is the National Association of Schoolmasters. Like the NEA and the AFT in the United States, the two English organizations actively lobby for legislation. About twenty-five members of Parliament receive a direct subsidy from NUT.[41]

Also, there is a close working relationship between the Department of Education and Science and NUT. This is similar to the relationship that exists between the Office of Education in the United States and professional organizations. The education department consults with NUT about proposed regulations, which provides a direct mechanism for NUT to influence educational policy and enhance its professional control of education matters.[42]

While professional control of education seems to be one aspect of the growing national control of education in England, there is a resistance to complete professional control. As in the United States, an apparent reason for stronger national control was to provide political elites with more power over educational policy. England has had a tradition of educator control, in which it differs from the United States. In a sense, the establishment of the Department of Education and Science became a means for forcing local educators to provide greater equality of educational opportunity and place educational policy in the context of the welfare state. In fact, George Male argues that the national government has clearly avoided complete professional control. This was evidenced, he claims, in the government's refusal in the 1960s to allow the establishment of a teachers' council that would have decided who would be allowed to teach and would have been controlled by teachers.

Also, in 1965, when the government established a five-year plan for economic development, teachers were not consulted about the educational parts of the plan. This would suggest that in England, educational policy has become primarily a function of decisions shared by national political elites and professionals in the Department of Education and Science and other organizations. Educational policy is not under the direct control of parents, students, or the general citizenry.[43]

In making the above conclusion, one must recognize certain traditions in English educational history that do not make this situation surprising. There has been a traditional lack of popular control in England and little call for popular control. Before the 1944 Education Act, the major legal authority was in the hands of the education committees of local education authorities. The Education Act of 1902 had created local authorities by combining local school districts into a countywide organization.[44] The official administrative agent of the local education authority is the chief education officer.

Traditionally, in this structure of control the real center of power was centered in the headmasters, or head teachers, of each school. Unlike their American counterpart, the school principal, the English headmaster based his authority on his knowledge of teaching and subject matter. English headmasters did not experience the professionalization of educational administration on the business model that occurred in the United States. Headmasters have had a tradition of independence from government pressures and parental pressures. Tradition has granted headmasters a great deal of discretionary power in running their schools.[45]

This situation has changed dramatically with the increasing involvement of the national government since 1944. The role of the chief education officer has been expanded in importance as local education authorities have had to respond to increasing numbers of national regulations and mandates. The chief education officer acts as an administrator for these national directives. At the same time, the power of the headmaster has been greatly reduced as more and more of the process of schooling becomes controlled by forces outside the school.

What is interesting in this comparison of the United States and England is that the shift in control from local units of government to national levels has been a product of attempts to use the schools to achieve equality of educational opportunity and equality of opportunity through the schools. As has been argued, this ideology gives the professional bureaucrat the central role in managing the social system. As this ideology has been instituted in both countries, control of the educational policies has tended to become centered in bureaucratic professionals. In the United States this has resulted in a decrease in the power of local boards of education. In England, it has resulted in a decrease of the power of the local educational authorities and the headmasters.

The headmasters' situation is interesting and invites speculation. Because headmasters never professionalized in the same manner as their American counterparts, one might speculate that their decline in influence came about because they did not have the tradition of functioning as expert administrators and social engineers. Certainly, the direction of English education since 1944 has been to use the school to provide equality of opportunity and engineer an end to poverty and major social-class differences. This is a trend for which neither tradition nor training has prepared the headmaster to take a leading role.

Professional Educators as Representatives

With the growth of professional bureaucratic control, the issue of representation, discussed earlier in this chapter, becomes crucial. How can educational professionals represent the interests of their clients and the public? And can professional self-interest be separated from the public interest? Neither question can be answered with any degree of certainty. All that can be done is to sketch an outline of the problems and summarize the fragmentary evidence available.

The major study of educator representation is Dale Mann's *The Politics of Administrative Representation*.[46] Mann's study is limited to professional educational administrators and consequently does not deal directly with educational professionals such as teachers, members of the central office staff, or members of state departments of education. But even with this limitation the study tells us something about the most political professional role in education in the United States. Unlike other educational professionals, the local school administrator must deal constantly with the political pressures of the community. In fact, the local administrator functions as a gateway for information and pressures from the local community to other professionals in the local educational structure. The manner in which the administrator operates that gateway often determines the relationship of other professionals to the community.

Mann defines three distinct kinds of representation. The first, the trustee administrator, makes decisions on the basis of what he thinks is in the public interest. Mann writes: "The trustee does what the trustee thinks is best for the children, community, clientele, and constitutents." Sometimes a trustee will make decisions that are opposed by elected representatives or community preferences. In these cases, the trustee decides that judgment based on professional knowledge is more in the public interest than the decision demanded by public pressures. Involved in this concept of representation is what I have called in this chapter "administrative elitism."[47]

The second kind of representation is what Mann calls "delegate representation." The delegate is almost the reverse of the trustee and gives major consideration to community pressures and preferences. Mann writes: "Delegates believe that they have been chosen to reflect accurately (not to interpret and not to replace) what the represented say they want and need." For the delegate representative there is a certain strain between the individual's professional training and the desire to be responsive to community desires. The attitude of the delegate representative is summarized by Mann in the statement of one inner-city principal that "'public education,' that's two words, and the emphasis has been for too long on the second one."[48]

The third kind of representation, and the one found least frequently by Mann, is the politico representative. The politico sometimes responds as a trustee and sometimes as a delegate. He shifts with the situation and the issues involved in a particular decision. We might expect the politico representative to occur more often. That is, we would not expect administrators to be committed to one kind of representation. Mann found just the opposite. Administrators do tend to become committed to one kind of representation.

Mann found that the majority of school administrators, 61 percent, functioned as trustee representatives. Only 30 percent functioned as delegates and 9 percent as politicos. Perhaps these findings are not surprising because the whole ideology of professionals supports the trustee kind of representation. The surprising finding may be that 30 percent of school administrators attempt to represent the pressures and desires of the public. What this means is that the majority of school administrators make decisions on the basis of their own experience and professional knowledge even when those decisions are in oppostion to community desires as expressed through elected school board members and other community pressure groups.[49]

One of the interesting findings in Mann's study is the variation in the kind of representation in relation to the social composition of the community. Mann compared the kind of representation provided by school principals with the kind of community served by the particular school. He divided communities into nonworking poor, nonworking and working-class poor, middle- and working-class poor, and upper-middle class and above. In urban areas populated by nonworking poor, he found 80 percent of the administrators functioning as trustee representatives. This suggests a high degree of paternalism on the part of administrators toward this social class. But, surprisingly, in urban areas with nonworking and working-class poor, only 48 percent of the administrators functioned in trustee roles, which was below the 61 percent average for all areas.[50]

Mann feels that the mixture of nonworking and working-class poor may create a tense situation in which working-class people feel threatened by those on welfare. This may lead to more community activity and pressure on school administrators, which may in turn affect the way they define their roles.

In urban areas with middle- and working-class poor, 64 percent of the principals were trustees; in upper-middle class and above areas, 75 percent were trustees. Thus the larger percentages of trustees were at both ends of the social scale. Mann argues that "school administrators serving such areas often feel that the poor are not capable of participation and thus must be 'saved' by the unilateral action of experts." Or the other hand, it might be the case that "the life style and personal career orientations of the upper-middle class predispose them to accept trustee decision-making."[51]

Mann's findings are limited to the functioning of local school administrators in the United States. But, as stated earlier, this is the professional educator role that is most subject to political pressure. Other professionals in education tend to be more insulated by the bureaucratic structure at local and national levels. One can only speculate about the percentage of trustees, delegates, and politicos among other professional educators. It would certainly be surprising to find a majority assuming the role of delegate representative. Both the ideology of professionalism and the insulation from public pressures would suggest that as one penetrates the educational structure, the percentage of trustee representation increases.

The other important question is whether or not professional interest can be separated from self-interest. Assume that the majority of professional educators in all educational institutions and government structures are functioning as trustees. The question for the public is whether decisions are being based on expert knowledge or self-interest. Is the ideology of professionalism and the growth of the professional administrative state really a cover for the economic and personal interests of the professionals making the decisions?

Obviously, no answer can be given to these questions that would cover all professionals in all situations. No study exists that concludes that professionals, particularly education professionals, act only in their own interest. It is not hard to accept the proposition that some educators, teachers and administrators, make personal sacrifices in the interest of their students. It would probably be possible to find legions of underpaid teachers and administrators whose sole purpose in life is to work for the good of their students.

On the other hand, the acceptance of the above propositions does not preclude the existence of professionals who act in their own interest; that is, many of their decisions are designed to enhance their status and economic well-being. In fact, some studies exist (and will be discussed below) that argue that self-interest is an important motivator among professional educators.

A major study dealing with this issue is Ernest House's *The Politics of Educational Innovation*.[52] One of House's major concerns is the failure of many educational innovations to be adopted by educators or to be fundamentally changed when educators put the innovation in practice. He argues that the only way to understand this problem is to view it in terms of the political structure of education and the self-interest of the professionals involved in that structure.

For instance, House finds a major difference between rates of adoption of educational innovations in local school districts in the

United States and the career orientation of the local superintendent. House divides superintendent roles into place-bound and career-bound. The career-bound superintendent is interested in moving up the hierarchy of superintendency. He views his present position as a steppingstone to a superintendent's position in a more prestigious and affluent district. The career-bound superintendent uses his present position to display his talents so that they get him a better job. The place-bound superintendent is primarily interested in remaining in his present job. His orientation is toward building strong local support so that he can be assured of continued tenure.[53]

It is in the career-bound superintendent's interest to introduce changes or educational innovations to gain recognition outside the district. Since the career-bound superintendent is interested in impressing other school districts and enhancing his career, he has to provide some evidence of leadership. An important form of evidence is to show an effect introduction of some educational innovation in a school district. The rate of innovation is higher for career-bound superintendents than for those who are place-bound.[54]

House also finds self-interest to be a factor when dealing with the politics of the central office staff. The central office staff is made up of those professionals who work directly under the superintendent in each school district. They serve as an administrative bridge between the superintendent and the principals of individual schools. This group includes professional administrators who deal with curriculum, personnel, special projects, and finance.

This bureaucratic structure often functions primarily to protect its self-interests. House gives examples of things that occur in the bureaucratic structure to allow the central office staff to exert maximum control. For instance, the technique of "'lining up the ducks,' where new administrative posts are only advertised publicly after the COS has already lined up a candidate."[55] Another technique is controlling information from the schools to the superintendent and board of education to protect staff interests and beliefs.

While the above example represents an almost endless list of techniques available for educational bureaucracies, there is one important point made by House in reference to our concern about professional self-interest. He argues that the introduction of educational innovations in a school district is often more dependent on the politics of the central office staff than on whether the innovation is beneficial to students in the school district. In fact, the structure of the bureaucracy often determines whether change will take place. The more centralized the central office staff, the less likely it is to accept educational innovations. House writes: "Centralization is usually negatively associated with innovation since it is assumed that ideas of the less influential will be vetoed because they may threaten the power structure and because there is less opportunity for circulation of ideas." House goes on to argue that "formalization is also negatively associated with innovation since individual initiative is stifled by rules and regulations. Structural flexibility and lack of specificity are more conducive to innovation."[56]

House's main argument about why teachers seem to be unwilling to accept educational innovations is that it is not in their interest. Teachers do not receive any special bonus or salary increases for being more innovative, nor can they expect any job advancement. Unlike career-bound school administrators, teachers do not have the opportunity of moving up an occupational ladder of teaching. Their only occupational advancement is to stop teaching and become administrators. Therefore, in terms of career advancement, there is no reason to become an innovator. And since most salary scales in the United States do not include merit raises for being innovative, there is no economic inducement for teachers to change.

In this regard, House's major recommendations are for the creating of an incentive structure for teachers. This would involve a differentiation among the teaching staff and differential rewards. This would mean a hierarchical structure among teachers. Another method he suggests, and the one he prefers, is to give teachers more power and influence over education: "This feeds professional ambition without changing vertical ambition and substitutes intrinsic rewards for more material ones."[57]

The picture of the politics of education painted by House is not one that would support the idea of the professional educator acting primarily in the interests of the student. It is a rather complex picture of professionals struggling to gain status and economic rewards and protect their positions. What House's study suggests is that when professional educators decide whether to adopt an educational innovation, their first concern is self-interest and not the interest of the student. But in all fairness to the legions of professionals who act primarily in the interests of their students, it should be mentioned that House's study is biased by his adoption of an economic model of self-interest to interpret his data. What House's study does show is that not all educational decisions are free of self-interest.

One of the more difficult issues is to separate professional concern about the public interest from self-interest. It is often the case that what a professional considers to be in the interest of the client is also in the interest of the professional. In these situations it is difficult to determine whether the major motivating force is client interest or professional self-interest. Certainly, if we were to consider the problem in terms of tension between two sets of interests, the best resolution for the professional would be to make decisions that are in the perceived interests of the client and in the self-interest of the professional. Or to state this another way, to do good and make money is to have the best of both worlds.

There is also the issue of the general interest of the profession. A professional group may want to impress the public or the government with the importance of its profession. Promoting the value of a profession can increase the status and income of individuals in the profession. Historically, we have an example of this phenomenon in the professionalization of psychology. Prior to World War I, psychology did not have a great deal of status. Psychologists expressed concern about this situation and consciously sought a means of proving themselves indispensable to American society. The opportunity came during World War I when psychologists had the opportunity to develop and implement IQ tests for the U.S. Army as a means of classifying manpower. Psychologists viewed the measurement and classification of human intelligence as the key to the enhancement of their profession. It would be through this means that psychologists would prove themselves indispensable to society.

Historian Russell Marks has written about the enhancement of the psychological profession by its involvement in efforts to develop mass IQ testing. Marks writes: "It legitimized the psychologists claim to authority in regulating human behavior and tied this authority closely to the needs of the state. The war experience had given the psychologists an unparalleled opportunity to select and control the population."[58]

One of the strongest statements about the importance of psychology was made by the leading psychologist and educator Charles Judd in 1923. This is the same Judd who tried to abolish school boards and turn complete control of education over to the experts. Marks quotes Judd as writing that the "most impressive characteristic of our democracy is its substitution of the authority of scientifically varifiable findings for the authority of arbitrary powers." Judd went on to state with a great deal of self-importance that the science of education should be supported because it provides the "central authority and the source of controlling powers in a democratic society."[59]

A more recent description of professional attempts at aggrandizement has been related by Richard Lehne is his study of school finance reform in New Jersey. In 1973 the New Jersey Supreme Court declared in *Robinson* v. *Cahill* that the existing method of funding public schools was in violation of the state's constitution. At issue was the inequality of expenditures between school districts in New Jersey. In the turmoil that followed the decision, Lehne found a number of specialized educational groups attempting to promote their own interests with the new financing plan. Lehne writes: "To select only one example from scores, the state association of guidance counselors contended that an adequate response to the judicial ruling would require the state to mandate student/counselor ratios in schools throughout New Jersey."[60]

The above examples suggest a complex web of interests. Self-interest can be tied to professional interests, and the interests of the profession can be related to individual interests. In the case of professional educators, all these interests are connected to the expansion of government into general welfare and social planning. As schools become primarily a function of government, increases in salaries, enhancement of the status of the profession, and advancement within the profession become dependent on government action. The example of the guidance counselors in New Jersey illustrates how professional expansion is related to state action.

But the example of the New Jersey counselors also demonstrates the difficulty of separating the public interest from professional interest. It might be that mandating a student/counselor ratio, which would increase the number of counselors in the schools, would be of benefit to students in New Jersey. One could say without much dispute that they would receive more counseling service if this were to occur. In this situation, professional counselors would probably be comfortable with their perception of a merger of public interests and professional interests. But it must be recognized that not all people would agree that it is in the public interest to increase government expenditures for more school counselors.

The difficult of separating decisions based on self-interest and professional interest from those made in the public interest is a fundamental problem in a society increasingly controlled by a bureaucracy populated by professionals. Not only does control slip from the hands of the general public but the professionals in government can justify all actions that are made independent of citizen control as in the public interest. If the public is convinced that the professional always acts in the public interest, then we might have a dictatorship of the professional in government.

This issue takes us back to the question of the ideology of equality of opportunity. As stated previously, this ideology places the professional expert and the school in the center of the social system and gives them prime importance in determining social policy. Whether this ideology is supported because of the self-interest of the professionals who assume control or because of a real public interest is impossible to determine. What can be said is that the ideology of equality of opportunity has justified the establishment and expansion of a welfare state in which major decision making is increasingly in the hands of professionals in bureaucratic structures. And the ideology of equality of opportunity and the welfare state have not ended poverty, redistributed income, or provided equal opportunity.

7

THE PRODUCTION
OF KNOWLEDGE AND
THE CONTROL OF EDUCATION

GOVERNMENT CONTROL AND SPONSORSHIP OF THE PRODUCTION AND dissemination of knowledge has been used to implement goals of manpower planning, equality of educational opportunity, and equality of opportunity. If educational systems are to achieve these social objectives, they must undergo major changes. To achieve these changes requires an expansion of research and development of new curriculums, methods of teaching, and institutional structures. These arguments have led to government involvement in educational research as a method of bringing about planned change in educational systems.

The production of new knowledge and ideas must be viewed as a form of control. As educational systems change, these new ideas often provide a framework for decision making. One element of modern government is the rise in importance of the professional researcher and expert who provides information and conducts studies for political decision makers. Torsten Husen, the great Swedish educator, says in an essay about meritocracy that modern society is witnessing the growing influence of experts and that "the rapidly growing top stratum will distil its own elite of experts—eminent scientists, technologists, economists, psychologists and so on—who will increasingly tend to do the research ordered by the body politic and also to furnish government agencies and politicians with the advice they feel they need."[1]

The conducting of research "ordered by the body politic" raises some serious questions about the control of modern institutions. The primary source of money for research on educational issues has been the government. The primary goal has been to produce research to serve particular social goals. In addition, there has been a concern about the dissemination of research to bring about change in educational institutions. Part of the effort has been to plan the dissemination of new knowledge gained from government-sponsored research.

Planned dissemination of research supported to serve political and social goals is a method of controlling the ideology of a society. This might not be an important issue if the "body politic" that controlled research represented some form of public demand, that is, if the government sponsored particular research studies because the public demanded more knowledge about a particular topic.

A public or consumer demand is not what determines the research. No mechanisms exist for the public to petition or demand sponsorship of educational research. In fact, as Richard Dershimer, former executive officer of the American Educational Research Association, writes: "Every research and development support program in education launched by the federal government was initiated by a small handful of persons, in other words, by a professional-bureaucratic complex." He goes on to claim of government-sponsored research programs in education that "many of these remain in existence today not because of any widespread public demand but because elements in the complex still support them."[2]

An attempt has been made to control educational change through research and dissemination, but most of the effort has encountered a great deal of difficulty because of the political structure of schooling. This has resulted in tension between educational researchers and the government bureaucracies that control research. In addition, government sponsorship of educational researchship has resulted in an expansion of the actual number of educational researchers. This corps of educational scholars has developed its own interests, which are sometimes in conflict with the desires of government bureaucracies.

This chapter considers these issues by exploring the expansion of educational research and the attempts to control educational change. Involved in this discussion is a consideration of models for the planned production and dissemination of new knowledge. This section is followed by a consideration of the control and politics of educational research.

The Expansion of Educational Research
and Methods of Dissemination

In the United States, three major legislative events marked the involvement of the federal government in educational research to implement social policy. The first event was the passage of the National Science Foundation legislation in 1950 for the purpose of increasing scientific and engineering manpower to strengthen the position of the United States in the cold war with the Soviet Union. The second event was the passage in 1965 of the Elementary and Secondary Education Act as part of the government's war against poverty. Included in this legislation were plans for the expansion of research and development in education to aid the public schools in achieving the social objectives of the poverty war. The third event was the establishment in 1972 of the National Institute of Education for the purpose of organizing research to aid schools in providing equality of educational opportunity.

The National Science Foundation's involvement in planned educational change has been primarily in curriculum development. To achieve its early goal of increasing scientific and engineering manpower, the National Science Foundation sponsored the development of new curriculums in science and mathematics. Part of the impetus for its early concerns was a belief that public schools were antiintellectual and did not provide proper training or motivation for students to enter scientific fields. Its general goals in school curriculums were, first, to develop new curriculums and, second, to implement them in public schools.[3]

In essence, what the National Science Foundation attempted to do was to establish a national curriculum under the sponsorship of the federal government. It should be noted that this endeavor has not been marked with a great deal of success, nor has it been free of criticism by elected officials. In fact, efforts at creating a national social science curriculum, *Man a Course of Study* (MACOS), resulted in severe congressional criticism in the 1970s and in limitations being placed on curriculum development and methods of marketing developed curriculums.[4]

Probably the best example of the early methods used by the National Science Foundation was its development and dissemination of what became known as the "new mathematics." In a sense the new mathematics was the National Science Foundation's greatest success story in terms of dissemination. The new mathematics spread like a brush fire through U.S. public schools in the early 1960s. Parents suddenly found their children's homework in mathematics incomprehensible. The spread of the new mathematics was not accompanied by long-term results. By the 1970s the new mathematics was being tossed out the door of the schoolhouse.

The model used by the National Science Foundation for the production and dissemination of the mathematics curriculum involved the establishment of a curriculum development team, the creation of a committee to monitor the textbook market, and the use of summer institutes to train teachers in the new curriculum. The curriculum development team, the School Mathematics Study Group, included an equal number of members from college departments of mathematics and high schools. The team began its work in the summer of 1958, and working only during the summers, completed its final revision of a textbook series in the summer of 1960. After the textbook series was completed, a committee was established and each year reviewed mathematics textbooks to determine if texts comparable to those of the School Mathematics Study Group were available, and if so, to remove the study group's text. The School Mathematics Study Group published its texts through the Yale University Press. During the 1960–61 academic year, 130,000 textbooks were sold, with sales increasing to 500,000 the following year. Within four years of the organization of the curriculum team, its material was being used by 20 percent of the intended market.

Much of the success of the National Science Foundation in disseminating its new curriculums was the result of a textbook industry starved for new materials. Textbook companies do not directly support the development of new curriculums. The National Science Foundation not only provided the new material but also placed pressure on the industry by its own publication and its monitoring of the market.

The efforts of the National Science Foundation were primarily directed toward the development and dissemination of new science curriculums. The major involvement of the federal government in educational research came with the passage of the 1965 Elementary and Secondary Education Act and its support of the concept of research and development in education. Prior to this legislation, the federal government had moved into educational research and development in 1964 when the Office of Education sponsored the establishment of four major educational research centers: the Center for Advanced Study of Educational Administration at the University of Oregon, the Learning Research and Development Center at the University of Pittsburgh, the Center for Research and Development for Learning and Reeducation at the University of Wisconsin, and the

Center for Research and Development on Educational Differences at Harvard University.[5]

Both the establishment of the research centers and the research component of the Elementary and Secondary Education Act involved a particular model for controlling educational change. This model charted a linear progression from basic research to packaging the research to marketing to the final phase of institutionalization in the public school system. It involved a conscious attempt to change public schools through government sponsorship of research and development.[6]

The research and development (R & D) model pictured local schools as passive receptors of educational innovations developed by an elite corps of educational researchers. The basic R & D model is often referred to as the Clark-Guba model, named after David Clark, director of the Cooperative Research Program in the U.S. Office of Education in the 1960s, and Egon Guba, who at the time was director of the Bureau of Educational Research and Service at Ohio State University.[7]

The Clark-Guba model contains four elements of planned educational change connected in a linear fashion. The first element is research, which advances knowledge and provides a basis for educational change. The next element is development, which involves invention and design. Invention takes basic research and applies it to solving a particular educational problem. Design takes the invention and fashions it into a package that can be used in the institutional setting of the school. After development of the educational innovation comes the third element, diffusion, which involves dissemination and demonstration. The diffusion part of the Clark-Guba model involves the conscious attempt to control educational change within local schools. Dissemination is to create a widespread awareness of the invention in its design package, and demonstration allows for the opportunity of examination and assessment. In the words of one study, dissemination "informs about the invention" and demonstration "builds conviction about the invention."[8] The fourth and final stage in this sequential model involves adoption. After building "conviction about the invention," the adoption stage provides for trials, installation, and institutionalization. The trial stage tests the invention in an educational situation, and installation "operationalizes the invention for use in a specific institution." The final part of the adoption phase, and the final part of the R & D model, institutionalizes the invention by making it "part of an ongoing program; converts it to a noninnovation."[9]

The Clark-Guba model puts the educational researcher in charge of educational change, and to a great extent in charge of future operations at educational institutions. It is an elitist model that pictures the professional researcher assuming expert control of the educational system. Ernest House argues in *The Politics of Educational Innovation* that the major problem with the model is that it views teachers and administrators in local educational systems as passive recipients of educational innovations. "In fact," he writes, "use of the paradigm is justified on the basis of the belief that the practitioner is passive and will not initiate innovation on his own."[10]

A government planning group, the Gardner Task Force, which was responsible for the research section of the Elementary and Secondary Education Act, had the same vision of the educational researcher. In fact, this government group envisioned the educational researcher completely overhauling the educational system of the United States. The report of the Gardner Task Force declared: "We must overhaul American education." The key to this overhaul was to be educational innovation. In rather revolutionary language, the report stated: "We now know, beyond all doubt, that educationally speaking, the old ways of doing things will not solve our problems. We are going to have to shed outworn educational practices, dismantle outmoded educational facilities, and create [a] new and better learning environment."[11]

The above statement has important implications for the concept of control of the educational system. It was a federal government report made by a task force composed of an elite group that included the president of the Carnegie Corporation, the editor of *Time*, the president of the Polaroid Corporation, the New York commissioner of education, the mayor of St. Louis, the president of the Educational Facilities Laboratories, the director of the Center for Advanced Study in the Behavioral Sciences, one school superintendent, two university presidents, and two university professors. The only elected official on the committee was the mayor of St. Louis. It was this elite group that planned a total overhaul of the educational system through government sponsorship of educational R & D.[12]

Besides research, the report believed that the overhaul of the American school system could be accomplished by "considerably greater emphasis on development and upon the dissemination of innovation." The report went beyond the issue of the immediate overhaul of the system and saw a process of ongoing change to meet the needs of a changing society. The report stated that "in this era of rapid change, we cannot depend on a single burst of innovation. We need a system designed to accomplish its own continuous renewal."

Not only was government-sponsored research and development going to change the educational system but it was also to maintain control over institutional change.[13]

The research and development effort blossomed in the 1960s and '70s as the federal government sponsored a series of new programs including regional educational laboratories, R & D centers, increased grants for educational research, and a massive dissemination network called the Educational Research (later changed to Resources) Information Center (ERIC). In 1972 many educational research efforts were placed in a newly established National Institute of Education (NIE). The expansion of R & D was reflected in federal government expenditures, which increased from an estimated $19.2 million in 1960 to $69.8 million in 1965.[14]

The expansion and domination of the federal government are clearly revealed when comparisons are made with research expenditures from other sources. In 1960 the combined state and local educational research expenditures were $7.76 million and foundation expenditures were $6 million. Compared with the $19.2 figure for federal expenditures, the federal government in 1960 provided more than 58 percent of the money for educational research. With the expansion of R & D in the 1960s the federal share actually increased. In 1965 state and local expenditures increased to $14 million and foundations increased their expenditures to $14.4 million. But these rates of increase were below that of the federal increase to $69.8 million. By 1965 the federal government was providing more than 71 percent of the money for educational research in the United States.[15]

These figures indicate not only the expansion of the R & D effort but the domination of R & D by the federal government. With 71 percent of the total money spent on research, the federal government could not help but have a major effect on the shape and direction of the production of new knowledge about educational systems. This was particularly true because the R & D effort was envisioned as resulting in an overhaul of the educational system and because it developed in the context of fulfilling the social policies of government.

The relationship between the federal government's involvement in educational research and social policy is clearly stated in the original 1972 legislation for the National Institute of Education. In proposing the NIE in a message to Congress in 1970, President Nixon stated: "The purpose of the National Institute of Education would be to begin the serious systematic search for new knowledge needed to make educational opportunity truly equal." The NIE was to set priorities for educational research and experimentation for "the attainment of particular national goals."[16] The 1972 legislation linked educational research to the providing of equality of educational opportunity. Title III of the legislation stated that the American educational system had not yet attained the objective of equal educational opportunity: "Inequalities of opportunity to receive high quality education remain pronounced. To achieve quality will require far more dependable knowledge about the processes of learning and education than now exists or can be expected from present research and experimentation in this field."[17]

The United States was not the only country to expand investment in educational research in an attempt to provide equality of educational opportunity and equality of opportunity. Torsten Husen details a similar growth in Sweden. Swedish educational research in the 1950s was dominated by concerns about matching the educational system with the manpower structure. (This was at the same time that concern in the United States focused on manpower needs, particularly in the sciences and engineering.) Swedish research "was essentially marketed as social engineering, which more or less amounted to telling people what they were good for. It could help to predict who was going to be able to cope with higher education or it could demonstrate aptitude for certain occupations."[18]

The emphasis changed in Sweden in the early 1960s when the Education Act of 1962 established nine-year comprehensive schools in place of separate schools. Like the introduction of the comprehensive school in England, this reform in Sweden was designed to provide greater equality of educational opportunity, which in turn was to result in greater equality of opportunity. The government of Sweden expanded its support of educational research with much the same rationale as that given in the United States. Husen writes: "The course of events reflects the expectations which government authorities put into educational research concerning desirable or necessary innovations within the educational system . . . we were told, the overriding task would be to renew the school's internal work . . . with research serving as one of the beacons."[19]

Not only was similar support of educational research for similar purposes taking place in different countries, but beginning in the 1960s there were international efforts at educational research. Torsten Husen's career in educational research reflects the growing cooperation among governments. In 1962 Husen became chairman of the International Association for the Evaluation of Educational Achievement (IEA), which had members from nineteen different countries. Since the 1960s this organization has been making comparative studies of the educational output of different countries. In 1970, Husen became chairman of the International Institute for Educational Planning, which has investigated effects of educational planning on other aspects of economic and labor planning.[20]

This description of Husen's career is meant only to be illustrative of the international growth of education research during the 1960s. Other examples of similar developments can be seen in England. In 1961 the Research and Intelligence Branch of the Department of Education and Science was established to provide increased funds for educational research. One of the primary research organizations in England is the National Foundation for Educational Research in England and Wales (NFER). Its budget and staff increased from £37,000 and 38 members in 1960 to £260,000 pounds and 120 members in 1967.[21]

English research interests have paralleled those of the United States. The NFER was established shortly after the passage of the Education Act of 1944, which was discussed in chapter 6. It was organized as an independent research organization by the newly created Ministry of Education, professional associations of teachers, local education authorities, and universities. This research organization is independent in terms of governance but not in terms of funding. Most of its money comes from the Department of Education and Science. A major project undertaken by the institute in 1966 was a study of the effect of the introduction of comprehensive schools. Like Sweden and the United States, NFER research reflected social concerns about equality of educational opportunity.[22]

In England the major organization concerned with curriculum development is the Schools Council (see chapter 6). Like the NFER, the Schools Council has its own independent governing council but receives most of its funds from the government. A majority of the members of the governing council are teachers.

The Schools Council approaches the issue of changing the curriculum in a manner similar to the early curriculum work of the National Science Foundation in the United States. There is a close working relationship with the private textbook industry to get new materials adopted and distributed. In addition, the Schools Council is interested in disseminating information to teachers and providing training in new curriculums. For this purpose the Schools Council has fostered the development of teacher centers as a method of inservice training and dissemination.[23]

The expansion of educational research during the 1960s was obviously welcomed by educational researchers in all countries as a recognition of their own importance. But this expansion took place in the framework of fulfilling general social and political objectives as defined by political organizations. By the 1970s this situation had begun to raise a number of important questions regarding the nature of research in relation to government objectives. The ethos and tradition of the science have been that science needs a climate that allows for the pursuit of truth without outside interference. Government support, while making research possible, tends to guide and control research endeavors. This tendency runs counter to the traditions of scientific research. Also, the expansion of R & D in education has been based on the assumption that it would provide controlled change of educational systems. In this case, research becomes an instrument of government policy.

Dilemmas of Government-Sponsored Research

The expansion of the educational research community and the traditions of science create an inevitable conflict between the needs and desires of government bureaucracies and the independence demanded by the researcher. By the 1970s government sponsorship of educational research in the United States expanded the research community and created groups of self-interested elites. For Richard Dershimer, the present struggle for control of research is between elite members of the research community and the federal bureaucracy. The elite within the educational research community tend to cluster around three major organizations: the Center for Advanced Study in the Behavorial Sciences, the National Academy of Education, and the American Educational Research Association.[24]

The Center for Advanced Study in the Behavorial Sciences was created by the Ford Foundation in 1964 to foster work in the behavorial and social sciences. One consequence of its organization was that it created a network of communication between leading scholars. While this served the interest of the advancement of knowledge, it also contributed to an informal structure between elites in the research community.

Probably the most elitist organization within the educational research community is the National Academy of Education. Formed in 1964, its original eight members were selected by a committee whose members were not eligible for membership. The original selection committee consisted of a group of former presidents of prestigious universities closely associated with major foundations and government. The selection committee included James B. Conant, John

Gardner, Clark Kerr, and Sterling McMurrin. To be the original members of the academy, they chose the elite of the educational community at that time. The original membership was made up of Jerome Bruner, Ronald Campbell, Lawrence Cremin, Lee Cronbach, William Frankena, Richard Hofstadter, Theodore Schultz, and Ralph Tyler. The purpose of the organization was not to issue a vast number of studies but to provide a "forum for conversation, debate, and mutual instruction. . . ." The National Academy of Education functions as another link in the network of leadership in the research community.

The American Educational Research Association originated as part of the National Education Association and until the 1960s was dominated by the parent organization. At that time the organization expanded its activities by creating a new journal, the *American Educational Research Journal,* and by making its annual meetings the major arena for the reading and discussion of educational research. Symbolic of its growing importance in the research community, the organization left the National Education Association. Because of the size of the organization, membership does not mean entry into the elite ranks of researchers, as does membership in the National Academy of Education. What is important is membership in the governing groups of the organization.

Richard Dershimer, who must be recognized as a member of this elite research community, strongly argues that an elitist model is essential for the advancement of research and that control of research must be in the hands of this elite group: "I am reaffirming the need for the elitist system that governs our community. I see no other way that the best minds can be kept at work in our field." From his perspective the major problem is that the elite within the research community has lost control of research to government bureaucrats. He gives two basic recommendations: "filling key government positions with persons from the R & D community and improving the policy-shaping procedures of the R & D community."[25]

What is interesting about Dershimer's proposals is that he does not suggest the removal of government bureaucracies from the control of research, but he argues that researchers should capture the bureaucracy and use it for their own purposes. Dershimer is explicit about how this should be accomplished: "As a first corrective step, we must do whatever we can to ensure that more key government positions are filled by persons from the R & D community itself." The "we" in this case refers to the elite members of the research community. For instance, on appointments to the National Institute of

Education, he writes: "Such appointees should be from the elite, or in a working relationship with the elite."[26]

For Dershimer, the capture of the government bureaucracy by the R & D community will require the internal development of administrators and politicians so that they can move into government organizations. In Dershimer's words: "We need to grow our own crop of bureaucrats who understand the value systems, the vicissitudes, the foibles, and the aspiration of researchers, but who develop a sympathy for and an understanding of the political world."[27] Dershimer's proposals reflect one of the ultimate consequences of government involvement in research: making the researcher a politician.

Dershimer's argument for elite control of research can be justified by scientific tradition. As mentioned previously, a large part of that tradition has stressed the researcher's freedom to pursue "truth" in any manner and direction that he deems best. Obviously, government involvement creates tension between the independence of the researcher and public policy. What Dershimer wants is for the government to provide the money and the R & D community to make the decisions about the research that will be supported. Of course, even in this situation the researcher must deal with the political world of science because the money will be controlled by the elite within the research community. Dershimer's model, like other elite models, assumes that researchers will not act out of self-interest but in the pursuit of knowledge.

The same image of the dedicated seeker of truth is included in the National Academy of Education's report *On Research for Tomorrow's Schools*. The study was issued as a report of the Committee on Educational Research of the academy. The membership of this committee would probably be considered by Dershimer as representative of the elite in the educational R & D community. It included James Coleman, Lawrence Cremin, Lee J. Cronbach, John Goodlad, Calvin Gross, David Jackson, Israel Scheffler, and Patrick Suppes.[28]

The study opens with a list of major problems facing education and portrays the researcher as "reshaping and revitalizing educational institutions and policies." The report presents the image of the dedicated scholar working, without self-interest, to improve American schools. In a self-serving manner, the committee report states: "The scholar is well equipped to provide many things education needs: dispassionate criticism; identification of missed opportunities and emerging problems . . . and painstaking elaboration of each rough preliminary idea into a detailed and practical method. Finally, education needs dispassionate evaluation . . . to make sure that it is educating as intended and to identify problems still unsolved."[29]

The problem with government funding, according to the report, is that it creates conflict between the needs of the political organization and the requirements of scholarship. The scholar is often unhappy that legislators do not place a high value on scholarly work. Part of the problem is that the politician does not understand the nature of the work or the end goal. Also, there is a conflict over time perspective. The politician wants results that can be used in the next election, whereas the scholar tends to work in an extended time frame. The government bureaucracy is caught between two sets of values. The scholar demands independence and time, and the politician demands results that can be displayed to the public quickly.[30]

An important concern expressed by the report is the potential control of government agencies over scholarly activities. The report states: "A research worker who obtains support from a mission-oriented agency finds his thinking shaped by that contact." The report describes ways in which the researcher supported by government money finds his thinking and research directed by government. The portrait in this case is not of the disinterested researcher but of the researcher interested in getting government money.

For example, according to the report, the researcher interested in getting money from a government agency "includes in his application a statement regarding the relevance his studies promise to have for the mission of the agency, and in his final report he may well trace out some implication of his results for the sponsor even though his study was not aimed toward 'practical' conclusions." The proposals, reports, and invitations by the particular government agency to meet other researchers, advise the agency, and read other proposals shape the thinking of the researcher and "the investigator's thoughts migrate toward topics, tangential to his original interest, that are of particular relevance to the agency. . . ."[31]

What is interesting in this description is that the report of the academy is not as concerned about the shaping of the researcher's scholarly interests as with the ability of a government agency to develop a strong reputation for research. In this case the concern is with the poor reputation of the Office of Education. What the report argues is that a major consequence of this shaping of scholarly interests is that "the prestige of the field, and hence its ability to attract additional investigators, grows as men of good reputation demonstrate their respect for the agency and its mission."[32]

One can take this description of the shaping of scholarly interests by government agencies and argue that it represents a powerful influence over the research being done in the United States. One might write ideally about dispassionate scholars, but in reality there is the competition for money and the political world of American research. Most researchers in the United States are located in colleges and universities and are often dependent on research money to support studies that will assure their tenure and promotion. It is not beyond the realm of imagination to think that some of these scholars might consciously, or even unconsciously, direct their research into areas where they can be assured of receiving support from the government or private foundations.

The National Academy of Education did express concern about the political directions given to research by making a distinction between decision-oriented research and conclusion-oriented research. Decision-oriented research is defined as the situation where "the investigator is asked to provide information wanted by a decision-maker: a school administrator, a governmental policy-maker, the manager of a project. . . ." Conclusion-oriented research "takes its direction from the investigator's commitments and hunches." Freedom is available only to a limited degree in decision-oriented research, whereas maximum freedom is granted the researcher doing conclusion-oriented research.

It is significant that the academy deals with research in terms of decision and conclusion orientation as opposed to "basic research" and "applied research." The reason given, and certainly it is a valid reason, is the difficulty of distinguishing between applied and basic research. But another reason, and an important one in terms of government control, is that concepts of applied and basic research are not usable when dealing with the researchers' relationship to the government bureaucracy. Concepts of decision-oriented and conclusion-oriented research deal directly with the degree of control exercised by the government over the actual research endeavor.

Like Dershimer's argument, the major concern of the report is with assuring control of research by the research community. The report does not deny the role of government in giving direction to the research that will be conducted. The report states, in relationship to conclusion-oriented research: "The educational decision-maker can, at most, arouse the investigator's interest in a problem."[33] While not explicitly stated in the report, this suggests that interest might be aroused by offering money for particular research. In the framework of conclusion-oriented research, the scholar might be enticed into investigating a particular area, but the questions asked and methods used should be under the control of the investigator.

One of the concerns of the academy report is the apparent lack of recognition by government of the importance of conclusion-oriented research. Politicians tend to demand immediate and definite results.

Yet, "the conclusion-oriented study is not planned with an eye to a definite and useful result. The main benefit is in the unforseen ideas it adds to society's intellectual capital."[34]

The blame for the neglect of conclusion-oriented research is not placed solely on the shoulders of government. The report argues that historical circumstances put the educational researcher in the position of being pressed "to carry out studies intended somehow to determine what professional educators should do."[35] Present support of educational research and historical circumstances have forced the educational researcher to deal primarily with decision-oriented research. What this means, of course, is that educational research and the researcher have become subordinate to the decision makers. The report is a plea for independence of educational research and control by the research community.

The academy's report did not deny the importance of decision-oriented research, but it did want to separate the researcher from responsibility for actual decisions. The report stressed: "The role of each study is to provide the decision-maker with information, not to tell him what to do."[36] The only function of decision-making research, it argued, is to give a statement of relevant facts and possible outcomes and alternatives. This research should only be part of the more general information decision makers must use in deciding on a course of action.

Another aspect of the relationship of government to educational research is that government policy does not seem to be informed by research opinion. This concern began to be expressed in the early 1970s with the apparent failure of education to end poverty and provide equality of opportunity. What began to be argued was that the massive amounts of money spent on education to solve social problems should be justified by some evidence that education could solve these problems. Most of the major educational programs sponsored by government in the 1960s and '70s have been sponsored without any evidence that they can achieve their objectives. In England, Douglas Pidgeon, deputy director of the National Foundation for Educational Research, points out that "research into comprehensive education should have been carried out prior to any policy decision to 'go comprehensive.'"[37] He does not feel that such criticism invalidates the research of the foundation into comprehensive schooling, but that criticism raises the issue of the role of research in informing public policy.

In the United States, the most eloquent spokesman for using research to inform policy has been Daniel P. Moynihan. Moynihan criticized the poverty programs of the 1960s for being based on the "conventional wisdom" that schooling makes a difference. What he felt exploded these common assumptions is the Coleman Report, which used national data to show little relationship between what people assumed is important in improving achievement in the schools and actual achievement. Moynihan felt that if these data had been available in the early 1960s and had been used in developing national policies, there probably would not have been as much emphasis on spending on education to achieve social objectives. He wrote in 1972 that "I for one would be willing to bet that the more we learn about formal schooling the less we will come to value it."[38]

Unlike the educational R & D community's belief that more research would result in an overhaul of education, Moynihan primarily saw educational research causing a reduction of educational funding for achieving general social goals. This position reflects Moynihan's general distrust of social scientists. He has argued that social scientists have been persuaded primarily by their political convictions and not by their research findings. Their political persuasions have been primarily liberal and radical, and consequently they support any program designed to aid the poor, even though no social science evidence exists to prove that such programs can achieve their objectives.

Moynihan's position has been in stark contrast to the research community's claim of lack of self-interest and ability to conduct dispassionate research. Social scientists, Moynihan has argued, are deeply committed to social change and tend to be at odds with the forces of personal wealth and political power. Their opinions on public issues have been shaped by their personal views and not their professional findings. His plea has been that social scientists not take sides on social issues but rely on the facts of their findings.[39]

As White House counselor and confidant to President Richard Nixon in the early 1970s, Moynihan became a leading advocate for the establishment of the National Institute of Education. He believed that the research findings of this institution could be used for the development of federal educational policy and programs designed to achieve that policy. This would avoid the problem of the past failure of educational programs because research had not been conducted before their implementation. The objective of the National Institute of Education, Moynihan stated, was "to bring 'big' science to bear on education, especially the problem of low achievement among students from low-income families."[40]

Moynihan believed the NIE would provide research that would inform policy, but the actual structure of the NIE has created a potential situation for policy controlling research. An investigation of the original organization and structure of the NIE demonstrates the dilemmas involved in government support of research. It also clearly demonstrates the potential for government to control the production of knowledge.

In organizational terms the NIE followed the typical pattern of educational institutions with an elite governing board and a bureaucratic structure that makes most of the decisions. What is important to keep in mind, as organizational features of the NIE are reviewed here, is that the major concern is with channeling research interests into particular fields by making available government funds for certain areas of research. The National Academy of Education had cautiously referred to this process as arousing "the investigator's interest in a problem." In other words, the NIE, by designating priority areas for research, creates the potential situation of guiding the production of knowledge about education by attracting researchers into those areas with offers of monetary support.

The group designated as formulating general policies for the NIE is the National Council of Educational Research. This group has the responsibility of advising the director of NIE and the assistant secretary for education on program development, methods of collecting and disseminating information, and submitting reports to the President and Congress on NIE's activities, educational research, and general educational issues.

The original membership of the National Council of Educational Research was a combination of elites from the education community and the business community. This again raises the question of representation and its meaning in educational organizations. Whose interests in research are represented by the following members of the National Council of Educational Research? The original chairman of the council was also chairman of the board of Texas Instruments, Inc., one of the leading manufacturers of electronic equipment and calculators and one of the pioneer developers of programmed calculators designed to teach young children basic arithmetic and spelling. Other members of the council who were selected from outside the education community were Ralph M. Besse, a Cleveland lawyer and chairman of the Cleveland Electrical Illuminating Company, and Carl Pforzheimer of Carl Pforzheimer and Company. In addition, there was a member from the Bell Telephone Laboratories, seven members from universities, two members from state departments of education, one superintendent of schools, and one principal of a public school. In 1975 the membership was changed and reduced; the president of the University of Illinois became chairman, Besse and Pforzheimer stayed on, four members came from universities and colleges, one member came from a state department of education, there was one principal of a public school, and another member was director of the National Enquiry into Scholarly Communication.[41]

The purpose of going through these early membership lists of the National Council of Educational Research is to show the lack of representation from what one might call "the general public" and the domination by professional educators. Those members from outside the research community have been drawn primarily from elite business groups. The membership is not dissimilar to the social composition of the Gardner Task Force, mentioned earlier in the chapter.

The research priorities of the NIE planning unit formed shortly before the passage of the legislation in 1972. The original legislation included vague language about attaining equality of educational opportunity and solving "the problems of" and achieving "the objectives of" American education. The task of giving substance to these statements was taken up by the NIE planning unit. In the words of the official history of the NIE: "A number of studies were commissioned to develop the proposed Institute's organizational structure. The concerns expressed in these papers, as well as Congressional debates and subsequent work of the NIE staff, are reflected in NIE's priority statements."[42]

Priority statements of the NIE define the areas it believes are most critical for the advancement of education. In effect, these areas define national goals for educational research. Since it is believed that educational research should have a direct effect on educational practice, priority areas can also be considered national goals for educational change. If this is taken one step farther, priority areas can be more simply called national goals for education.

For example, consider the original priority areas of the NIE for educational research and change. There were five priority areas: essential skills, productivity, education and work, problem solving, and diversity. In addition, the NIE received money for its internal development and for the dissemination activities "to increase the quantity and quality of 'consumer' information about R & D. . . ."[43]

The goal-setting aspect of priority areas is highlighted when one considers the substance of each area in relationship to actual funding. The original priority area receiving the largest amount of funding was education and work. The goal of this priority area was to "improve our understanding of the relationship between education and work." The research to be supported was designed to emphasize the manpower model in education and provide information to adapt the school to the needs of the labor model. The NIE said it would support research that would improve definitions and concepts such as careers, job satisfaction, and economic return. In addition, it called for research to assess "the ability of educational institutions to adjust to changes in labor market demands for specialized manpowers." It also supported continuing "to improve curriculum materials that increase children's career awareness and how to provide young people with work experience that offers both specific skills and an understanding of career options."[44]

The second-best-funded priority area was diversity, which included a wide range of subjects, such as experimental schools, vouchers, multicultural education, and education for the handicapped. The general goal was to support research that would help schools adapt to a diverse population. Diversity in this case referred to racial and ethnic differences and differences caused by physical problems.

Following diversity, in terms of funding, was productivity. Support of research in this area was justified with the interesting statement that while there had been an actual increase in school expenditures per pupil of 35 percent since 1950, "there is no indication that education is 35 percent 'better'—by whatever measure—today than it was in 1950."[45] The goal of productivity research was to discover ways to provide quality education at a price the nation could afford.

The lowest priority areas on the funding scale were essential skills and problem solving. Essential skills called for the support of research to assist educators to provide children with basic skills in reading and mathematics. Problem-solving research involved investigating organizational features of local school systems and their ability and capacity to adapt to educational innovation. In one sense, this priority area recognized the early failure of R & D to overhaul the educational system. The statement defining this priority area begins: "Many observers question whether Federal efforts to assist schools in dealing with their problems over the past decade have been effective."[46]

In 1977 these priority areas remained essentially the same with two name changes: Diversity became "educational equity" and included research into the educational needs of women and school desegregation, and essential skills became "basic skills." The order of funding shifted; basic skills received the highest amount followed by productivity, education and work, educational equity, and problem solving.[47]

These priority areas can be restated as national educational goals meant to tighten the relationship between the school and the labor market and define schooling primarily in terms of gaining a career and an occupation. In addition, schools should become more inexpensive to operate, teach basic skills, and have the capacity to change to meet the needs of a diverse population.

At first glance, the reader might not object to these as national educational goals. Problems appear when one considers what is not included. For instance, given that the United States was faced with serious economic and energy problems throughout the 1970s, one might ask why there was no research priority for understanding ways of increasing critical skills and abilities in the understanding of economic systems. It would seem reasonable that since government had apparently been unable to solve these problems, a major goal would be to turn out a future citizenry that could develop imaginative solutions. Another major problem of the 1970s was the decline in participation in local and national elections. This would seem to call for research into how to help students understand the political forces of modern society and the methods that might be used to change and influence government. The other major problem, and one that has been present throughout the twentieth century, is the possibility of war and international tensions. What about research into methods of teaching students to understand and work for peace?

When one compares the above suggestions with the actual priority areas of the NIE, a distinct feature of the NIE activities emerges. None of the NIE priority areas has anything to do with the schools educating active citizens. The primary emphasis is on the passive citizen. The major goal relates to helping students find a job. While the NIE has been interested in teaching basic skills, this has not been in the context of producing active political citizens.

The priority areas of the NIE fit into the general liberal-professional model of society where the school functions to lead people into careers in the labor market. Heavy support is given to professionals to determine how schools should reorganize and how they can reduce costs. Professionals are not given the political power to accomplish these goals, but it is assumed that their models for changing schools will provide the direction for American education. What are basically political problems, and thus could be decided in the political arena, become areas for expert investigation.

As mentioned, politicians like Daniel Moynihan considered the most important function of the NIE to be the support of research that would inform public policy. To a certain extent, this is what the National Academy of Education report would call decision-oriented research. The concern was that research about the effectiveness of programs would be conducted before the actual programs were implemented.

While NIE's priority areas did represent fields of concern to policy makers, by the late 1970s some priority areas seemed to be functioning more like programs than like research about policy. For instance, the proposed program plan for the NIE in 1977 states, in reference to education and work: "Activities in this area of long standing concern to the public will help students (a) make better choices in their careers, (b) improve their mastery of skills to enter and progress in jobs, and (c) leave and re-enter occupational education throughout their lives." The plan goes on to state in words that are clearly program-oriented and not research-oriented that "work experience in various settings and improved counseling and information are the principal strategies we have chosen." Specifically, one listed program highlighted for 1976 was "initiate a series of approximately 30 five-minute TV spots to give children ages 4 to 10 a better understanding of the broad range of careers they might consider."[48] This hardly resembles Moynihan's original plea for "big science" to be brought to bear on education.

It is important to briefly analyze the above quotes from the NIE planning document. First, it should be noted that there is reference to the "long standing concern to the public." Although a concern about creating work-oriented education programs may be a concern to a majority of the population, there is no means by which majority desires can directly influence NIE policy. It is not altogether clear what public is being referred to in this statement. Outside influence is brought to bear on NIE policy through the National Council for Educational Research, Congress, and the administration. As has been argued in previous chapters, it is difficult to determine whose interests and desires are being represented. NIE's policies are so far removed from the control of the majority of the population that one must understand the above statement to be NIE's interpretation of what the public is concerned about. One wonders, for instance, if the majority of the population would vote to provide money for making thirty five-minute TV spots for the career education of children between four and ten years of age.

More important in the priority area of education and work, the NIE seems to operate exactly opposite to the Moynihan argument that research into the effects of different policies should be conducted before implementation. As discussed in previous chapters, there is no proof that the manpower model in education or career education works in terms of reducing unemployment and finding people jobs. There is no proof that mass programs in vocational education work in terms of preparing people for employment. It may be true that changes in occupational structure and shifts in the labor market make it impossible for schools to provide programs that will give people skills that are actually in demand when they graduate. In other words, vocational education may make it more difficult for people to get jobs because their training is too specific. There is no proof that career education helps people make "better" career decisions. The attempt to create a curriculum about careers may actually hinder the thinking about careers because the perspective of the curriculum and those who develop it is actually more limited than the real-life situations in the labor market. Maybe the study of literature is a better preparation for career decisions and employment preparation because it introduces students to a broad range of life experiences and provides critical skills. The point of this discussion is that from the perspective of someone like Moynihan, these issues need to be dealt with by research before the implementation of programs.

Trying to separate research from actual government policy has been one of the major dilemmas in the relationship between the research community and the government. Dershimer's writings and the policy statements of the National Academy of Education have given expression to the desire by many researchers to be free of the controlling influence of politicians and government bureaucrats. On the other hand, these same researchers demand increased government support of research. Politicians seem able to justify this support of research only in terms of its being able to solve major national problems. Bureaucrats are then given the responsibility of interpreting the intent of Congress in supporting research and monitoring the work of researchers. This becomes a control of research in terms of public policy. The NIE is an example of where support of research becomes indistinguishable from implementation of public policy.

Government-Sponsored Research and the Control of Education

The example of the NIE demonstrates the thin line that exists between government support of research and policy designed to exercise control. Certainly, the R & D model of the 1960s was specifically stated in terms of renewal and planned change in education. Obviously, in this model, support of any particular research was tantamount to designating that area as a target for change in

American education. Research policy is national policy regarding education. The same thing is true of the NIE. The concept of a priority area means that the area is considered worthy of emphasis in American education. In this case, research could lead to the expansion of existing school programs or the addition of new programs in priority areas.

What this means is that government research policy can control education in several ways. First, by making available funds for particular research, the government attracts scholars to those areas of inquiry. Scholars competing for government research grants write proposals and shape their research according to their interpretation of the kinds of proposals the government will fund. Once the research is supported, the scholar will be in the business of producing new knowledge and information. The scholar will incorporate this research in papers delivered at professional meetings, in articles in journals, and in books. Often the scholar, through professional organizations, will come into contact with other scholars sponsored by the government to do similar research. This situation may lead to the creation of a community of scholars around a common area of interest. Graduate students will also be induced into research, either by their faculty adviser (who is receiving research support) or by the availability of research money. All this research effort might eventually be included in textbooks on education that will affect the thinking of undergraduates. In this manner, as it did with career education in the 1970s, government support of research can lead a whole group of scholars to a lifelong commitment to a particular area of study.[49] The scholar's prestige and general self-interest can become associated with a field, and this can lead him to become an effective lobbyist for future support of such research and the expansion of programs in the area.

Second, the designation of priority areas for educational research is also the designation of national goals for education without having to state them as national goals. The NIE is a perfect example of this situation. In the NIE, support of programs and support of research take place within a designated priority area. At the same time, the NIE engages in a major program of dissemination of information about these priority areas. In this process are combined the production, development, and distribution of knowledge.

If research policy is considered as national policy for education, then the issue of who controls research policy becomes extremely important. Hiding national goals for education in research policy is a method of removing those goals from popular debate. Certainly in the United States a great deal of controversy would be generated at the idea of the federal government having national educational goals. It would even create popular debate if the federal government openly implemented national educational goals.

The establishment and implementation of national goals as research goals has limited potential for popular debate. In fact, by hiding educational goals in research policy, major debates take place within the research community and the bureaucratic structure of government. It also results in a struggle for power between the professional research community and the government bureaucracy. Neither group seems interested in popular control of government research policy.

It is important to understand that the issue is not popular control of the activities of the researcher involved in the investigation of a problem. What is at issue are the consequences of centralized forces such as the federal government having a major influence on research pursued by investigators. This influence over the production of knowledge could determine the parameters of educational debate for many years. For instance, heavy government funding of research and programs in basic skills and education and work results in the production of a large amount of new knowledge about these areas, the creation of a corps of researchers, and educational bureaucrats at all levels who have a self-interest in the perpetuation of funding and recognition of these fields, and in the creation of school curriculums that attempt to implement this growing body of knowledge.

What can occur is that the parameters of discussion about education are defined by the new knowledge and the self-interest of researchers and bureaucrats. Discussions defined by these parameters primarily center on what programs will best achieve the goals of relating education to work and the teaching of basic skills. Discussions that will tend not to occur are about whether these are proper objectives for public schooling or whether they should be related to other parts of the curriculum. As mentioned, there are inherent weaknesses in attempts to link the school to the needs of the labor market. In terms of basic skills, there is the important question of which skills will be linked to other areas of the curriculum. Few people would quarrel with the goal of teaching reading, but serious issues arise about what is to be read in school. While support has been provided for work and education, little has been provided for research into the teaching of literature, art, political science, economics, and music. If there is a growth of new knowledge in basic skills and work and education, but not in other areas, this could result in basic skills being primarily related to the teaching of material related to work and education.

The above discussion exemplifies how government funding of research and programs can define the objectives and the functioning of schools. Another possible consequence is the determination of future actions by school administrators. In chapter 6 there was a discussion of the "career-bound" superintendent, the educational administrator who wanted to move up the occupational ladder. It was suggested that one way school administrators could gain recognition and prove their administrative ability was by introducing new educational programs. The upwardly mobile school administrator could prove his worth by displaying knowledge about what is new in education and by implementing new ideas.

This suggests certain dynamics for change that are inherent in the school structure. This does not mean that change will be introduced successfully, but that discussions and attempts at the introduction of new ideas will be part of the techniques used by some upwardly mobile school administrators. If government funding of educational research is having a major influence on the new knowledge being produced, then it will have an indirect effect on the new ideas and programs entertained by upwardly mobile school administrators. The upwardly mobile school administrator is seldom a source of original ideas. The administrator must search through the marketplace of ideas to find those that are conducive to his thinking and seem adaptable to the school system. If the marketplace is dominated by ideas produced by government support, then the administrator will most likely choose within those parameters. The marketplace of ideas does not determine selection. The determining factors will probably be the politics and dynamics of the particular school system. What the marketplace does is to determine the parameter of ideas from which the individual selects.

It would be difficult to measure how much the ideas a population has about education result from the research supported by government and the methods of dissemination. What should be recognized is that a clearly stated objective of R & D policy is to influence change in educational systems. It is also true that governments have mainly provided money to support research in certain priority areas. At issue are the effectiveness of this process in bringing about change and the control of educational systems by controlling the production and dissemination of knowledge. The latter issue raises questions about the nature of popular control of educational systems and of ideology. If Richard Dershimer is right and control is primarily in the hands of a professional-bureaucratic complex, then the ideology of that group could become the ideology of society.

8

THE
ECONOMICS
OF SCHOOLING

DISCUSSIONS ABOUT THE FINANCIAL SUPPORT OF SCHOOLING HAVE centered on social, economic, and political purposes. Translated into the language of economists, these purposes are identified as "public benefits," "neighborhood effects," and "externalities." Economists use these terms to distinguish public and private reasons for supporting schools. Private benefits would include increased personal income, personal satisfaction gained through learning new skills and acquiring new knowledge, and increased political and social power gained through education. Private benefits can be used as a justification for personal investment in education. Public benefits, or externalities of schooling, would include increased economic growth, political stability, efficient use of manpower, and reduction of crime. As noted in previous chapters, these represent major social and economic purposes of schooling. Public benefits, or externalities, can be used to justify public investment in schooling.

To understand the role of public benefits in the debate about the financial support of schooling, consider the arguments of two individuals widely separated in time and economic perspective: nineteenth-century common school crusader Horace Mann and twentieth-century economist Milton Friedman. Mann argued for general public support of common schools in terms of their supposed public benefits. Friedman has justified a different method of financing education through vouchers but has reiterated Mann's argument of the supposed public benefits of schooling.

The problem facing Horace Mann in the nineteenth century was to provide a convincing argument that all adult members of a community should give financial support to common schools even if they had no children or sent their children to private schools. If schooling provided only private benefits, such as increased income or personal satisfaction, there would seem to be little justification for all members of the community to pay for the support of a common school. Purely private benefits from schooling would support the argument for the private or personal payment for education.

Mann justified public financial support of schooling primarily in terms of economic benefits. He argued that property values depended on the existing community and improvements made in that community. A present owner of property was merely a trustee of wealth inherited from a previous owner that would be passed on to a future owner. Generations were interdependent; each must make improvements in property. The value of property also depended on the quality of the surrounding community.

What this meant was that the interrelationship between generations and within communities made it possible to isolate individual wealth from the wealth of the community and previous generations. If schooling increased the skills and abilities of one individual, then all individuals in the community would benefit and all future generations would benefit. According to this reasoning, even if an individual had no children or sent his children to private schools, he still benefited economically from common schools because an educated generation increased the value of his property. Therefore, the public benefits of schooling justified taxing all members of the community to provide financial support for schools.[1]

It is important to point out that Mann's argument for public benefits does not necessarily justify free schools or government provision of schooling. As will be discussed later in the chapter, a number of economic and historical issues are involved in the rise of free and universal schooling. What is important for this part of the chapter is to understand how a public benefits argument can justify taxing all members of the community to support the education of only a few members of the community. Mann wrote in reference to the successive generations of citizens of Massachusetts that "the property of this Commonwealth is pledged for the education of all its youth, up to such a point as will save them from poverty and vice and prepare them for the adequate performance of their social and civil duties."[2]

Mann believed that the public benefits argument justified both public support of schooling and government provision of schooling. By contrast, Milton Friedman, in his original argument for a voucher plan, used the public benefits argument to justify government subsidy of education but not government provision of education. It is important to understand the distinction between subsidy and providing schooling. A subsidy can help individuals purchase an education. There do not have to be government-owned and -operated schools. Through direct subsidy, the government can assist individuals to attend privately operated schools without actually building and operating public schools.

Friedman in his early proposal in the 1960s for vouchers argued that government intervention in education could be rationalized in terms of the public benefits derived from education's contribution to the maintenance of a stable and democratic society. This public benefit, neighborhood effect, justified government action to require that each person receive "a minimum amount of schooling of a specified kind."[3] On the other hand, Friedman did not believe that the private benefits gained from vocational training justified government intervention. The only justified forms of intervention, according to Friedman, were forms that produced significant neighborhood effects as public benefits.

While Friedman believed neighborhood effects justified government financing of education, he did not justify "the actual administration of educational institutions by the government, the 'nationalization,' as it were, of the bulk of the 'education industry.' . . ." What he proposed was that the government subsidize education by providing parents with vouchers "redeemable for a specified maximum sum per child per year if spent on 'approved' educational services."[4] Through a system of vouchers, parents would purchase education for their children from private institutions. Neighborhood effects would be guaranteed by the government regulating private schools to assure that schools met certain minimum standards and had certain minimum content.

A voucher system would promote competition between schools and teachers and provide a major step for improving the quality of education in the United States. In addition, vouchers would allow for a child to receive an education primarily as a result of parental choice and not the choice of government officials. Competition would also increase the possibility of creating more economically efficient systems of education.

A major argument against private systems of schooling, and an argument strongly voiced by Horace Mann, was that it leads to social-class divisions. The poor attend one school and the rich another. The ideology of the common school has stressed mingling rich and poor within one school as a means of promoting social unity.

Friedman's response to this argument was that, in reality, public schools created class divisions in education because of their organization into school districts. In Friedman's words: "Under present arrangements, stratification of residential areas effectively restricts the intermingling of children from decidedly different backgrounds."[5] In addition, parents can still send their children to private schools. Except for parochial education, he argued, only a limited few can afford private schooling, thus resulting in further stratification. Government-provided schooling actually restricts the possibilities of social-class intermingling.

His example was of a black resident of an inner city trying to obtain a high-quality education for his gifted child. The existing structure of government schooling made it almost impossible for this disadvantaged person to send the child to a school outside the inner city. Friedman stated that if this resident "attached enough importance to, say, a new automobile, he can, by dint of saving accumulate enough money to buy the same car as a resident of high-income suburbs. To do so, he need not move to that suburb." On the other hand, "let a poor family in a slum have a gifted child and let it set such a high value on his or her schooling that it is willing to scrimp and save for the purpose. Unless it can get special treatment, or scholarship assistance, at one of the very few private schools, the family is in a very difficult position."[6]

Because good schools are in high-income neighborhoods, it is difficult for a poor family to save extra money for a child's education and afford the expense of moving to a wealthy suburb.

Since the time of Friedman's original voucher proposal, attempts have been made in the courts to rectify the problem of inequalities between school districts. As we shall see later in the chapter, there has been an attempt to provide equality of educational opportunity in terms of assuring equality of expenditures between school districts. What is important at this point is the contrast between Mann and

Friedman with regard to the nature of government support of schooling.

Friedman's voucher proposal incorporated a belief that the basic choice about education should be in the hands of parents and those who operate the schools. He believed, like Mann, that education provided enough public benefits to warrant government subsidy, but he felt there was no reason for the government to provide education. An important question arises when one follows the logic of Friedman's argument. What happens if there are not enough public benefits to justify government subsidy of education?

Currently, Friedman has apparently abandoned his belief in the public benefits of education. It should be remembered that his earlier argument was based on the assumption that education contributed to the maintenance of a stable democratic society. In making his claim of public benefits he had no proof that schooling did accomplish this goal. There was also no proof that without government subsidy of schooling, parents educating their children through private means would not achieve the same goal.

Writing in 1976, Friedman recognized that the "case for . . . government financing of schooling based on supposed externalities is seriously flawed. The flaw is present in my own treatment of these issues in *Capitalism and Freedom*. . . ."[7] The error Friedman feels he made was not to distinguish between average externalities and marginal externalities. The essential issue is how much additional education is required to provide a given amount of public benefits. For instance, to use Friedman's example, if 99.7 percent of all children are going through elementary school, 90 percent through high school, and 50 percent through college, then how much additional education of the population is required to reduce crime? In this situation one would have to be able to prove a concrete relationship between years of schooling and a decline in the crime rate. As Friedman suggests, there is no proof that educating one more individual at each level of schooling would reduce crime.

Friedman's argument leads to another issue: Would private financing of education by parents provide the same externalities, or public benefits, as government-subsidized education? In this regard Friedman emphatically states, "I have never found any plausible argument for any net positive externalities from schooling that would not be satisfied if 90 percent, to take an arbitrary figure, received elementary schooling—the three R's. I have yet to see a plausible argument for any net positive externality from additional schooling." If private interest is able to provide this much schooling, he writes, "there is no case from externalities for either compulsory schooling or the governmental financing of schooling."[8] In other words, in terms of public benefits, there is no justification for government intervention in education.

Private or Government Financing of Schooling?

The arguments of Milton Friedman and Horace Mann represent two ends of the spectrum on school financing. It is sometimes hard today, when there is almost universal government support of schooling, to appreciate the continuing importance of this debate. In fact, one is struck by the peculiar nature of government-financed schooling only when consideration is given to other possible areas of government support. For instance, what about free and compulsory eating? This is a favorite example used by the English economist E. G. West to illustrate some of the economic issues surrounding school finance.

As West argues, it seems strange that contemporary governments provide free and compulsory schooling but not free and compulsory eating establishments; there would seem to be more proof of the beneficial effects of diet than of the beneficial effects of schooling. West writes: "It is difficult to envisage, however, that any government, in its anxiety to see that children have minimum standards of food and clothing, would pass laws for compulsory and universal eating, or that it should entertain measures which lead to increased taxes and rates in order to provide children's food 'free' at local authority kitchens or shops."[9]

West's illustration highlights the uniqueness of government-provided schooling in terms of other services provided by government. Most governments provide some food programs for the poor either by subsidizing the purchase of food or by free meals. Usually there is no direct subsidy for the rich or the middle class for the purchase of food. Nor, in Western countries like the United States and England, are there government-run grocery stores that prescribe the purchase of only certain food items. There are attempts to guide eating habits through informational programs, and there is food inspection. But there does not exist the same control over eating habits as there is over the consumption of education.

The contrast between government services related to education and food also illustrates the possible range of government involvement in the financing of education. At one end of the scale is no government involvement and at the other end of the scale is complete government provision of education with private schools being illegal. Between these two extremes are a variety of options. Beginning with no government involvement, the next step on the scale is government inspection and regulation against fraud and harmful products. Following this would be inspection, regulation, and subsidy to those unable to purchase the product or service through private income. In this case there would be a selective form of subsidy. Regulation, inspection, and selective subsidy have tended to be the limit of government involvement in food but not in education. The next step on the scale would be inspection, regulation, and a full subsidy for the purchase of the product or service. In terms of food this would mean that the government subsidize grocery purchases by all members of the population, rich and poor.

The next step is government regulation, inspection, and partial provision of the product or service. In terms of food this would mean government-operated grocery stores offering free food and privately operated grocery stores selling food. This, by the way, represents the current situation regarding education in the United States. Private grocery stores would probably continue to exist because of particular dietary habits of certain members of the population and the preferences of the rich for specialty foods that might not be available in government stores. In the same manner private schools continue to exist alongside free public schools because of particular religious, philosophical, and social-class preferences.

The interesting question about these options is this: Why in countries like the United States and England have governments provided free schooling to all children? Why, for instance, don't these governments subsidize only the education of those who cannot afford to purchase schooling and let those with enough private means pay for schooling directly? Why provide free education for all children, including the children of the rich?

History provides some answers, but the answers raise unsettling issues regarding the current government financing of schooling. First, consider the historical situation of moving on our scale of options from no government involvement in education to government subsidization of the poor. Our example here will be New York City, the subject of a study by the historian Carl Kaestle. Kaestle found that in New York City in the 1790s, prior to government funding of education, 80 to 90 percent of the population received some form of schooling in private schools. Schooling at that time was not a continuous experience. Children might be sent to school to learn to read, then removed from school when parents felt that good had been accomplished. Said Kaestle: "Schooling was such a discontinuous and informal procedure that a 52 percent enrollment rate might occur in a given year even if 80 or 90 percent of the population got some schooling during their childhood."[10]

Kaestle also found that a system of private schooling did not result in students being divided according to social class. Private schools had sliding rate scales geared to the financial situation of the parents. Kaestle found by studying amounts paid in tuition and occupations of parents that most private schools enrolled a broad spectrum of children from different social classes. These private schools were common schools in the sense that they mixed children from different social backgrounds.

The historical irony of this situation is that when the government of New York provided money for education, it was used to support charity or "free" schools for the poor. At the time, private school teachers felt they should receive the subsidy since they were already providing a common education. The other option was to provide the poor with a direct subsidy so that they could purchase an education for their children from the existing private schools. By supporting charity schools, the government in effect segregated children of the poor from children of other groups in society and destroyed the common school quality of the private system. Later in the nineteenth century, during what was called the "common school movement," the argument was that existing public schools were only for the poor and that public schooling had to be extended to all members of society so that children of rich and poor could mingle in the same schoolhouse.

Kaestle's study raises some important issues. For instance, it is often argued that government provision of schooling is necessary because many members of society would not receive an education with a system of private schooling. It is also argued that government provision of schooling is necessary because of social-class segregation that might occur in a system of private schooling. Kaestle's study raises serious doubts about both these arguments. There would seem to be little historical support for the argument that large numbers of the population would be without schooling if the system were financed through private sources. E. G. West's study of schooling in nineteenth-century England also reaches the conclusion that most children received an education when there were only private schools. This does not mean that these schools were of high quality or that *all* children received an education. But from West's point of view, the situation at best could only justify subsidizing the poor to purchase an education from a system of private schooling.[11]

Why, then, did free public schools come into existence? The historical studies are sketchy in answering this question. There were of course the claims of public benefits, or neighborhood effects. These arguments were used to justify the establishment of free public schools. But for an economist like E. G. West, these arguments must be viewed only as a justification for other interests involved in the creation of free government schooling. After all, there was, and is, no proof that free government schooling provides more public benefits than a system of private schooling does.

West investigated the historical issue of free government schooling by examining the elimination of the rate-bill system in New York in the 1840s. It is important to understand that when common schools were instituted in the early nineteenth century, they were not free to all children. They were funded in part by the government and in part by rate bills based on the number of days attendance with poor parents exempt from payment. Thus, a system of government-provided education was supported partially through taxes and partially through user costs.

A major problem with this system, West found, was collecting payments from parents. This problem often caused a delay in paying teachers' salaries. This issue of collection led to a campaign by public school teachers and social officials for free public schooling. The actions of the teachers and administrators fit into what West calls the "economic theory of democracy." Within the framework of this theory it is argued that people working in a service provided by the government, in this case educators, can afford to bring more influence on a government policy related to that service because their incomes depend on that policy. The average citizen has interests spread over a number of government services and cannot devote as much time to a single government issue such as education. Those in the service of government tend to try to maximize their benefits on policies regarding their incomes. In West's terms, the educator "may be prompted by the desire to help others as well as by the desire to help himself and his family. . . . And what people do is a better guide than what they say."[12]

From this perspective, educational rhetoric about the reduction of crime and poverty and increased political stability was a rationalization for an attempt to improve the economic advantage of those employed in government schools. There was no proof that benefits would result from free schools. West argues: "The suppliers of educational services to the government, the teachers and administrators, as we have seen, had produced their own organized platforms by the late 1840s; it was they indeed who were the leading instigators of the free school campaign."[13]

West believes that the interests of teachers and administrators in government service were enhanced by reducing the problem of salaries dependent on the collection of rate bills but also by the creation of a monopoly situation. The creation of free public schools made it difficult for private schools to exist. Even with rate bills, there was still some option available to parents to choose private schooling. With compulsory taxation providing free schools, private schools would be hard-pressed to compete.

The obvious result of the provision of free public schools was a decline in the number of private schools. Few parents wanted to pay taxes to support free public schools and then pay again to send their children to private schools. West gives figures from the office of the New York State Superintendent that show an increase in the number of students in private schools from 48,451 in 1863 to 68,105 in 1867. In that year, legislation was passed in that abolished rate bills. In 1871, four years after the passage of the legislation, private school enrollment had decreased to 49,691.[14]

E. G. West's studies of the evolution of government financing of education in the United States and England have raised some important issues about the various options regarding government intervention in schooling. In his study of English education, *Education and the State*, West finds little justification in the supposed public benefits of education for the provision of free government schooling. For instance, in terms of crime reduction, one could make the reverse argument and claim that education had a negative effect. According to English statistics, "the last year of compulsory education was also the heaviest year for juvenile delinquency and that the tendency to crime during school years was reversed when a boy went to work." West's point is not to prove that education breeds crime but to highlight the difficulty of claiming any relationship between more education and less crime in a society. The same difficulty exists in trying to prove that free government schools are necessary to "make democracy work."

West argues that in the early nineteenth century, the English were able to achieve political literacy despite efforts by the government to discourage it. His example is early-nineteenth-century England when the government put "severe taxes on paper in order to discourage the exercise of the public's reading and writing abilities." The government was concerned about the public distribution of what were viewed as revolutionary pamphlets, such as Tom Paine's *Rights of Man*. Despite this effort by the government, and the lack of free government schools, between two thirds and three quarters of the population was literate. In West's words: "Here then we have the paradox of a public managing to educate itself into literacy competence from personal motives and private resources, despite the obstacle of an institution called government which eventually begins to claim most of the credit of the educational success."[15]

West finds little evidence to support other public benefit claims of free government education. His response to those who see government schools promoting common values is that the idea of common values is meaningful only if it refers to values held in common by all members of a society. Common values cannot be determined by a group of educational experts. "In so far as education is supposed to be a useful vehicle for transmitting these values," West writes, "it can be only that kind of education which represents the diffused wishes of the populace."[16]

West also rejects the use of schooling as a means of manpower planning because of the difficulty of economic forecasting. He gives as an example the failure of the English government to accurately predict patterns of fuel consumption over a ten-year period. In addition, the failure of manpower planning was proved in England's attempt to produce more scientists in the 1950s in reaction to the number of scientists being produced in the Soviet Union. This was the same phenomenon that took place in the United States during this period. West states that "any assessment of the effectiveness of the subsequent British manpower planning schemes must take into account that the British 1961 Census of Population showed that out of a total of about 260,000 scientists and technologists, 50,000 were in jobs that did not make full and direct use of their qualifications."[17]

The above arguments deal with justifying the provision of free government schooling by claims of public benefits or externalities. You will recall from our scale of options that one important thread that runs through most of these possibilities is a concern about the education of the poor. Two of the options are either subsidizing the education of children in private schools or providing free government schooling. One argument for support of free public schooling for all children is that it is a means of financing the education of the poor. This argument must now be separated from concerns about public benefits or neighborhood effects. In other words, without making any claims that the education of the poor will reduce poverty and crime and improve economic efficiency, can free public schooling be justified purely in terms of helping the children of the poor obtain an education?

A central issue with regard to this question is the nature of the taxes collected to support free government schools. There is obviously some economic justification for providing free education to the children of the poor, but there seems to be little economic justification for providing a free education for the middle class and the rich. The argument given in the nineteenth century was that if only the poor received a free education, their education would be viewed as charity schooling. And, of course, as West stated, the campaign for free schools for all children was primarily motivated by the self-interest of public school teachers and administrators.

The issue regarding taxes is whether free education for all children has resulted in the poor actually subsidizing the education of the middle classs and the rich. So far we have been discussing options with regard to government involvement in and financing of education. Obviously, the provision of free government schools does not mean that they are free of cost to all citizens. The major financial difference between a private system of schooling and free public education is that an individual pays the cost directly to the private school and indirectly, through taxes, to the free public school.

In a fashion similar to our scale of options on government involvement in education, we will now set up a scale of options on government collection of money to support its involvement in education. At one end of the scale will be a tax system that redistributes costs from the poor to the rich and at the other end of the scale a tax system that redistributes costs from the rich to the poor. In the middle of the scale will be a system of taxation that provides no redistribution.

In terms of the support of free schools, a tax that did not redistribute costs would be of little advantage to any user of the schools. All users of the school would be taxed in some manner to support the cost of operating the system. A redistribution of costs would imply that the rich and the middle class would be taxed more than the poor to help subsidize the education of the poor. Without some redistribution, this process would not take place. All that would be accomplished for the poor is that education would be more expensive because of the added cost of the collection and distribution of taxes. It should always be kept in mind that there is an added cost in the maintenance of a free government system of education and that cost is the administration of the tax system.

There is a redistribution effect if all citizens are taxed and not just those citizens who are users of the public schools. This was and is a controversial issue for people with no children or with children in private schools. Horace Mann's argument about the interdependence of wealth was one justification for charging all members of the community for the education of only some members.

It is important to understand that redistribution in this case does not necessarily provide redistribution of cost according to the income or wealth of the taxpayer. The poor who are without children or who send their children to private schools (this sometimes happens in the United States in parochial schools) still pay taxes to provide a free education for the poor, the middle class, and the rich who attend free public schools.

One goal of a free public education is supposed to be to shift the costs from the poor to the middle class and the rich. There is at present a great deal of controversy about the degree to which systems of taxation actually accomplish this goal. In our scale of options, the ideal in terms of justifying the existence of free public education would be to move from the end where costs of education are redistributed from the rich to the poor to where costs are redistributed from the poor to the rich. The degree of this redistribution of costs depends on the kinds of taxes collected.

A discussion of the issues surrounding taxation leads to an arena where there is a great deal of disagreement and confusion among experts. One problem in the United States is the complexity of the tax structure regarding education. Varieties of taxes are raised at local, state, and national levels and distributed from each level to cover costs of education in free public schools. Adding to the complexity of the situation is the fact that different states have adopted different methods of raising and distributing money.

It is not possible in this chapter to give full consideration to the varied methods of funding schools in the United States. Even if extended research and discussion were given over to this topic, I have little confidence that any definitive conclusions could be reached. This situation should be of concern to the average citizen who pays for public education. Any taxpayer should know how the cost of a public service is distributed throughout the population. There is always the nagging question whether an individual is paying more for a public service through taxation then he would pay through direct payment for the service from private sources.

Another way of approaching the problem of the redistribution of costs of schooling is to consider the issue in terms of possible alternatives that might directly aid the poor who are unable to provide the full cost of educating their children. One argument justifies the existence of free public schools because certain members of the population cannot afford school costs. An interesting thing about this argument is that it does not necessarily lead to justification of a free public school system.

One obvious way of improving the ability of the poor to assume the costs of education is to increase their income. A direct method government can use to increase the income of the poor is to reduce or eliminate regressive taxes that the poor must pay. A "regressive tax" is one that absorbs a larger percentage of the income of the poor than the income of the rich. A "progressive tax" operates in the opposite fashion and takes a larger percentage of the income of the rich than the income of the poor. A standard assumption of modern welfare governments has been that the most just tax is a progressive tax because the rich have a larger discretionary income. The poor must devote a large percentage of their incomes to basic items like food and housing. In terms of redistribution of the costs of schooling, it would seem logical that a major concern would be to rely on progressive taxation to achieve that goal.

Nevertheless, some of the available evidence suggests that in the United States, taxes raised to support public schools are primarily regressive taxes. E. G. West demonstrates that, at least in terms of 1960 census figures, the percentage of income going to taxes to support public education paralleled levels of income with the poor paying the highest percentage and the rich paying the smallest percentage. In these figures income is divided into ten increasing levels with the lowest-income level of whites paying 7.83 percent of their income to support public schooling. The percentage declines as one moves up income levels with the highest-income level of whites paying only 2.63 percent of their income and nonwhites paying 3.08 percent of their income. In absolute dollars the lowest-income levels in 1960 paid $117 to support public schooling. (It should be remembered that this amount is in 1960 dollars.) If we consider a low income in 1960 to be below $4,000, then this income group paid taxes in absolute dollars of $140.[18]

These figures are startling when we consider them in terms of the actual percentage of costs of public schooling assumed through taxes by low-income families. In 1960, according to the National Center for Education Statistics, the average expenditure per child in public elementary and secondary schools was $375.14.[19] This means that a family with an income of $4,000 with one child in 1960 was paying more than 36 percent of the cost of educating that child in a public school through a system of regressive taxation. The percentage being paid by the lowest-income group was 31 percent. Although many poor families had more than one child in the public schools, there were also many low-income families without children, particularly among the elderly, who were paying for the costs of public schooling.

Analyses of particular taxes also support the idea that low-income groups are paying a good percentage of the costs of free government education. In the United States one of the main sources of revenue for public schools is the local property tax. These taxes are paid directly by property owners or indirectly by renters of property. Whether as a homeowner or as an apartment-house dweller, low-income families feel the effect of property taxes. In fact, low-income families pay a higher percentage of their incomes for property taxes than do upper-income families. According to 1970 figures, families with incomes of less than $2,000 paid 16.6 percent of their income in property taxes. The percentage of income paid in property taxes declined in the following pattern: family incomes of $2,000 to $2,999 paid 9.7 percent; family incomes of $3,000 to $3,999 paid 7.7 percent; and family incomes of $4,000 to $4,999 paid 6.4 percent. Moving to the top of the income scale, families with incomes between $15,000 and $24,999 paid only 3.3 percent of their income in property taxes, and those with incomes over $25,000 paid only 2.9 percent.[20]

While these figures do not give an accurate indication of how much of the cost of free public schooling is assumed by each member of society, they do indicate that all taxpayers, including low-income families, assume part of the cost of public schooling. Low-income families also might be paying a higher percentage of their incomes to support public schools than upper-income groups pay. This situation seems to contradict any justification of providing free public schooling in terms of redistribution of costs.

An alternative way of viewing this situation is to have public schools charge a tuition and at the same time eliminate all regressive taxes that affect low-income families. As was argued earlier in the chapter, if the issue is that low-income families do not have enough money to purchase an education, then provide some mechanism to increase their incomes. The most direct method that government could use to increase the incomes of poor people is to eliminate the regressive taxes they pay. Besides increasing incomes, this action would eliminate the hidden costs of collection and distribution of tax monies. Why charge tuition? In the first place, there seems little justification for middle- and upper-income families to receive a free public education. In the second place, this might provide an opportunity for poor families to use an option that has traditionally been reserved for middle and upper-income families. This is the option of choosing a private school.

The best argument for public schools charging some tuition, but not necessarily a full-cost tuition, has been given by E. G. West. West has suggested several alternative means of financing education. One of his first proposals was made in the 1960s in *Education and the State*. His most recent proposal has been made in the context of the peculiar problems regarding public financing of private schools in the United States. To fully understand and appreciate this proposal, it is necessary to give a brief description of the reasoning behind his earlier alternative for financing education in England.

West proposed that government financing of education should be limited to providing direct government grants for education to poor families through a negative income tax. He reasoned that history indicated that with no free public education, at least 950 out of every 1,000 families would provide an education for their children. Thus, if the concern was that all children receive an education, then the issue was one of providing for the children of the fifty families that did not choose education. The situation did not justify free public schools for all children. Now West reasoned that twenty of these fifty families did not provide their children with an education because of poverty. The government's obligation in this case, West argued, was to increase their incomes by eliminating regressive taxes. Second, the government could provide a subsidy through a negative income tax so that they could purchase an education. The remaining thirty families might not provide an education for their children because of a combination of poverty and irresponsibility, or just through neglect. In these cases, West proposed that the state impose selective compulsion on these families in the same manner that government intervenes in other forms of child neglect. He argued that governments do not need to establish elaborate machinery for the enforcement of compulsory education on all members of the population. The issue is simply families that are negligent. Governments do not have compulsory eating laws, but they do intervene when parental neglect causes malnutrition.[21]

The major problem with West's proposal in the United States is the First Amendment of the Constitution, which forbids government involvement in the establishment of religion. A direct government subsidy that would allow parents to choose between private schools could be used to pay tuition at a religious school. In the United States, the courts have considered this as government support of a religious institution and therefore in violation of the constitutional requirements of the First Amendment. West has recently proposed that public schools charge partial tuition to help parents choose private education without violating the First Amendment.[22]

To understand the boundaries established around school finance by the First Amendment, it is necessary to review one of the more recent court cases. In 1972 New York passed into law three programs that were to relieve the costs of private schooling to the poor and provide some maintenance of the private school system. The first part of the law provided direct grants to nonpublic schools that enrolled large numbers of pupils from low-income families. These grants were to be used for the maintenance and repair of facilities and for equipment to ensure the "health, welfare and safety of students." It was assumed that this would be constitutional because of previous rulings by the U.S. Supreme Court that had made a distinction between government aid to benefit the child and government aid to benefit religious institutions. The first Supreme Court case of this kind, *Cochran* v. *Louisiana State Board of Education* (1930), dealt with a Louisiana law that permitted the purchase and distribution of textbooks to all schoolchildren. Under this law, textbooks were provided to children attending private religious schools. The Supreme Court ruled that the law did not involve the support of religious institutions but existed for the benefit of children.[23] The same constitutional reasoning has allowed states to provide free transportation for parochial school students. It was assumed that the same reasoning would allow for state grants to maintain buildings in the interests of the welfare of the children.

Two programs provided for tuition reimbursement. One program provided a tuition reimbursement of $50 for each elementary school child and $100 for each high school student to families with annual incomes below $5,000. The other program provided tax relief for families failing to qualify for a tuition reimbursement. This tax relief took the form of a tax deduction on the state income tax with the allowed deduction decreasing as income increased.

The U.S. Supreme Court, in *The Committee for Public Education and Religious Liberty* v. *Nyquist* (1973), found all three provisions of the New York law in violation of the First Amendment. The maintenance and repair grants were considered to have the primary effect of subsidizing religious activities. The tuition reimbursement plans were ruled in volation of the Constitution because they also involved state subsidization of religious institutions. It is in the context of these rulings that West has proposed an alternative financial plan for financing schools in the United States.

What West proposes is a return to rate bills in public schools, or in different terms, the introduction of partial tuition charges. Concurrent with the establishment of partial tuition payments would be the elimination of certain regressive taxes. There would also be savings involved in the elimination of the costs of collecting and distributing these taxes.

Within the framework of West's proposal, the increased money resulting from the elimination of regressive taxes would function like the tuition subsidy in the New York law but without raising the issue of government support of religious institutions. The Supreme Court could hardly argue that the elimination of taxes was a subsidization of religious institutions. In fact, such a change would seem to promote the other religious clause of the First Amendment, which is the right to the free exercise of religion. The combination of reduction of taxes and partial tuition charges to support public schooling would increase the choices families could make about the school their children would attend. Families could pay tuition at a public school or at a private school. While not giving all families an equal choice of private schooling (because public schools would still be receiving some support from taxes), it would increase the possibility of choice among low-income families—choice that does not now exist because they have no control over tax money going to the support of education.

You will recall that a low-income family with one child is paying approximately 30 to 40 percent of the cost of education of that child in public schools through regressive taxation. West's proposal would return that money to low-income families in order to let them make a decision about how it should be used for education. The present method of funding public schools reflects a paternalistic attitude by the government in relation to low-income families. Essentially, money is taken from them by regressive taxes and returned to them through an elaborate bureaucratic structure. West writes that the present system, in which private school users pay twice for an education through taxes to support public schooling and then tuition to support private schooling, must be considered anti-poor because it reduces the choices of the poor. And for users of parochial schools in New York, the average income of those families is below the average of all families in the state.

West proposes to introduce this plan by having state governments decree that all future increases in school costs be paid by the users of the schools through tuition. This tuition would be a user tax. He writes that if redistribution of income to meet user costs by the poor is necessary, there are superior methods for doing this than those now used to support public schooling. "These include a negative income tax system, increases in welfare payments and decreases in regressive taxes and excises."[24]

West's proposals for England and the United States raise

provocative issues about present systems of government financing of education. These issues can be restated in the following set of questions:

1. If there are no measureable public benefits from free public schooling (as opposed to private purchase of education), why should the government provide this service?
2. If the issue is the ability of low-income families to pay for an education, why not provide a direct income subsidy (rather than government schools) to those families so that they can purchase an education?
3. Why is public schooling free to those income groups who could afford to purchase an education for their children?
4. If low-income families actually pay part of the cost of public schools through regressive taxes, why not increase their choices and incomes by returning that money through elimination of those taxes?
5. Who actually benefits financially from a system of free public schools when costs are apparently increased by the expense of collection and distribution of an elaborate system of government taxation?

Free Public Schools and Equality of Educational Opportunity

The questions dealing with government provision of education and the distribution of costs provide the background for an issue that has had major importance as public schools in different states have been forced by the courts to reorganize their systems of school finance to provide equality of educational opportunity. The other side of the issue of distribution of costs of schooling is distribution of tax money to support public schooling. While the poor have been assuming part of the cost of schooling through regressive taxes, they have been receiving an unequal part of the tax money for supporting public schools when compared with middle- and upper-income families. Any claims that free public schools were established to help the poor are contradicted when one looks at the evidence regarding the distribution of costs and government support.

The single most important action by states in the creation of the inequality of educational opportunity in school finance was the division of state educational systems into separate school districts. Beginning in the early nineteenth century when Massachusetts established school districts, state governments have been able to effectively separate poor, middle-income, and rich children by creating separate school districts wherein children receive a free education. They must pay tuition if they attend public schools outside the district. In addition, the primary source of public school revenue has been the property tax, which is collected and distributed in each separate school district.

A discussion of the consequences of school districting destroys any pretense that public schools were organized to integrate different social classes and racial and ethnic groups. School districting has allowed for the separation of rich communities from poor communities and for the segregation of races based on residential patterns. School districting has allowed upper-income groups to provide superior free public schools for their children in terms of the amount of money spent per child. It has permitted the white population to force minority groups to send their children to separate schools.

School districting has placed severe limitations on the ability of individuals to choose an education for their children. For example, again consider an elaboration of West's analogy to eating. In terms of eating, it would mean that a person not only would be taxed to support free meals served at a local government restaurant but also would be allowed to eat for free only at a government restaurant in his own eating district. There would still be private restaurants and grocery stores, but these options would be available only to those who could afford the double burden of paying taxes for free public eating and purchasing private food. Because of the taxes to support free public eating, it would be difficult for low-income families to purchase private food.

Now, if states were divided into eating districts and if those districts were based on residential patterns, it would mean that the poor would be together for the purposes of eating. They would be forced to pay the majority of costs for free public food through property taxes and would be forced to eat only in their own district restaurants. If they wanted to eat in another district's government eating establishment, they would have to pay as if they were buying private food.

Imagine what would happen under these conditions. In wealthy eating districts, more money could be collected from local property taxes, which when combined with money from state and federal governments, could hire better cooks and purchase better food than could be had in low-income eating districts. Eating district A might be able to offer residents a choice of fine continental cuisine, whereas eating district B could only offer a couple of plain but officially labeled "wholesome" dishes. If residents of district B complained about their free food and its possible negative effects on health, officials of the state department of eating and the local eating district could reply that they were doing everything to increase the standards of food selection and the training of cooks. If these same families demanded the right to choose eating establishments, the official reply could be that government nutritionists were better able than individuals to determine what was good food. The low-income residents of district B would be forced to eat their free food while casting envious glances across district lines at their neighbors sitting at tables with real linen covers and gulping down tasty food.

The above analogy does not exaggerate the effects of the organization of school districts in the United States. What is amazing is that a major attack on the system did not take place until the late 1960s. The landmark court case that brought national attention was *Serrano* v. *Priest* (1971). This decision by the California Supreme Court found that the California method of financing resulted in inequality of educational opportunity. The case involved the two sons of John Serrano, who lived in a poor, mainly Mexican-American, community in Los Angeles. The local school had seen rapidly increasing class sizes and a consequent shortage of textbooks and supplies. Local school authorities told John Serrano that the financial situation in the school would not improve. The only option for the Serrano family was to move to another school district. The California Supreme Court's decision stated that "plaintiff contends that the school financing system classifies on the basis of wealth. We find this proposition irrefutable. . . ."[25]

At the heart of this discriminatory system of financing schools is the fact that property tax rates vary within states according to the wealth of the taxing area. And this variation generally involves higher rates in low-income districts than in high-income districts because the amount of money generated from property taxes is related to property values. Areas with high property values and a low tax rate can generate as much revenue as areas with high tax rates but low property values. In school districts with low-income housing and a declining industrial area, there is constant pressure to increase property tax rates just to maintain a constant level of expenditures per pupil. On the other hand, areas with high property values can actually decrease tax rates and still maintain a constant level of expenditures. Of course, the situation of declining tax rates does not occur too often because of continuing inflation.

As mentioned earlier, the property tax is primarily a regressive tax. When this regressive tax is combined with the process of school districting, it creates extreme inequalities in both the payment of taxes and the distribution of revenues. Low-income families pay higher rates and receive less revenue for their efforts. In the *Serrano* case, the California Supreme Court gave as an example that "Baldwin Park citizens, who paid a school tax of $5.48 per $100 of assessed valuation, were able to spend less than half as much on education as Beverly Hills residents, who were taxed on $2.38 per $100."[26]

Litigation involving school finances is occurring in state court systems because of a ruling by the U.S. Supreme Court, *Rodriguez* v. *San Antonio Independent School District* (1973), that the right to an education is not protected by the Constitution. The Court declared: "The consideration and initiation of fundamental reforms with respect to state taxation and education are matters reserved for the legislative processes of the various states."[27] As we shall see later in the chapter, this process of reorganizing school finance systems is resulting in greater centralization of the control of education in educational bureaucracies at the state level.

In the context of providing equality of educational opportunity, the major goal of school finance reform is to provide an equal distribution of government revenues to support education. In attempting to overcome the problems resulting from the combination of regressive taxes and districting, there has been an intensification of discussions about who should control the actual expenditure of tax money. School finance reform provides an opportunity for shifting from the school district as the basic unit to either a single educational structure in each state or to the individual family. In other words, the possibility exists for either centralization or decentralization of control.

The strongest advocates of decentralization of control in the legal developments surrounding school finance reform have been the lawyers who provided the original legal framework for the *Serrano* decision. John Coons and Stephen Sugarman provided the basic thesis against existing systems of educational finance in *Private Wealth and Public Education* (1970). This volume contained the legal arguments against existing school finance systems and suggested alternative approaches. The most important alternative has received more elaborate treatment in their recent volume, *Education by Choice: The Case for Family Control* (1978).

Unlike Milton Friedman and E. G. West, Coons and Sugarman believe that schooling provides important public benefits. Because they believe in the public benefits, they are less willing to minimize government support of education. This is an important and major distinction. As suggested earlier, the public benefits argument is the major justification for government subsidization of education or government provision of schooling.

The most important public benefit stressed in *Private Wealth and Public Education* is equality of opportunity for the poor. The authors accept the idea that equality of opportunity should be built around a system of schooling. They write: "In short, the sine qua non of a fair contest system—of equality of opportunity—is equality of training. And that training is what public education is primarily about." In what could be described as a classic statement of the doctrine of equality of opportunity through education, they state: "There are, we hope, loftier views of education that coexist, but in a competitive democracy those views represent dependent goals that can be realized only upon a foundation of training for basic competence in the market."[28]

Their stress is on maintaining fair competition in the marketplace. Keeping the competition fair is the function of the school, and this process, in the minds of the authors, enhances social mobility. "Social mobility as a value plays a potent role . . . and public education must be seen in its special relation to the underclasses to whom it is the strongest hope for rising in the social scale."[29]

From their perspective, inequality in educational expenditures defeats the goal of equality of opportunity. They accept a strong relationship between quality of education and educational expenditures. In fact, they write: "Money is the only measure applicable in every element in the educational process—salaries, plant, equipment, and so on: all educational goods and services are objects of purchase." If the poor have less money spent on their education, then they are receiving a lower-quality education than their more privileged cohorts in another school district. If they receive a lower-quality education, then that circumstance, combined with the economic disadvantages of their background, compounds the problem of competing in the market.

In previous chapters there has been lengthy discussion of the problems inherent in the argument for equality of opportunity through schooling and the difficulty of proving that schooling increases social mobility. In addition, there is the general issue of the value of the whole ideology of equality of opportunity. But rather than restate all those arguments, let us consider the full implication of the school finance issue for writers like Coons and Sugarman who accept the ideology of equality or opportunity.

For them, the inequality of school expenditures results in public schooling having a negative effect on equality of opportunity. First, the children of low-income families are disadvantaged by a system of regressive taxation that reduces family income to support public schools. Second, even though the poor pay higher tax rates to support public schooling, they have less money spent on the education of their children than do middle- and upper-income groups who pay lower tax rates. If money means quality education, then they are receiving inferior educational opportunities.

This means that within the framework of equality of opportunity the public schools are creating more inequality and making it more difficult for the children of the poor to compete in the market. The public schools are disproportionately, in terms of the rest of the population, reducing the income of the poor through taxes and providing their children with inferior training. This argument, if one accepts the ideology of equality of opportunity and the assumption that money is directly related to quality education, has important implications for schooling in the United States. What it suggests is that because of districting and regressive taxation, the public schools in the twentieth century have primarily denied or hindered equality of opportunity. In the framework of this argument, the public schools, rather than having been a force for increased opportunity and social mobility, have had the opposite effect. The argument also suggests that this effect continues in states that still collect school revenues primarily through regressive taxes and provide unequal funding of schools.

After identifying equality of opportunity as the chief public benefit of schooling, *Private Wealth and Public Education* describes in detail all the inadequacies in existing attempts by state governments to provide for some equality in educational expenditures. This part of the study provides important background information for litigation in school finance cases. This section of the book can provide the reader with a good introduction to the complicated nature of school financing in various states.

The authors' solution to the problem of inequality of educational opportunity involves a more equitable means of distribution of tax money and a plan to shift the control of schooling from the educational bureaucracy to individual families. The plan is called "power equalization," and the basic structure of the plan is applicable at different levels of government. The central idea is that the amount of government subsidization of education should be related to income and desire.

What this would mean for existing school districts is that the state government would distribute money to local school districts on the basis of the rate at which the local district taxed itself and the amount of money yielded by that rate of taxation. For instance, a school district with low property values but a rate of taxation equal to wealthier school districts in the state would be given money by the state government to make its effort in the form of the rate of taxation yield the same amount as the wealthier school districts in the state.

Power equalization, the authors believe, would provide for equalization in school financing and at the same time allow a certain amount of freedom at the district level. They say that "the units should be free, through the taxing mechanism, to choose to share various amounts of the state's wealth (by deciding how hard they are willing to tax themselves)."[30]

The plan would call for the selection of a key district in the state to be used as a standard for determining the amount of money a given rate of taxation should yield. On the basis of this key district the state would establish a table that would show what each percentage of taxation should yield. If a school district taxed itself at a given rate, and that effort yielded an amount below the amount for the rate in the state table, then the state would give that school district enough money to bring it up to the amount given in the table. The authors write: "If the table decrees that a 2 percent entitles a district to $1,200 per pupil when the tax actually produces that $1,200 only in the richest 10 percent of the districts, the state has committed itself to making up the difference in many districts and in other words, to a substantial aid program."[31]

The revolutionary nature of the power equalization formula is in the argument that it should be applied at the family level to subsidize the purchase of education. With power equalization at the family level, the basic unit of educational spending would be the individual family. The family would choose its children's education from whatever public-private schools might come into existence. The term "public-private" is used to describe schools that would be privately operated (for profit or not) and would receive government money in the form of subsidization of the purchase of education.

The difference between "family power equalization" and Milton Friedman's voucher system is in the recognition of the differing value placed on education by families and the problems facing low-income families. Like power equalization at the district level, family power equalization would mean that state subsidization would be based on a combination of family effort and income. For instance, the state might establish a table based on the top 10 percent of incomes in the state that relate the percentage of income spent on education to an actual amount yielded from these upper-income levels. If, according to these tables, a family that spends 5 percent of its income on education should be spending $1,500, then if that 5 percent effort actually only produces $500, the state would subsidize the family with a $1,000 educational grant.

One of the interesting aspects of this proposal is that it separates families with children from families without children in the determination of the amount of money that should be spent on education. In the district power equalization proposal all voters, including those without children, would participate in determining the tax rate. With family power equalization, only the individual family with children would determine the percentage of income. The assumption is that families without children have little interest in spending large amounts on education. With family power equalization, there would be an actual increase in the amount of public money spent on education because of the removal of this disinterested part of the population from the decision-making process.

The family power equalization formula received more elaborate treatment by Coons and Sugarman in their 1978 book, *Education by Choice: The Case for Family Control.* This work was published eight years after their original work and reflected an increased commitment to assuring that changes in political control in education accompanied school finance reform. Also, during that eight-year period, a variety of other school finance proposals had appeared on the scene and had provided some alternatives to family power equalization. Four of these models, according to Coons and Sugarman, provide for equal educational opportunity within specific definitions of that concept. One model, family power equalization, most adequately meets their criteria for equality of educational opportunity.

To understand their argument more fully, consider the three models they reject. The first is what they call the "Uniform Grant Model (UGM)," under which all children would receive a scholarship or voucher of equal value. Equality in this model would mean equality of spending. All children, rich or poor, would receive equal amounts from the state. The authors write: "UGM approximates uniformity in spending, a quality often seen as a political advantage, and certainly one common definition of equal educational opportunity."[32]

The second proposal is the "Needs Adjustment Model (NAM)," which was originally proposed by Theodore Sizer and Phillip Whitten in 1968. In the words of Coons and Sugarman, the "original idea was to compensate for the discrimination inherent in the unregulated

Friedman model by making larger grants ($1,500) to the poorest families . . . and progressively reducing the grant to zero for families of average income." This system would make the child from a low-income family more attractive to schools because of the larger grant that child would bring to the school. Coons and Sugarman dismiss the model because it would never, in their opinion, be supported by the middle class.

One variation of the NAM is to give all children a basic grant with children from low-income families receiving larger amounts. Schools would not be allowed to charge tuitions beyond the grant given by the government. This would make it impossible for upper-income groups to purchase schooling at higher tuition rates. In fact, the children of the poor would be more attractive to schools and provide for the purchase of higher-quality education. Also, within this model, educational need is defined in terms of family income. There would be a resulting balance between educational need and school income. In the words of Coons and Sugarman: "The consequence for all schools could be seen as the equalization, not of spending, but of the true quality, because two major determinants of quality education—dollars and the abilities of the students—would be 'in balance' in every school."[33]

The major objection Coons and Sugarman have to this model is their lack of assurance that the money a student brings to a school will be directly used for the education of that particular child. For instance, children from low-income families may bring more dollars to the school, but there is no assurance that the extra money will not be spread evenly throughout the school population. On the other hand, if school spending is regulated so that the money is spent on those particular children, then, according to Coons and Sugarman, children with larger government grants may not be as attractive.

The third model they consider is the "Cost Adjustment Model (CAM)," which allows for educational spending on the basis of variation of costs according to such factors as regional differences in costs of living that result in higher teacher salaries, differences in costs between different educational programs (e.g., vocational education and academic programs), and other factors that might affect cost. What this means is that there would have to be an official determination of the nature of cost variations, with educational vouchers varying according to official decisions.

The major drawback the authors see in this model is that it would result in a great deal of political turmoil. "A legion of educational factions," they write, "would arise to lobby particular dollar adjustments in recognition of their special burden or special contribution."[34] In addition, there would be the practical problem of determining and justifying differences in cost in educational programs.

Their fourth model is a more elaborate statement of family power equalization, which is now called the "Quality Choice Model (QCM)." In this model each family could choose variously priced schools whose tuition would be allowed to vary within a given range. The family would choose a school and pay part of the tuition directly; the rest would be subsidized by the government, using the power equalization formula. To solve the problem of families with more than one child, all "extra" children would receive full subsidization from the government. Coons and Sugarman view this system as working like the federal food stamp program where families determine how many stamps they would want to purchase and use. But, as the authors point out, there are several important differences. The food stamp program only allows for support of a minimum budget, and the program is available only to the poor. If QCM were applied to the food stamp program, all income levels including the rich would receive subsidized food stamps.

The authors argue that while some people might object to subsidizing food for the rich, the situation is different for education because the rich already receive government subsidization. At least under QCM, the authors reason, the rich and the upper-middle class will for the first time be forced to pay some tuition to the public schools. This would at least provide some change in the current situation of providing tuition-free education to families that can afford to pay full cost.

The concept of equality of educational opportunity takes on a specific meaning with QCM. The authors state that "its objective is not to equalize school spending, school offering, or school quality but only each family's economic ability to select cheaper or more expensive schools; it aims to make the family's choice depend only on its interest in education . . . and its evaluation of what its child will gain from a particular school."[35] In other words, equality becomes equality of ability to choose an education.

One irony of current trends in public school finances in the United States is that they seem to be moving in a direction opposite to that hoped for by those who played a primary role in launching the national reform of inequality in educational finance. Rather than school finance reform having resulted in greater family control through choice, as advocated by Coons and Sugarman, it seems to have resulted in a greater concentration of control of educational systems in state departments of education. The reason for this is that most school finance reform has required an increased involvement of state departments of education in the monitoring of local school districts to assure that the legislative goals of school finance reform are being achieved.

The best example of this situation is in New Jersey. After a state supreme court ruling, *Robinson* v. *Cahill* (1973), forced the state to restructure its system of financing schools, Richard Lehne provided an excellent study of the political turmoil and its impact on education. This court case originated in concerns about the inequality of school expenditures between districts in New Jersey. The state supreme court, in deciding this issue, focused on the educational mandates of the New Jersey constitution. The actual wording of the constitution had important consequences for the development of later plans to remedy the disparities in educational expenditures.

The education clause of the New Jersey constitution states: "The legislature shall provide for the maintenance and support of a thorough and efficient system of free public schools for the instruction of all the children in this state between the ages of five and eighteen years." The key words in the clause are "thorough and efficient system." It should be noted that many other states have similar wording in their constitutions.[36]

The New Jersey Supreme Court accepted the premise that the amount of money spent on an education was related to the quality of education. This is an unproven assumption. There had been some discussion in the court case about neighboring New York City, which maintains a very expensive system of public schooling that provides educational services of questionable quality. The New Jersey Supreme Court stated that "we accept the proposition that the quality of educational opportunity does depend in substantial measure upon the number of dollars invested. . . ."[37] Within the reasoning of the court, a "thorough and efficient system . . . for . . . all children" required equality of education expenditures.

The ruling of the New Jersey Supreme Court thus required not only a reform of school finance in the state but also an obligation on the part of state government to assure that all children were receiving a thorough and efficient education. This created two separate but related sets of issues that had to be dealt with by the state government following the court decision. One issue was the method to be used to collect and distribute taxes at the state level to assure equality of education as related to school finance. This resulted in a great deal of turmoil in the state legislature over the method of taxation. The basic problem was a fear by state legislators of the political reaction of voters if new taxes were instituted. At one point in the struggle, the New Jersy Supreme Court was forced to close all public schools in the state for a short period to force the legislature to act.

The second issue was defining the meaning of "thorough and efficient system of education" and implementing a method by which the state could determine if a local school system was providing such an education. The problems inherent in defining a thorough and efficient education are exemplified by changes in the wording of that section of the legislation finally passed in 1976. Richard Lehne reports that in the original administration bill the thorough and efficient section was worded as follows: "Sufficient instruction to assure the attainment of reasonable levels of proficiency in the basic communications and computational skills. . . ." The legislative committee change the phrase "sufficient instruction to assure" to "instruction intended to produce." In terms of school staff, the administrative version called for "sufficient qualified personnel to enable all pupils to develop to the best of their abilities. . . ." This was changed to the more conservative standard of requiring only "qualified instructional and other personnel. . . ." The change of language by the legislative committee reflected a concern about future litigation over the meaning of "sufficient instruction" and "sufficient qualified personnel." The obvious problem was that no one knows what constitutes sufficient instruction and personnel.[38]

The consequence of *Robinson* v. *Cahill* and the resulting legislative action has been the opposite of the school finance reform hoped for by Coons and Sugarman. The struggles and educational decisions have been shifted to the state government. In New Jersey it is now the state legislature that determines the allocation of school finances. In curriculum and instruction, it is now the state department of education that determines if local school districts are providing a thorough and efficient education. Rather than have family choice, the decision-making process became more concentrated and removed from the actual users of public schools.

Lehne has found that this process has created a great deal of bureaucratic control and red tape. Under the Public School Act, which was passed in 1976, local school districts are required "to define specific educational goals, to shape their programs to meet these goals, to assess their accomplishments, and to take whatever corrective actions were necessary."[39] The New Jersey Department of Education has undergone significant changes in order to handle the monitoring of the actions of local educational units. In the past, the department was primarily divided into subject-matter experts. The department now has been reorganized so that staff members primarily function as planners and evaluators. In other words, the primary function of the department has become that of planning educational systems and evaluating local actions. It polices the actions of local school districts to assure that they conform with the intent of the legislation.

The increased role of the education department is reflected in complaints from local school districts. The major complaint is the tremendous amount of information that must be submitted to the department of education to prove compliance with state requirements. One of the objections, Lehne writes, is that the "costs of bureaucratic procedures will outweigh any conceivable benefits." From the perspective of local educators, this process will become even more costly and controlling. Lehne writes that educators expect there will "be ever-more-strict enforcement of an ever-growing number of detailed regulations."[40]

In addition, the planning process required by the state department of education is absorbing increasing amounts of time and money. As Lehne points out, there is no proof from the past history of government that elaborate systems of government planning have improved the delivery of public services. The variables of human demand and choice are beyond the control of the planners. Lehne argues: "In most cases, planning is a feeble instrument, which barely affects the market forces, institutional dynamics, and patterns of public preference that shape the provision of human services." In terms of complaints about educational planning in New Jersey, Lehne reports cricitism that "extensive planning requirements consume valuable administrative resources, demand widespread citizen participation, and necessitate multiple official clearances, all of which take time from delivering public services to citizens."[41]

The pattern that seems to be emerging in New Jersey is that the obligation of state government to assure equality of educational financing has resulted in increased costs in terms of planning and policing local educational systems. This cost is in addition to the cost required for the collection and distribution of educational revenue. There is no proof that the increase in cost resulting from the expansion of bureaucratic control and planning will result in increased quality of education. What seems to have been created is a new layer of administrative control at the state level, which will absorb increasing amounts of educational revenue.

Also, the increased activity of evaluators and planners on the state level means increased educational costs at the local level. The time and effort required to report to the state and meet state guidelines will require either more administrative personnel at the local level or the allocation of larger percentages of time by local administrators to do the paperwork required by the state. This could lead to a whole new layer of administrators at the local level whose primary responsibility will be handling state requirements in reporting and participating in planning.

A major indication of the shift in the location of decision making in the educational structure as a result of school finance reform is the change taking place in the goals and structure of state education associations. Since state government is now the prime distributor of money and the determiner of programs in New Jersey, state-level organizations of education associations have had to become politicized so that the interests of their members can be represented in the state-level struggle over educational policy and money.

Lehne cites several examples of the politicalization of the state's education organization. For instance, two formerly weak organizations, Personnel Guidance Association and the Association for Adult Education, found that they had to become more active in the political process to advance the interests of guidance and adult education. Lehne writes: "The unsettling debates about the *Robinson* program convinced both groups that they had to become directly involved in politics for the first time." The two organizations were forced by circumstances to change their methods of operation and their relationship to the state department of education. As Lehne states: "In their communications with the department, the associations began to advocate positions rather than simply express professional judgments."[42]

Similar things began to happen with well-established organizations. It is reported that members of the staff of the principal's organization now devote more time to dealing with the state legislature. The state school board association has shifted the emphasis of the work of their staff members to problems of government relations. As Lehne summarizes the changes: "New Jersey education associations have adopted a more politicized stance not only in relation to the formal institutions of government but in their dealings with their own members as well."[43]

This example of changes in New Jersey that resulted from school finance reform strongly suggest that choice and control will be less and less in hands of families and more and more a function of politics and lobbying at state levels. The hope that Coons and Sugarman had, that ending inequalities resulting from districting would result in greater individual control and choice, does not seem to be occurring as events unfold.

A study of history would not make this result surprising. The same argument E. G. West used in regard to the abandonment of rate bills for free public schooling can be applied to the present situation. Professional educators would support school finance reform not only because of equality of educational opportunity but also because greater state involvement in school finance eliminates the problem of local voter rejection of tax increases to support schools. During the 1970s, many schools across the country closed because local voters rejected increases in property taxes. Transferring the burden of taxation to the state eliminates the potential for local voters controlling local school revenue. Like the rate bill, which created problems of collection, local property taxes as the primary means of financing schools introduce an element of financial uncertainty and an element of control by the local population. School finance reform that results in changes similar to those in New Jersey ends these problems.

It would also seem at this stage of history, although there is no proof, that school finance reform that moves in the direction of the New Jersey pattern will greatly increase the administrative costs of education. The relationship between states and local school officials becomes more complex and demanding, which will result in increased staff members at both levels. As noted by Lehne, none of this increased administrative activity means that the quality of education will increase. If taxes continue to be regressive, low-income families will be paying more to assure that they receive an equal share of educational expenditures. It will also mean that they will pay a higher percentage of the costs than will upper-income groups. This would be a strange price to pay to gain equal treatment.

The Demand for Education

One problem resulting from the centralization of educational financing is the ability to determine what should be the supply of education. In traditional free marketplace economics, supply is usually considered a function of demand by the consumer. Cost of product is determined by the combination of supply and consumer demand. This becomes distorted when supply and cost are separated from consumer demand, as they are in government-provided schooling. The only influence the consumer can have on cost and supply is through political agents like an elected state representative or votes on tax issues.[44]

It is difficult for a vote to have the same effect on cost and supply as direct purchase of a product does. A vote is usually given for a broad range of issues or a political personality. Voting does not allow for much discrimination between products. One candidate might reflect your views about environmental issues but not about education, and another candidate might have your educational views but not your environmental concerns. How do you vote in this case? How does the candidate know which issues you are voting to support? The same is true of a tax levy. You might vote for a tax levy in hopes of improving the general educational system but be dissatisfied by the kind of education your children are receiving. How does the local school district interpret your vote?

Voting does not allow for discrimination between items or supply accurate information about demand for individual items. In the case of education it is difficult with government schools for the consumer of education to convey information regarding consumer demand. For instance, consider the issues of teacher to student ratio and counselor to student ratio. Both factors contribute to a major share of the cost of education. Now it is obviously in the self-interest of teachers and counselors to maximize their numbers and increase the number of teachers and counselors per student. On the other hand, elite school boards that represent a section of the community interested in maintaining low costs and low taxes might want to increase the number of students served by teachers and counselors. Power in this situation is in the hands of the board of education. In response, teachers through their unions make this item part of the collective-bargaining negotiations with the school board. This adds to the cost of whatever is decided because teachers must pay to support their unions and boards must pay their negotiators. While teacher and counselor ratios may be only part of a total package, they do require time for discussion. This is an item of cost. The actual decision about ratios and costs will become a function of the negotiations.

The consumer has no direct influence on this important decision affecting cost. It could be that most users of the schools would like to maximize the number of teachers per student but minimize the number of counselors. But even if the consumers of education increase the number of teachers, there has to be some limit on cost. A parent might be willing to pay for one teacher for every fifteen students but not for one teacher for every ten students. On the other hand, a parent might have found counselors of limited value and be willing to support only a limited number.

Consider this issue as it relates to the expansion of the educational bureaucracy discussed in chapter 5. The major characteristics of this expansion have been increased numbers of administrators per teachers and consolidation of school districts. The question in terms of bureaucratic expansion is: Would the consumer of education directly pay for the costs of more administrators? The issue of school district consolidations highlights another aspect of the problem of regulating costs without direct consumer influence. According to Walter Garms, James Guthrie, and Lawrence Pierce in their study of school finance, the actual cost per student increases after a school district has more than 20,000 students. They write: "Large school districts, those with more than 15,000 to 20,000 students, suffer from higher per student costs resulting from additional administrative burdens, increased allowances for maintenance and vandalism, higher security costs, etc."[45] If schools operated in a free market situation, schools would reach an optimal size and, at least theoretically, their growth would stop because an increase in size would result in an increase in cost to the consumer. The regulation of cost by the consumer is not possible in government-provided education.

With government-provided schooling, rather than government subsidization of the purchase of schooling, control of costs and particularly control of individual items become extremely difficult. How many and at what cost should schools provide pencils, books, teachers, administrators, counselors, and all the other items that make up the cost of public schooling? As the governance and financing of education become more complex, there is less chance for consumer demand to influence the cost and supply of education. Milton Friedman suggested in the discussion at the beginning of this chapter that the cost of public schooling could not be justified in terms of public benefits. In the present discussion, the cost of public schooling cannot be justified in terms of consumer demand.

9

THE ROLE OF THE SCHOOL
IN THE MODERN WORLD:
A SUMMARY

THE MAJOR HINDRANCE TO THE COMPLETION OF THE liberal revolutions of the eighteenth and nineteenth centuries has been the rise and expansion of the modern school. At the heart of these revolutions was a belief that liberty and progress depended on freedom of thought and conscience. Control of the consumption and production of knowledge by government-operated schools is contradictory to these goals. The political structure of schooling determines the content and nature of the ideology of what is taught in school. If the school has an effect on what people know and how they think (if it doesn't, there is no jusitification for the existence of schools), then the school has a significant effect on the future political actions of its students. If those that control the political structure of schooling have a clearly defined political ideology, then that ideology will provide the framework that will limit the thoughts and expressions of future citizens.

If government-operated schools teach no particular ideology, as is often claimed in the United States, then the future citizen may be being prepared for future nonparticipation in the political system. In a country like the United States, where the school is called the cornerstone of the democratic system, recent years have seen a marked decline in citizen participation in political activities.

In the four presidential elections between 1960 and 1976, the percentage of eligible voters who actually voted decreased from 63.8 percent in 1960 to 54.4 percent in 1976. Not only has actual voting decreased in the United States, but many no longer bother to register to vote. In the words of Curtis Gans, director of the Committee for the Study of the American Electorate: "The level of participation in America, while never as high as in some European democracies, is lower today than in any democracy in the world except Botswana."[1]

It is possible that the public schools have slowly killed political activism in the United States. The dream of nineteenth-century common school reformer Horace Mann was to teach a political consensus in the schoolroom that would result in the reduction of political strife in society. In fact, the school might have been successful in achieving that goal. Even to suggest that teaching be limited to a consensus of values is to prescribe a political ideology that blurs distinctions between fundamental political doctrines.

Of course, common school reformers were facing the practical problem of establishing a public school that would not be alienated from particular sectors of society because it taught a particular political doctrine and would not be destroyed by being drawn into political controversies. This meant, as Mann suggested, that all controversial political doctrines and discussions be avoided in the schoolhouse. In practice this has meant the teaching of political doctrines in an objective manner with controversial doctrines taught only as a means of condemnation. Communism, anarchism, socialism, fascism, and libertarianism are often brought into the classroom only to make sure that students do not give them serious consideration. The passion of politics is lost in claims of neutrality and objectivity, and meaningful political distinctions are lost as what are considered extreme doctrines are condemned and a consensus of political values is taught.

It is interesting to consider that if government-operated public schools had existed in the eighteenth century, there might not have been an American Revolution. The Revolution was born in a sea of political passion and controversy. Bernard Bailyn has shown in his prize-winning book, *The Ideological Origins of the American Revolution,* that the breeding grounds for revolution and the ideas about future government could be found in the large number of political pamphlets that were widely distributed throughout the colonies. Because of the importance of these pamphlets in developing American political thought, American revolutionary leaders believed that the key to a free society was a free press. Revolutionary leaders saw the shaping of an active and passionate citizenry in the reading of a free and controversial press. Colonists were noted for their high degree of literacy even though a common government-operated public school did not exist.[2]

The American Revolution was not fought for government-operated public schools but for political liberty and freedom of thought and conscience. The establishment of a common public school system that intends to teach a consensus or a particular political doctrine must be viewed as contradictory and inhibiting to that tradition. In terms of the arguments presented in this volume, the importance of the school increased in the nineteenth century as a means of providing political stability and cohesion. The doctrines of nationalism, political cohesion, and acceptance of authority became central to the goals of expanding public systems of education and mitigated the expansion of political liberty and freedom of conscience.

But the death blow to political activism might be the ideology of equality of opportunity. Here is an ideology that does not see society as involved in a struggle over political power but as a social process allowing everyone to find his place in a hierarchy of occupations. The important thing in this ideology is not political liberty or freedom of thought; it is to give everyone an equal chance to compete for places in an occupational structure. Political activism is replaced in this ideology with a stress on social intervention by government to assure the fairness of competition.

The emphasis on occupational training that results from the ideology of equality of opportunity contributes to political inactivity by creating specialized ignorance. Within the ideology of equality of opportunity the school assumes the role of providing equality of opportunity by being the initial distributor of talent. Rather than have equality of opportunity be a function of individuals with equal educations competing in the marketplace, the sorting of individual talent takes place with the guidance of professional experts in the school. This sorting leads to a differentiation of curriculum and a specialization of training. One obvious result is a decline in general education and in the preparation for understanding the social and political dynamics of society. That is, as society becomes professionalized, there is an increasingly tighter fit between the schools and intitial entry into the labor market; the individual gains increasingly specialized knowledge in school at the expense of understanding the dynamics of the entire society in which that knowledge will be put to use. Specialized ignorance may not only contribute to a lack of political activity but may be a preparation for becoming a pawn of the elites who control society.

The ideology of equality of opportunity may also contribute to a decline in political activity by creating an image of government as a benign institution working to increase fair play in the social system rather than as a place where people struggle for power and benefits. It is this benign image that is essential for justifying the position of professional elites in their control of the social system. With the growth of the administrative state, there has been a transfer of decision-making power from political representatives to a professionalized bureaucracy. This transfer of power is justified by claiming that the professional expert can represent the true interests of the people. The professional is pictured as a model of Christian charity doing good and working in the interests of the people. Surrounded by the rhetoric of equality of opportunity, the professional expert is portrayed as warring against the evils of poverty and breaking down the barriers of ignorance and disadvantaged family backgrounds to allow the poor to enter the mainstream of competition in the occupational structure. The beauty of this picture is that it does not threaten the middle class or the rich; nor does it threaten the economic rewards received by the professional class. The war is not against inequality of income but against inequality of competition. The only sacrifice asked of privileged members of society is financial support of the institutions and professionals who will be leading the battle. This benign image of the modern welfare state does not call for greater political activism on the part of its citizens, but only for greater social cooperation.

It is of course in the interest of the professional elites who control the modern welfare state to eliminate concern about political liberty and struggle from the social system. It is in their interest to emphasize the model of an ideal society run by philosopher-kings who are dedicated to working for the good of all people. Nothing portrayed the attempt to kill politics and remove political content from schooling in the interests of a professional elite better than the accountability movement in education during the 1970s. This movement demonstrated how the quest for power by modern professional elites was premised on a decline of political activity by the citizenry of the welfare state.

The accountability movement began in the United States in the late 1960s when there was political turmoil in public schools and a demand for community control of the schools was surfacing. The community-control movement sought greater control by community members over professional and elite actions in the school at the same time that the accountability movement was demanding greater professional control.

The model for accountability, as the name implies, was the public accountant, who would report to the public the specific accomplishments of the educational system. The U.S. commissioner of education, Sidney Marland, stated his hope in 1972 that "perhaps within the next ten years—there could well be a nationwide accounting process or institution which would act like a certified public accountant in business, objectively assessing the success and failure of our schools and reporting the findings to the public. . . ."[3]

In the accountability model, the educational professional assumed the role of stewardship over the public interest in education. It is the obligation of the educational system to report to the public or make a public accounting of failures and successes. There is no room in this model for direct public control of the educational system, nor is there any consideration that actual public control over the content of education is important. It is assumed that professional educators will reduce the learning process to a series of specific behavorial objectives that can and will be measured by standardized tests and that test results will be reported to the public. The accountability movement placed the professional educator in control of the system and reduced the role of the public to that of responder to reported results.

The goal of removing control of the educational system from the public and placing it in the hands of professional experts was specifically stated in a book that provided the major national statements and impetus for accountability, Leon Lessinger's *Every Kid a Winner: Accountability in Education* (1970). Lessinger, a former associate commissioner of education, called for the establishment of public auditors who would be called into schools to provide for public accounting of a school system's accomplishments. One of the book's subsections, "Accounting for Competence as Well as for Cash," reflects the tenor of Lessinger's argument. The individuals who would assume control of this whole process were to represent a new profession, which he called "educational engineers."[4]

The argument for a new profession of educational engineers demonstrates part of the argument made in chapter 7 regarding government involvement in the consumption and production of knowledge. In this case, Lessinger sees his new profession as originating in the federal government's support of educational research and development during the 1960s. He writes, with regard to the role of educational engineer: "How has this field grown? With the advent of massive federal aid to education. . . . Like agriculture, business, and medicine before it, the educational enterprise began to call on array of new talent representing a mix of disciplines. . . ." He argues that because of federal involvement a whole new profession has been created that is directly related to federal funding. He writes: "Thus, over the past decade, an increasing amount of money in education has gone to people with expertise in such fields as systems design and analysis (for 'management by objectives'), quality control, operations research, instructional technology, facilities design, performance contracting, and accomplishment auditing."[5] It was this combination of expertise that was to produce the educational engineer.

In the light of the arguments made in chapter 7, this is a clear demonstration of the government creating a set of professional experts who develop their own interests and attempt to promote those interests by placing themselves in charge of the educational system. You will recall that the research and development movement of the 1960s was premised on the idea that federal funds provided for educational research would control change in educational systems. The nature of this change and control over the change were to be in the hands of the researcher. As noted by Lessinger, this involvement of the federal government created an expanded corps of educational researchers. It was this corps of researchers that was to combine its skills to produce the new profession of educational engineer and take charge of the educational system under the banner of accountability.

Thus it can be argued that one reason, not necessarily the only or major reason, for the accountability movement was the self-interest of this corps of professionals that had its expertise and research methods authenticated by the federal government. Involved in this self-interest was an intellectual and professional stake in reducing education to specific behavioral objectives and management objectives. One can argue that a major result of federal involvement in research was the spread of the idea into all areas of education, including the accountability movement, that education should be reduced to competency-based objectives that could be measured by professional experts.

The major threat to the accountability movement was community control of the schools and recognition of the political significance of the content of education. If the content of education was considered apolitical, then educational engineering would not require community involvement or control. For instance, in the context of accountability, educational engineers could enter a school system and establish a reading program with specific behavioral objectives that could be measured and reported to the public. The assumption was that the most important concern was reading skill and not the political and social content of what was read. But this line of reasoning is in opposition to concerns that sparked the community-control movement. Minority groups that argued for community control were concerned not only about their children not learning how to read but also about the racial and political content studied in the school and the racism that existed among some teachers.

Illustrative of the response of the accountability movement to demands of community control is the manner in which Lessinger deals with the problem in *Every Kid a Winner*. Writing from the perspective of the late 1960s, Lessinger states: "Across the spectrum of national concerns we hear a new cry for participatory democracy. . . . In the school systems we hear a rash of demands for participation in decision making: teacher power, student power, black power, parent power. . . ." He argues that some educators see only two possible responses to this situation. One is to protect and defend their prerogatives to run the schools. And the other, he states in language that reveals his generally negative attitude toward community control, is to "throw open the process of governance to a populist chaos in which every citizen claims expertise about education on the grounds of having gone through school or of having a child there."[6]

For professional experts like Lessinger, community or popular control of schools not only threatens their control of the educational system, but also creates "populist chaos." Lessinger offers a middle way between professional defensiveness and populist chaos by proposing an analogy from medical practice. He argues that if someone had to wait several hours for treatment in the emergency ward of a hospital, he would have the right to complain about incompetence. "We are not invading the physician's professional domain," he writes, "but simply claiming that an institution should meet the human needs it was established to serve."[7] He also argues that we respect the skills of a surgeon and do not rush into a operating room demanding democratic control.

In other words, the proper role of the nonprofessional in education is not to control but to complain about inadequate delivery of services. In Lessinger's words: "To a somewhat greater extent than in an operating room, these critics of the school may even have ideas about how the problem might be solved; but in each case the professional has to do the work himself. If a surgeon needed technical help, he would consult not a layman but a specialist."[8]

The medical model allows Lessinger to avoid the issue of the political content of education. Surgery in an operating room is not a political act, nor is there any political content to an operation. On the other hand, education involves a content, and the content of education is not neutral and cannot always be determined from a position of expertise. There is no such thing as an expert opinion about what is the best social, economic, and political content to include in the curriculum of the school. The determination of the best content of schooling is not a judgment based on expertise but on the values held by individuals. The demand for participatory democracy alluded to by Lessinger is a demand to control the content of schooling. Lessinger's model allows the educational engineer to determine the content of schooling based on his values, while the role of the public is reduced to complaining about the delivery of services as accounted for by educational engineers.

The accountability movement illustrates the intersection of the political structure of schooling with the political content of schooling. Professional control is based on a model of government in which the primary issue is satisfactory delivery of services and not the struggle over power and benefits. This model attempts to neutralize politics and present the picture of an apolitical government service operated by professional experts. The role of the citizen is to cooperate and help the government provide services and at the same time to complain if those services are not delivered adequately. When this model of governance is placed on the school, it creates a curriculum that appears to be apolitical. But this apolitical curriculum has a political content. The political content becomes precisely a political ideology that does not emphasize political struggle and mass participation but presents an image of government that is supportive of professional control.

The accountability movement is but one element of the continuing evolution of the role of the school in the modern world. One can feel sure that people in the eighteenth century would not have been able to envision its important and central role in twentieth-century social systems. It probably would have been equally difficult for nineteenth-century citizens to realize that an institution they were creating to control and stabilize the political system would in the twentieth century become both an institution for controlling political ideology and a major arena for political struggle.

For instance, in the United States since World War II, the school system has become the focal point for most of the struggles around social policy. The civil rights movement, the war on poverty, the internal struggle over the war in Vietnam, and the declining economic system of the 1970s all focus on the role of the modern school. And in all cases the school has not been able to deliver on its promise. It has not integrated society, eliminated poverty, or ended unemployment through career and vocational education.

But more important than the above issues is the role of the school in controlling the ideological content of society. This, after all, was the major purpose of schools when public systems of education were expanded in the nineteenth century. The importance of this function of schooling has not declined in the twentieth century but has become hidden in an ideology of equality of opportunity that, as has been argued throughout this volume, supports a particular form of political control. Both control and ideology intersect in the modern school. The political structure of schooling determines its political content, and if the school does influence the ideology of its students, then the political structure of schooling influences the political ideology of society.

If the above is true, then the next most important step in advancing the liberal revolutions of the past is to separate the control of ideology from the political structure. This means separating the school from government and allowing for complete freedom of expression and conscience. It may be that only in this manner will society be able to advance its thinking and solve what seem to be unsolvable economic and social problems in the modern world. Government control of schooling not only means control of ideology but also a stifling of the development of new political and social ideas. Intellectual growth depends on freedom of thought.

The discussion of the economics of education in chapter 8 demonstrates the feasibility of separating the school from government. In fact, it may be to the advantage of the poor and the middle class to pay directly for education rather than indirectly through an expensive system of taxation. If people can choose their own food, they can certainly choose their own education. The next most important step society can take in the interest of social improvement and freedom is to separate school and government by eliminating public systems of education.

NOTES

Chapter 1. Political Theories of Education: Nationalism, Representation, and Bureaucracy

1. A good recent study is M. Kent Jennings and Richard G. Niemi, *The Political Character of Adolescence* (Princeton: Princeton University Press, 1974). The authors divide good citizenship into participation in system, allegiance to system, social-interpersonal behavior, and moral ethical behavior. Much of their categorization is based on Gabriel Almond and Stanley Verba, *The Civic Culture* (Princeton: Princeton University Press, 1963).
2. For a discussion of the issue of nationalism and the claims of fascism to represent the will of the people, see George Mosse, *The Nationalization of the Masses* (New York: New American Library, 1975), pp. 1-20.
3. Homer D. Babbidge, ed., *Noah Webster: On Being American. Selected Writings, 1783-1828* (New York: Praeger, 1967), pp. 3-19.
4. Noah Webster, "Dissertations on the English Language, 1789," in ibid., pp. 93-108.
5. Noah Webster, "An Examination into the Leading Principles of the Federal Constitution Proposed by the Late Convention Held at Philadelphia, 1787," in ibid., p. 53.

6. Noah Webster, "Sketches of American Policy, Part IV, 1785," in ibid., p. 45.
7. Noah Webster, "Americans, Unshackle Your Minds . . .," in ibid., p. 85.
8. Ibid., p. 83.
9. Jean-Jacques Rousseau, "Political Economy," in *The Minor Educational Writings of Jean Jacques Rousseau*, ed. William Boyd (London: Blackie and Son, 1910), pp. 42–43.
10. Ibid., pp. 44–45.
11. Ibid., p. 45.
12. Jean-Jacques Rousseau, "Considerations on the Government of Poland," in ibid., pp. 141–42.
13. Ibid., pp. 145–46.
14. William Boyd, ed. and trans., *The Emile of Jean Jacques Rousseau* (New York: Teachers College Press, 1956), pp. 164–65.
15. Johann G. Fichte, "The Nature of the New Education," in *Addresses to the German Nation*, trans. R. F. Jones and G. H. Turnbull (Chicago: Open Court, 1922).
16. Adam Smith, *The Wealth of Nations* (New York: Modern Library, n.d.), pp. 735–39.
17. Lawrence Cremin, ed., *The Republic and the School: Horace Mann on the Education of Free Men* (New York: Teachers College Press, 1957), p. 93.
18. Ibid., p. 97.
19. Ibid., p. 94.
20. Ibid., p. 97.
21. Ibid., p. 92.
22. John Stuart Mill, *Utilitarianism, Liberty, and Representative Government* (New York: Dutton, 1951), p. 88.
23. Ibid., p. 217.
24. Ibid., pp. 218–19.
25. Ibid., p. 219.
26. Joseph Cronin, *The Control of Urban Schools* (New York: Free Press, 1973).
27. A general history of the social reconstructionist movement in the United States can be found in Charles Bowers, *The Progressive Educator and The Depression* (New York: Random House, 1969). George Counts' "Dare the School Build a New Social Order?" was the first major statement of the reconstructionist program.
28. Dan C. Lortie, *Schoolteacher: A Sociological Study* (Chicago: University of Chicago Press, 1975), pp. 113–14.

Chapter 2. Political Theories of Education: The Economic State

1. John Dewey, "My Pedagogic Creed," in *Dewey on Education,* ed. Martin S. Dworkin (New York: Teachers College Press, 1959), p. 30.
2. A. S. Makarenko, *The Collective Family: A Handbook for Russian Parents* (New York: Doubleday Anchor, 1967), p. 32.
3. Ruth Gamberg, *Red and Expert: Education in the People's Republic of China* (New York: Schocken, 1977), p. 27.
4. Adam Smith, *The Wealth of Nations* (New York: Modern Library, 1978), pp. 734–35.
5. Karl Marx, *Capital: A Critique of Political Economy* (New York: Modern Library, 1936), p. 461.
6. Ibid., p. 462.
7. Karl Marx, "Alienated Labor," in *Marx's Concept of Man,* ed. Erich Fromm (New York: Fredrick Ungar, 1961), p. 98.
8. Ibid., pp. 102–3.
9. Ibid., p. 103.
10. Marx, *Capital,* p. 534.
11. Ibid.
12. John Dewey, "School and Society," in Dworkin, *Dewey on Education,* p. 46.
13. John Dewey, *Democracy and Education* (New York: Free Press, 1966), p. 260.
14. Dewey, "School and Society," p. 49.
15. Dewey, "My Pedagogic Creed," p. 21.
16. Dewey, *Democracy and Education,* p. 87.
17. Maurice Shore, *Soviet Education: Its Psychology and Philosophy* (New York: Philosophical Library, 1947), p. 129.
18. Jann Pennar, Ivan Hakalo, and George Bereday, *Modernization and Diversity in Soviet Education* (New York: Praeger, 1971), pp. 34–39.
19. Shore, *Soviet Education,* p. 173.
20. Ibid., p. 191.
21. Ibid., p. 193.
22. Pennar et al., *Modernization and Diversity,* pp. 43–53.
23. See Urie Bonfenbrenner, Introduction, in Makarenko, *The Collective Family,* pp. ix–xix.
24. A biography and study of Makarenko can be found in James Bowen, *Soviet Education: Anton Makarenko and the Years of Experiment* (Madison: University of Wisconsin Press, 1965).
25. Anton Makarenko, *The Road to Life* (Moscow: Foreign Languages, 1955), 3:265.

26. Ibid.
27. Ibid., p. 267.
28. Makarenko, *The Collective Family*, p. 14.
29. As quoted by John N. Hawkins in *Mao Tse-tung and Education* (Handen, Conn.: Linnet, 1974), p. 73.
30. Ibid., pp. 74-78; Gamberg, *Red and Expert*, pp. 63-68.
31. Hawkins, *Mao Tse-tung*, p. 78.
32. Gamberg, *Red and Expert*, pp. 23-27.
33. *Quotations from Chairman Mao Tse-tung* (Peking: Foreign Languages, 1967), pp. 261-62.
34. Ibid., p. 262.
35. Ibid., p. 170.
36. Ibid., p. 174.
37. Quoted by D. I. Chambers in "The 1975-1976 Debate over Higher Education Policy in the People's Republic of China," *Comparative Education* 13, no. 1 (March 1977): 3.
38. Edward Krug, *The Shaping of the American High School* (New York: Harper & Row, 1964), pp. 249-83.
39. Joel Spring, *Education and the Rise of the Corporate State* (Boston: Beacon, 1972), pp. 91-126.
40. *Cardinal Principles of Secondary Education* (Washington, D.C.: National Education Association, 1918).
41. Spring, *Education and Corporate State*, pp 1-21.
42. For a history of national educational policy after World War II, see Joel Spring, *The Sorting Machine* (New York: Longman, 1976).
43. Document quoted in Martin Carnoy and Jorge Werthein, "Socialist Ideology and the Transformation of Cuban Education," in *Power and Ideology in Education*, ed. Jerome Karabel and A. H. Halsey (New York: Oxford University Press, 1977), pp. 573-89. Also see Samuel Bowles, "Education and Socialist Man in Cuba," in *Schooling in a Corporate Society*, ed. Martin Carnoy (New York: Longman, 1972).

Chapter 3. Education and the Welfare State

1. For general descriptions of the development and purposes of the welfare state, see Gaston V. Rimlinger, *Welfare Policy and Industrialization in Europe, America and Russia* (New York: Wiley, 1971); and Melville J. Ulmer, *The Welfare State: U.S.A.* (Boston: Houghton Mifflin, 1969).
2. Morris Janowitz, *Social Control of the Welfare State* (Chicago: University of Chicago Press, 1977), pp. 2-3.
3. Ibid., p. 7.

4. Rimlinger, *Welfare Policy*, pp. 112–93.

5. National Association of Manufacturers, "Reports of the Committee on Industrial Education, 1905, 1912," in *American Education and Vocationalism: A Documentary History 1870–1970*, ed. Marvin Lazerson and W. Norton Grubb (New York: Teachers College Press, 1974), pp. 88–100.

6. T. W. Schultz, "Investment in Human Capital," in *Economics of Education*, ed. M. Blaug (Middlesex, England: Penguin, 1968), 1:14–16.

7. Ibid., pp. 22–24. Also T. W. Schultz, "The Human Capital Approach to Education," in *Economic Factors Affecting the Financing of Education*, ed. Roe L. Johns et al. (Gainesville, Fla.: National Educational Finance Project, 1970), pp. 29–33.

8. Theodore W. Schultz, "Education and Economic Growth," in *Social Forces Influencing American Education*, ed. Nelson Henry (Chicago: University of Chicago Press, 1961), pp. 48–51.

9. Ibid., p. 63.

10. Ibid., p. 82.

11. Theodore W. Schultz, *Investment in Human Capital: The Role of Education and of Research* (New York: Free Press, 1971), p. 56.

12. Ibid., p. 69.

13. Gary S. Becker, *Human Capital: A Theoretical and Empirical Analysis, With Special Reference to Education* (2nd ed.; New York: Columbia University Press, 1975), pp. 156, 201–2.

14. Ibid., p. 166.

15. Ibid., pp. 205–12.

16. Ibid., pp. 208–9.

17. Martin Carnoy, "The Cost and Return to Schooling in Mexico" (Ph.D. dissertation, University of Chicago, 1964), and *Education as Cultural Imperialism* (New York: Longman, 1974).

18. Samuel S. Bowles, "The Efficient Allocation of Resources in Education: A Planning Model with Applications to Northern Nigeria" (Ph.D. dissertation, Harvard University, 1965); and Samuel Bowles and Herbert Gintis, *Schooling in Capitalist America* (New York: Basic, 1974).

19. Schultz, *Investment in Human Capital*, p. 46.

20. Martin Carnoy, *Educational and Employment: A Critical Appraisal* (Paris: International Institute for Educational Planning, 1977), p. 11.

21. Philip H. Coombs, *The World Educational Crisis: A Systems Analysis* (New York: Oxford University Press, 1968), pp. 17–34.

22. Ronald Dore, *The Diploma Disease: Education, Qualification and Development* (Berkeley: University of California Press, 1976), pp. 4–5.

23. Ibid., p. 5.
24. Coombs, *World Educational Crisis*, p. 53.
25. Dore, *Diploma Disease*, p. 4.
26. Coombs, *World Educational Crisis*, p. 52.
27. Dore, *Diploma Disease*, p. 76.
28. Carnoy, *Education and Employment*, p. 11.
29. Richard B. Freeman, *The Overeducated American* (New York: Academic, 1976), p. 53.
30. Ibid., p. 26.
31. Ibid., pp. 16–21.
32. Ibid., p. 40.
33. Carnoy, *Education and Employment*, pp. 64–66.
34. Ibid., pp. 73–86.
35. Janowitz, *Social Control*, pp. 52–58.

Chapter 4. Social Mobility and the Bureaucratic Society

1. A general description of historical changes in the occupational structure and the causes of social mobility can be found in Seymour Lipset and Reinhard Bendix, *Social Mobility in Industrial Society* (Berkeley: University of California Press, 1959), pp. 11–76; and in Peter Blau and Otis Duncan, *The American Occupational Structure* (New York: Wiley, 1967), pp. 418–32.
2. See T. B. Bottomore, *Classes in Modern Society* (New York: Vintage, 1966).
3. A good historical description of this process can be found in Burton J. Bledstein, *The Culture of Professionalism: The Middle Class and the Development of Higher Education in America* (New York: Norton, 1976). A sociological treatment of this phenomenon can be found in Magali Sarfatti Larson, *The Rise of Professionalism: A Sociological Analysis* (Berkeley: University of California Press, 1977).
4. Sociologists talk about two kinds of competition in educational systems. Ralph H. Turner, "Modes of Social Ascent through Education: Sponsored and Contest Mobility," in *Education, Economy, and Society*, ed. A. H. Halsey et al. (Glencoe, Ill.: Free Press, 1961), argues that the American educational system is like a sporting contest where players compete for prizes. The sponsored mobility of the English system is characterized by controlled selection by an elite.
5. Bledstein, *Culture of Professionalism*, pp. 38–39; and Larson, *Rise of Professionalism*, pp. 9–18.
6. Larson, *Rise of Professionalism*, p. 15.
7. Ibid., p. 136.

8. Ibid., p. 179.

9. For a general discussion of the educational policies and politics of these early labor groups, see Edward Pessen, *Most Uncommon Jacksonians: The Radical Leaders of the Early Labor Movement* (Albany: State University of New York Press, 1967).

10. A good introduction to the issue of equality of educational opportunity in relationship to school desegregation and finance is Charles Tesconi and Emanuel Hurwitz, ed., *Education for Whom?* (New York: Dodd, Mead, 1974).

11. For a history of the war on poverty, see Joel Spring, *The Sorting Machine: National Educational Policy Since 1945* (New York: Longman, 1976), pp. 186–230.

12. Ibid., pp. 205–30.

13. For a good description of the social and political philosophy of early leaders of the testing movement, see Clarence J. Karier, "Testing for Order and Control in the Corporate Liberal State," in *Roots of Crisis* (Chicago: Rand McNally, 1973), pp. 108–38; and idem, *Shaping the American Educational State* (New York: Free Press, 1975), pp. 161–33.

14. See Arthur R. Jensen, "How Much Can We Boost IQ and Scholastic Achievement? *Harvard Educational Review* 39, no. 1 (Winter 1969).

15. A history of the IQ debate can be found in Edgar Gumber and Joel Spring, *The Superschool and the Superstate* (New York: Wiley, 1974), pp. 87–115.

16. Lipset and Bendix, *Social Mobility*, pp. 1–2.

17. Ibid., pp. 72–75.

18. Ibid., p. 127.

19. Ibid., pp. 127, 143.

20. Blau and Duncan, *American Occupational Structure*, p. 1.

21. Ibid., p. 7.

22. Ibid., p. 6.

23. Ibid., pp. 426–29.

24. Ibid., pp. 402–3.

25. Ibid., p. 431.

26. Ibid., pp. 429–30.

27. Christopher Jencks, *Inequality* (New York: Harper & Row, 1972), p. 254.

28. Ibid.

29. Ivan Illich, *Deschooling Society* (New York: Harper & Row, 1970).

30. The clearest and most forceful statement of this position can be found in Samuel Bowles and Herbert Gintis, *Schooling in Capitalist America* (New York: Basic, 1976).

31. Richard B. Dobson, "Social Status and Inequality of Access to Higher Education," in *Power and Ideology in Education*, ed. Jerome Karabel and A. H. Halsey (New York: Oxford University Press, 1977), p. 257.
32. Ibid., pp. 254–57.
33. Ibid., pp. 257–69.
34. Lester C. Thurow, "Education and Economic Equality," in Karabel and Halsey, *Power and Ideology*, p. 333.
35. Ibid.
36. A. H. Halsey, "Towards Meritocracy? The Case of Britain," in Karabel and Halsey, *Power and Ideology*, p. 184.

Chapter 5. Professionalism and Bureaucracy in Education

1. For general definitions of professionalism, see Everett C. Hughes, "Professions," and Bernard Barber, "Some Problems in the Sociology of the Professions," in *The Professions in America*, ed. Kenneth S. Lynn (Cambridge, Mass.: Houghton Mifflin, 1965), pp. 1–35; and Magali Sarfatti Larson, *The Rise of Professionalism: A Sociological Analysis* (Berkeley: University of California Press, 1977), pp. 2–19.
2. Dan C. Lortie, *Schoolteacher: A Sociological Study* (Chicago: University of Chicago Press, 1975), p. 160.
3. James Lynch and H. Dudley Plunkett, *Teacher Education and Cultural Change* (London: Allen & Unwin, 1973), pp. 71–116.
4. Thomas Alexander, *The Training of Elementary Teachers in Germany* (New York, Teachers College Press, 1929), pp. 1–27.
5. Willard S. Elsbree, *The American Teacher: Evolution of a Profession in a Democracy* (New York: American Book, 1939), pp. 311–59.
6. H. C. Dent, "An Historical Perspective," in *The Training of Teachers*, ed. Stanley Hewett (London: University of London Press, 1971), pp. 12–27.
7. Merle Borrowman, *The Liberal and Technical in Teacher Education: A Historical Survey of American Thought* (New York: Teachers College Press, 1956), p. 61.
8. Lynch and Plunkett, *Teacher Education*, p. 38.
9. Ibid., pp. 34–35.
10. Arthur G. Powell and Theodore R. Sizer, "Changing Conception of the Professor of Education," in *To Be a Phoenix: The Education Professoriate*, ed. James Counelis (Bloomington: Phi Delta Kappa, 1969), p. 61.
11. Ibid., pp. 62–64.
12. Ibid., pp. 62–66.

13. Elsbree, *American Teacher*, p. 297.
14. Ibid., pp. 296–305.
15. Lynch and Plunkett, *Teacher Education*, p. 73.
16. Joel Spring, *Education and the Rise of the Corporate State* (Boston: Beacon, 1972), pp. 62–91.
17. Borrowman, *Liberal and Technical in Teacher Education*, pp. 107–10; and Lawrence Cremin, *The Transformation of the School* (New York: Vintage, 1961), pp. 90–179.
18. Lynch and Plunkett, *Teacher Education*, pp. 130–37.
19. The war on poverty is described in Joel Spring, *The Sorting Machine: National Educational Policy Since 1945* (New York: Longman, 1976), pp. 186–230.
20. Lynch and Plunkett, *Teacher Education*, p. 134.
21. General articles by Thorndike on the science of education can be found in Geraldine Joncich, *Psychology and the Science of Education* (New York: Teachers College Press, 1965).
22. B. F. Skinner, *The Technology of Teaching* (New York: Appleton-Century-Crofts, 1968).
23. Spring, *Sorting Machine*, pp. 113–28.
24. Lortie, *Schoolteacher*, p. 228.
25. Ratios calculated from statistics given in W. V. Grant and C. G. Lind, *Digest of Education Statistics 1976 Edition: National Center for Education Statistics* (Washington, D.C.: U.S. Government Printing Office, 1977), p. 36.
26. Ibid.
27. Ibid., p. 55.
28. Ibid., p. 59.
29. Ibid., pp. 59, 62.
30. Ibid., p. 36.
31. A good introduction to different theories of bureaucracy is in Nicos P. Mouzelis, *Organization and Bureaucracy: An Analysis of Modern Theories* (London: Routledge & Kegan Paul, 1967), pp. 7–79.
32. Ibid., pp. 10, 19, 36–37.
33. Ibid., pp. 36–37.
34. Ibid., p. 10.
35. This general history of the NEA and AFT is based on Joel Spring, *American Education: Introduction to Social and Political Aspects* (New York: Longman, 1978), pp. 167–89.
36. Spring, *American Education*, pp. 183–86.
37. Spring, *Education and Rise of Corporate State*, pp. 6–8.
38. See Miriam Wasserman, *The School Fix, NYC, USA* (New York: Outerbridge & Dienstfrey, 1970), pp. 185–391.

39. A description of this lobbying effort can be found in *American Teacher* 63, no. 1 (September 1978): A2–A5.
40. This discussion took place at the national convention of Citizens for Educational Freedom in Cincinnati, Ohio, 21 October 1978.
41. Charles W. Cheng, "Teachers Unions and the Power Structure in American Education" (paper presented at the Conference on the Power Structure in American Education, San Francisco, 9–11 November 1978), pp. 31–39.
42. David F. Noble, *America by Design: Science, Technology, and the Rise of Corporate Capitalism* (New York: Knopf, 1977), pp. 257–320.
43. Raymond Callahan, *Edcuation and the Cult of Efficiency* (Chicago: University of Chicago Press, 1962), p. 208.
44. Ibid., p. 199.
45. Ibid., pp. 200–204.
46. Noble, *America By Design*, pp. 224–56.
47. Spring, *Education and Rise of Corporate State.*
48. Clarence Karier has provided the best description of the role of testing in what he calls "the educational state." There is very close agreement on these points in Karier's work and that of previously cited work by Spring and Noble. See Clarence Karier's *Shaping the Educational State* (New York: Free Press, 1975), pp. 161–244.

Chapter 6. The Control of Schooling

1. Peter Bachrach, *The Theory of Democratic Elitism* (London: University of London Press, 1969), p. 2.
2. A general study of the theory of polyarchy can be found in Robert A. Dahl, *Polyarchy: Participation and Opposition* (New Haven: Yale University Press, 1971).
3. Bachrach, *Democratic Elitism*, p. 8.
4. Ibid.
5. Ibid.
6. There are several major studies of these elitist goals in school board reform. The most complete study is Joseph Cronin, *The Control of Urban Schools* (New York: Free Press, 1973), pp. 39–123. Also see David Tyack, *The One Best System* (Cambridge, Mass.: Harvard University Press, 1974), pp. 126–67; and Joel Spring, *Education and the Rise of the Corporate State* (Boston: Beacon, 1972).
7. Tyack, *One Best System*, p. 126.
8. Ibid.
9. Spring, *Education and Rise of Corporate State*, p. 86.
10. Ibid., pp. 86–87.

11. The following are the major studies of this issue in the United States: Scott Nearing, "Who's Who in Our Boards of Education?" *School and Society* 5 (20 January 1917): 89–90; George Counts, *The Social Composition of Boards of Education* (Chicago: University of Chicago Press, 1927); and the most recent study, Harmon Zeigler and Kent Jennings, *Governing American Schools: Political Interaction in Local School Districts* (North Scituate, Mass.: Duxbury, 1974).

12. Zeigler and Jennings, *Governing American Schools*.

13. Hanna Pitkin, *The Concept of Representation* (Berkeley: University of California Press, 1967), p. 195.

14. Ibid., p. 198.

15. Ibid., p. 205.

16. Tyack, *One Best System*, pp. 144–46; and Cronin, *Control of Urban Schools*, pp. 100–109.

17. Tyack, *One Best System*, p. 146.

18. Cronin, *Control of Urban Schools*, p. 138.

19. Ibid., pp. 138–39.

20. Joel Spring, *The Sorting Machine: National Educational Policy Since 1945* (New York: Longman, 1976), pp. 96–113.

21. Zeigler and Jennings, *Governing American Schools*.

22. Ibid.

23. Ronald F. Campbell and Tim L. Mazzoni, Jr., *State Policy Making for the Public Schools* (Berkeley: McCutchan, 1976), pp. 28–133.

24. Ibid., pp. 134–216.

25. Laurence Iannaccone, *Politics in Education* (New York: Center for Applied Research in Education, 1967).

26. Ibid.

27. Ibid.

28. Spring, *Sorting Machine*, p. 227.

29. This situation is described in Richard Lehne, *The Quest for Justice: The Politics of School Finance Reform* (New York: Longman, 1978).

30 Spring, *Sorting Machine*, pp. 176–85.

31. Stephen Bailey, *Education Interest Groups in the Nation's Capital* (Washington, D.C.: American Council on Education, 1975).

32. At the time of the writing of this manuscript a cloak of secrecy had been cast around the functioning and procedures of this organization. What is meant by "secrecy" in this case is a lack of public announcements or attempts to inform the public. The organization is obviously not secret to those leaders that belong to it.

33. Samuel Halperin, "The Political World of Washington Policymakers in Education," (paper presented at the Conference on

the Power Structure in American Education in San Francisco, November 1978), p. 25.

34. Ibid., p. 23.
35. George A. Male, *The Struggle for Power: Who Controls the Schools in England and the United States* (Beverly Hills: Sage, 1974).
36. Ibid., p. 73.
37. "Education Act. 1944," in *Educational Documents: England and Wales 1816-1967*, ed. J. Stuart Maclure (London: Chapman & Hall, 1968), pp. 222-26.
38. Male, *Struggle for Power*, p. 43.
39. Ibid., pp. 48-51.
40. Ibid., p. 49; and David Wardle, *English Popular Education 1780-1970* (Cambridge, England: Cambridge University Press, 1970), pp. 156-57.
41. Male, *Struggle for Power*, pp. 109-19.
42. Ibid., pp. 86-88.
43. Ibid., pp. 63-64.
44. "The Education Act. 1902," in Maclure, *Educational Documents*, pp. 149-53.
45. Male, *Struggle for Power*, pp. 109-119.
46. Dale Mann, *The Politics of Administrative Representation* (Lexington, Mass.: Lexington, 1976).
47. Ibid., pp. 15-25.
48. Ibid., pp. 25-29.
49. Ibid., p. 38.
50. Ibid., p. 53.
51. Ibid., pp. 52-53.
52. Ernest R. House, *The Politics of Educational Innovation* (Berkeley: McCutchan, 1974).
53. Ibid., pp. 37-44.
54. Ibid., p. 41.
55. Ibid., pp. 45-47.
56. Ibid., p. 49.
57. Ibid., p. 97.
58. Russell Marks, *The Idea of I.Q.* (manuscript, 1978), p. 49.
59. Ibid., pp. 60-61.
60. Lehne, *Quest for Justice*, p. 98.

Chapter 7. The Production of Knowledge and the Control of Education

1. Torsten Husen, *The Learning Society* (London: Methuen, 1974), pp. 100-101.

2. Richard A. Dershimer, *The Federal Government and Education R&D* (Lexington, Mass.: Lexington, 1976), p. 2.
3. Joel Spring, *The Sorting Machine: National Educational Policy Since 1945* (New York: Longman, 1976), pp. 1–52, 93–140.
4. Joel Spring, *American Education: An Introduction to Social and Political Aspects* (New York: Longman, 1978), pp. 146–51.
5. Dershimer, *Federal Government and Education*, p. 59.
6. The best general discussion of this model can be found in Ernest House, *The Politics of Educational Innovation* (Berkeley: McCutchan, 1974), pp. 204–49.
7. Ibid., p. 215; and Dershimer, *Federal Government and Education*, pp. 59–60.
8. House, *Educational Innovation*, p. 218.
9. Ibid.
10. Ibid., p. 223.
11. Dershimer, *Federal Government and Education*, p. 64.
12. Ibid., pp. 63–64.
13. Ibid., p. 65.
14. Lee J. Cronbach and Patrick Suppes, eds., *Research for Tomorrow's Schools: Disciplined Inquiry for Education* (London: Collier-Macmillan, 1969), p. 205.
15. Ibid.
16. Office of Public Information, *NIE: Its History and Programs* (Washington, D.C.: U.S. Government Printing Office, 28 February 1974), p. 3.
17. Ibid., p. 6.
18. Torsten Husen, "Two Decades of Educational Research in Sweden," in Husen, *Learning Society*, p. 173.
19. Ibid., p. 170.
20. W. Kenneth Richmand, "Foreword," in ibid., pp. vii–xiii.
21. W. D. Wall, "The Work of the National Foundation for Educational Research in England and Wales," in *Educational Research in Britain*, ed. H. J. Butcher (London: University of London Press, 1968), p. 18.
22. Ibid., pp. 22–24.
23. Jack Wrigley, "The Schools Council," in *Educational Research in Britain 2*, ed. H. J. Butcher (London: University of London Press, 1970), pp. 21–35.
24. A brief history and description of these organizations can be found in Dershimer, *Federal Government and Education*, pp. 132–37.
25. Ibid., p. 142.
26. Ibid., p. 137.
27. Ibid., pp. 138–39.

28. Cronbach and Suppes, *Tomorrow's Schools.*
29. Ibid., p. 4.
30. Ibid., pp. 240–42.
31. Ibid., p. 243.
32. Ibid.
33. Ibid., pp. 20–21.
34. Ibid., p. 23.
35. Ibid., p. 269.
36. Ibid., p. 26.
37. Douglas Pidgeon, "The National Foundation for Educational Research in England and Wales," in Butcher, *Educational Research in Britain 2,* p. 4.
38. Daniel P. Moynihan, "Can Courts and Money Do It?" *New York Times,* 10 January 1972, reprinted in Miriam Wasserman, *Demystifying School* (New York: Praeger, 1974), pp. 226–30.
39. See Daniel P. Moynihan, "On the Education of the Urban Poor," in *Coping: Essays on the Practice of Government* (New York: Random House, 1973), pp. 167–94.
40. Moynihan, "Can Courts Do It," pp. 226–30.
41. Office of Information, *NIE,* p. 9.
42. Ibid., p. 7.
43. Ibid., pp. 16–17.
44. Ibid., pp. 26–30.
45. Ibid., p. 30.
46. Ibid., p. 47.
47. National Institute of Education, *Preliminary FY 1977 Program Plan Executive Summary* (undated).
48. "Education and Work Program," in ibid., p. 1.
49. The story of the early spread of career education can be found in Spring, *Sorting Machine,* pp. 233–37.

Chapter 8. The Economics of Schooling

1. Horace Mann, "Tenth Annual Report (1846)" in *The Republic and the School,* ed. Lawrence Cremin (New York: Teachers College Press, 1957), pp. 62–77.
2. Ibid., p. 77.
3. Milton Friedman, *Capitalism and Freedom* (Chicago: University of Chicago Press, 1962), p. 86.
4. Ibid., p. 89.
5. Ibid., p. 92.
6. Ibid.

7. Milton Friedman, "Are Externalities Relevant?" in *Nonpublic School Aid*, ed. E. G. West (Lexington, Mass.: Heath, 1976), p. 92.
8. Ibid.
9. E. G. West, *Education and the State: A study in Political Economy* (London: Institute of Economic Affairs, 1970), pp. 13–14.
10. Carl F. Kaestle, "Common Schools Before the 'Common School Revival': New York Schooling in the 1790's," *History of Education Quarterly* 12, no. 4 (Winter 1972): 476. This study is also in Kaestle's *The Evolution of an Urban School System: New York City, 1750–1850* (Cambridge, Mass.: Harvard University Press, 1973), chap. 2.
11. West, *Education and the State*, pp. 126–209.
12. E. G. West, "The Political Economy of Public School Legislation," in *Studies in Education, No. 4* (Menlo Park: Institute of Humane Studies, 1977), p. 19. This article was originally published under the same title in the October 1967 issue of *Journal of Law and Economics*.
13. Ibid., p. 20.
14. Ibid., p. 25.
15. West, *Education and the State*, pp. 35, 43.
16. Ibid., p. 71.
17. Ibid., p. 98.
18. E. G. West, "An Economic Analysis of the Law and Politics of Nonpublic School 'Aid,'" in Friedman, *Nonpublic School Aid*, pp. 13, 25.
19. National Center for Education Statistics, *Digest of Education Statistics: 1976 Edition* (Washington, D.C.: U.S. Government Printing Office, 1977), pp. 36–37.
20. Walter Garms, James Guthrie, and Lawrence C. Pierce, *School Finance: The Economics and Politics of Public Education* (Englewood Cliffs, N.J.: Prentice-Hall, 1978), p. 141.
21. West, *Education and the State*, pp. 199–209.
22. West, "Economic Analysis," pp. 1–28.
23. For a general discussion of school cases, see Joel Spring, *American Education* (New York: Longman, 1978), pp. 244–30. A general discussion of the *Nyquist* can be found in West, "Economic Analysis."
24. West, "Economic Analysis," p. 25.
25. Spring, *American Education*, p. 227.
26. Ibid.
27. Ibid., p. 228.
28. John E. Coons, William H. Clune III, and Stephen D. Sugarman,

Private Wealth and Public Education (Cambridge, Mass.: Harvard University Press, 1970), p. 3.

29. Ibid., p. 4.
30. Ibid., pp. 201–2.
31. Ibid., p. 207.
32. John E. Coons and Stephen D. Sugarman, *Education by Choice: The Case for Family Control* (Berkeley: University of California Press, 1978), p. 194.
33. Ibid., pp. 195–97.
34. Ibid., p. 197.
35. Ibid., pp. 198–203.
36. Richard Lehne, *The Quest for Justice: The Politics of School Finance Reform* (New York: Longman, 1978), p. 49.
37. Ibid., p. 50.
38. Ibid., pp. 143–44.
39. Ibid., p. 174.
40. Ibid., p. 176.
41. Ibid., p. 175.
42. Ibid., p. 182.
43. Ibid., p. 183.
44. See Garms, Guthrie, and Pierce, *School Finance,* pp. 61–71, for a general discussion of supply and demand for education.
45. Ibid., p. 65.

Chapter 9. The Role of the School in the Modern World: A Summary

1. Curtis Gans, "The Cause: The Empty Voting Booths," *Washington Monthly,* October 1978, pp. 27–30.
2. Bernard Bailyn, *The Ideological Origins of the American Revolution* (Cambridge, Mass.: Harvard University Press, 1967).
3. As quoted by Don Martin, George Overholt, and Wayne Urban in *Accountability in American Education: A Critique* (Princeton: Princeton Book, 1976), p. 71.
4. Leon Lessinger, *Every Kid a Winner: Accountability in Education* (New York: Simon & Schuster, 1970), pp. 23–41.
5. Ibid., p. 119.
6. Ibid., p. 128.
7. Ibid., p. 129.
8. Ibid.

INDEX